Exploring the Basic Income Guarantee

Series Editor

Karl Widerquist
Georgetown University in Qatar
Doha, USA

Basic income is one of the most innovative, powerful, straightforward, and controversial proposals for addressing poverty and growing inequalities. A Basic Income Guarantee (BIG) is designed to be an unconditional, government-insured guarantee that all citizens will have enough income to meet their basic needs. The concept of basic, or guaranteed, income is a form of social provision and this series examines the arguments for and against it from an interdisciplinary perspective with special focus on the economic and social factors. By systematically connecting abstract philosophical debates over competing principles of BIG to the empirical analysis of concrete policy proposals, this series contributes to the fields of economics, politics, social policy, and philosophy and establishes a theoretical framework for interdisciplinary research. It will bring together international and national scholars and activists to provide a comparative look at the main efforts to date to pass unconditional BIG legislation across regions of the globe and will identify commonalities and differences across countries drawing lessons for advancing social policies in general and BIG policies in particular.

All proposals submitted to the series undergo documented single-blind peer review by subject-matter experts (SME). In addition, all manuscripts are reviewed by SME prior to acceptance through a documented single-blind process.

Roberto Merrill • Catarina Neves
Editors

Determining the Value of Universal Basic Income

Political Feasibility, Ecological Impact, Economic Realities, and Research Methodologies

palgrave
macmillan

Editors
Roberto Merrill
Escola de Letras, Artes e Ciências Humanas, Departamento de Filosofia
Universidade do Minho
Braga, Portugal

Catarina Neves
Ethics Institute
Utrecht University
Utrecht, Utrecht, The Netherlands

ISSN 2662-3803 ISSN 2662-3811 (electronic)
Exploring the Basic Income Guarantee
ISBN 978-3-032-04003-9 ISBN 978-3-032-04004-6 (eBook)
https://doi.org/10.1007/978-3-032-04004-6

This work was supported by Universidade do Minho.

This Palgrave Macmillan imprint is published by the registered company Springer Nature Switzerland AG.
The registered company address is: Gewerbestrasse 11, 6330 Cham, Switzerland

Contents

Notes on Contributors

Sara Bizarro teaches philosophy at the University of New Orleans in the United States. She holds a Masters and a PhD in Philosophy from the University of Lisbon. She has worked on several projects involving Basic Income. In 2019, she published *Unconditional Basic Income, A Defense of Freedom*, with Roberto Merrill, Gonçalo Marcelo, and Jorge Pinto (in Portuguese: *Rendimento Básico Incondicional, Uma Defesa da Liberdade*, Edições 70). This book won the First Place Essay Prize attributed by the Portuguese Philosophy Society in 2019. She also published "The Fourth Industrial Revolution, Unconditional Basic Income, Inequality and Emancipation" (in Portuguese, "Quarta Revolução Indústrial e RBI, Desigualdade ou Emancipação"), with Gonçalo Marcelo, *Análise Social*, 2019. She has participated in the organizing committee for the 17th BIEN World Congress, Portuguese Parliament, and ISEG in 2017 and organized the Guaranteed Income Workshop, University of New Orleans in 2024. She is a founding member of RBI-P (Association for Unconditional Basic Income, Portugal), a Lifetime member of BIEN (Basic Income Earth Network), and a Member and Volunteer at USBIG (United States Basic Income Guaranteed). Her current research interests lie in Ethics, Social and Political Philosophy, and the Philosophy of Film.

Carla Guapo Costa is a Full Professor with tenure at the School of Social and Political Sciences (ISCSP) at the University of Lisbon and a researcher at the Orient Institute and the Center for Administration and Public Policies, funded by the Portuguese Ministry of Education, Science, and Innovation. Currently, she is the Head of ISCSP's Pedagogical Council, and the Coordinator of the Centre for European Research and Documentation at the University of Lisbon, where she conducts research on European issues. She holds a PhD in Economics from the Institute of Economics and Management (ISEG) at the same university, and she is also an Auditor in National Defence, certified by Portugal's Institute for National Defence. Her main research areas are international political economy and geoeconomics. She has authored several books and papers in both national and international journals. She has worked on consultancy missions for Portuguese-speaking African countries (São Tomé and Príncipe and Angola) and the former Portuguese colony in East Asia, Timor-Leste, focusing on sustainable development and geoeconomics. She is currently a lecturer at the Royal College of Defence Studies, in London, where she debates on geoeconomics and economic security.

Evelyn L. Forget is Distinguished Professor of Economics and Community Health Sciences at the University of Manitoba in Winnipeg (Canada). Her research examines the health and social implications of poverty and inequality, and she is often called upon by governments, First Nations, and international organizations to advise on poverty, inequality, health, and social outcomes. Her most recent books are *Basic Income for Canadians: From the COVID-19 Emergency to Financial Security for All* and (with Hannah Owczar) *Radical Trust: Basic Income for Complicated Lives*. She is a Fellow of the Royal Society of Canada and an Officer of the Order of Canada and has received an honorary D.Sc. from Queen's University and an honorary DCL from St. John's College, both in Canada.

Pedro Vaz Goulart is Associate Professor at the School of Social and Political Sciences (ISCSP), Universidade de Lisboa, and its Economics Group Coordinator. He holds a PhD from the International Institute of Social Studies of Erasmus University Rotterdam. He is a specialist in child labour, education and labour, economics for non-economists, and participation and local development, themes on which he has led several funded research projects. His over 50 publications include articles in *Economics of Education Review*, *Economic History of Developing Regions*, *European Journal of Development Research*, *European Urban and Regional Studies*, *Journal of Educational Research*, *Social Indicators Research*, or *Social Science History*. Pedro has (co-)edited volumes on "Global Labour in Distress" (Palgrave), "Participation for What?" (Hivos, Oxfam-Novib), and "South-South Globalization" (Routledge). He has also published chapters in relevant volumes (e.g. *The World of Child Labour*, ME Sharpe;

South-South Globalization, Routledge; *Child Labour's Global Past*, Peter Lang; *The Wiley Blackwell Encyclopedia of Family Studies*). Pedro is committed to publish in Portuguese language to disseminate knowledge to relevant stakeholders. He has been consulted by national and international media, government, and academic peers. He has served at several EADI committees, and he is a co-editor of the EADI Global Development Series at Palgrave.

Michael W. Howard is Emeritus Professor of Philosophy at the University of Maine (USA). He is the author of *Self-management and the Crisis of Socialism* (2000) and the editor of *Socialism* (2001). He is the co-editor (with Karl Widerquist) of *Alaska's Permanent Fund Dividend* (2012) and *Exporting the Alaska Model* (2012). He is a Senior Consultant Editor of *Basic Income Studies.* He was the president of the US Basic Income Guarantee Network (2008-2022) and is currently co-chair of the Maine Basic Income Security Committee. He is the author of over 60 articles and book chapters in social and political philosophy on such topics as socialism, workplace democracy, climate justice, and basic income.

Soomi Lee is a Professor in the Public Administration Department and the Director of the Master of Public Administration program at the University of La Verne in the United States. Her research encompasses public policy, public finance, and urban economics. Her publications have appeared in journals such as *Urban Studies*, *Urban Affairs Review*, *Regional Studies*, and *Basic Income Studies.* Lee has served on the executive board of the United States Basic Income Guarantee Network and led the organizing committee for the 2019 North America Basic Income Guarantee Congress held in New York City. Her research on basic income focuses on the political, financial, and program design aspects.

Roberto Merrill is Assistant Professor in Philosophy and Head of Department of Philosophy at the School of Arts and Humanities at the University of Minho, where he also coordinates the MA in Political Philosophy. He is also a researcher at the Centre for Ethics, Politics and Society (CEPS), where he coordinates a project funded by the Portuguese Government on UBI (website here: https://ubiexperiments.weebly.com/). He is a member of the Executive Committee of the Research Committee on Political Philosophy of the International Political Science Association. Dr. Merrill's research interests within political philosophy include liberal neutrality, perfectionism, and value pluralism, as well as contemporary theories of distributive justice. He published in 2019 a book on *Unconditional Basic Income, A Defense of Freedom* (Prize by the Portuguese Society of Philosophy for best essay in philosophy for 2018–2019) and in 2022 a book on *Basic Income Experiments: A Critical Examination of Their Goals, Contexts, and Methods*, Palgrave Macmillan. He is currently working on a book manuscript on pre-distribution and property-owning democracy.

James P. Mulvale (MSW, MA, PhD, RSW) is a Professor in the Faculty of Social Work and a Member of St. Paul's College at the University of Manitoba (Canada), which is located on Treaty One territory and the homeland of the Red River Métis Nation. He teaches courses on social welfare policy, social work research, community development, and social work theory and epistemology. He has written extensively on basic income in the Canadian political context and on the ecological and moral rationales for a universal and unconditional guarantee of economic security for all. His additional research interests include digital pedagogy in social work education, green social work theory and practice, and the intersections between moral philosophy and social welfare. He was a founding member of the Basic Income Canada Network in 2008, has provided leadership in provincial basic income groups in Manitoba and Ontario, and currently participates in a strategic planning group for the Canadian basic income movement.

Catarina Neves is a postdoctoral fellow at Utrecht University, currently working on the *Visions for the Future Project* with Ingrid Robeyns. Catarina teaches the *Ethics of Institutions* course in Utrecht University's Masters in Applied Ethics together with Ingrid Robeyns. She has a PhD in Philosophy from University of Minho, with a thesis on Unconditional Basic Income entitled "Acknowledging the gift: how an unconditional basic income encourages reciprocity". Her project was funded by FCT—Foundation for Science and Technology in Portugal (reference SFRH/BD/144495/2019). She is also the co-author of a book on basic income experiments—*Basic Income Experiments. A Critical Examination of Their Goals, Contexts, and Methods* (2022)—published by Palgrave Macmillan.

Thiago Monteiro de Souza is a PhD candidate at the University of Minho and a researcher at the Centre for Ethics, Politics and Society (CEPS). His main topic of study is Unconditional Basic Income and its political-ecological perspectives. Thiago was born and raised in Rio de

Janeiro, Brazil. He moved to Lisbon, Portugal, in 2019 to pursue his postgraduate studies. In 2022, he commenced his PhD program at UMinho with a research project titled "The moral, political and ecological value of the UBI: a critical examination of pilot experiences". Thiago's PhD project is funded by the Portuguese Foundation of Science and Technology (FCT) and is associated with the Universidade Federal Fluminense (UFF) in Niterói, Rio de Janeiro, Brazil. His current research is centred on normative debates regarding the environmental value of the UBI, and he is drawing correlations with the empirical findings from the UBI policy of Maricá, a municipality in the state of Rio de Janeiro. His primary research interests include Unconditional Basic Income, Post-productivism, Environmental Crisis, and Ecological Republicanism.

List of Figures

List of Tables

CHAPTER 1

Introduction

Roberto Merrill and Catarina Neves

The idea of Unconditional Basic Income has experienced a surge in popularity in recent years (Van Parijs, 1995; Birnbaum, 2012; Noguera et al., 2013; Widerquist, 2013, 2017; Van Parijs & Vanderborght, 2017). This is fuelled by the growing awareness of the challenges posed by inequality, automation, climate change, and the limitations of current social welfare systems. A UBI is thus offered as an alternative that can help solve these global issues (Zelleke, 2005; Van Parijs, 2013; Merrill et al., 2019; Pinto, 2020; Langridge et al., 2023). This edited book features recent work on some normative and empirical debates about Unconditional Basic Income. It draws from several disciplines, with contributions from philosophy, political science, and economics, while exploring UBI's potential to reshape the political, economic, and ecological landscape of the twenty-first century.

Unconditional Basic Income (hereinafter UBI, or Basic Income) can be defined as a proposal that argues for a universal dividend. Concretely, it argues that all citizens from a particular political community should receive

R. Merrill (✉)
Escola de Letras, Artes e Ciências Humanas, Departamento de Filosofia, Universidade do Minho, Braga, Portugal

C. Neves
Ethics Institute, Utrecht University, Utrecht, Utrecht, The Netherlands

R. Merrill, C. Neves (eds.), *Determining the Value of Universal Basic Income*, Exploring the Basic Income Guarantee,
https://doi.org/10.1007/978-3-032-04004-6_1

a regular, unconditional cash payment (Van Parijs & Vanderborght, 2017). It is thus an individual transfer of resources across one's life. Moreover, it is often argued that the cash transfer's amount should be equal to or above the poverty line, with some proposals, arguing for a value that should be as high as possible (Van Parijs, 1995). In this edited volume, most authors use the term Unconditional Basic Income (or the abbreviation UBI) or Basic Income, while one author uses Universal Basic Income. While we have a preference for the use of the word *unconditional*, given that we believe it best captures what is the most radical feature of UBI—the fact that it is 'obligations free', throughout the book these three concepts are used interchangeably.

While sounding radical, UBI is not a new idea, dating back to the eighteenth century,[1] Moreover, there is a rich academic literature on the topic, especially within political philosophy, covering a range of topics: UBI's distributive impacts; its contested role in the project of gender justice (Zelleke, 2011); the discussions around fair cooperation and basic income (Van Parijs, 1991; Birnbaum, 2012; White, 2003); or the debates around its economic feasibility, including its potential funding mechanisms and impact on labour markets (Widerquist, 2013). The latter explores how UBI could be funded through several mechanisms, including progressive taxation, carbon dividends, and other innovative financing models.

But despite the prolific literature on the topic, UBI has never enjoyed the same level of mainstream attention as in recent decades. And much of this revival in contemporary policy debates is owed to the growing body of empirical research that emerged in the last decade, from pilots conducted in Finland, Kenya, India, Namibia, or the more recent ones in the United States. These have been instrumental in shifting the discourse on UBI from a utopian vision to a policy proposal. This book is part of this trend, and hence the authors of the several chapters discuss evidence from most of these experiments.

It is worth clarifying that despite the growing number of so-called UBI pilots or experiments, there is significant variance among them, not only in terms of research methodology (i.e. randomized control trials versus saturation studies; duration of the experiment), but also in the definition

[1] While Thomas Paine and Thomas Moore discussed the idea of an unconditional cash transfer, only later, through Thomas Spence, did the idea of a universal and unconditional cash transfer was formulated. See Basic Income Earth Network for more details on the history of Basic Income. At: https://basicincome.org/history/ [accessed on February 2025].

of basic income they apply. Hence, while some experiments seem to target a sample that represents the entire population (e.g. such as the saturation study in Namibia), some target particular groups (e.g. like the Finnish experiment, which targeted the long-term unemployed). Moreover, some explicitly target lower-income groups and are thus framed as guaranteed income pilots, instead of basic income, as in the case of most experiments in the United States. Hence, when the discussion on evidence takes place in this volume, we should be attentive that the term 'basic income experiments' is an umbrella term that covers a range of pilots, trials, and experiments that vary in methodology, but also in how they resemble the UBI definition mentioned above.

The Contributions in This Volume

Despite this diversity in debates and work on UBI, there is still a range of issues that merit additional scrutiny, namely the political feasibility and the ecological dimensions of basic income. Both remain underexplored, particularly the ecological dimension, especially when it comes to its implications for addressing the growing environmental crises, such as climate change, biodiversity loss, and resource depletion (there are some noteworthy exceptions, see Van Parijs, 2013; Pinto, 2020; Langridge et al., 2023) . For a UBI to feature as an important policy proposal for the future, with action guiding force, it requires that such topics are addressed. Secondly, for UBI to be politically feasible, evidence from experiments is key. However, while the political debate has largely used data from experiments, there is still a pressing need for comprehensive debates on the methodologies around experiments, and how results are communicated.

This edited volume seeks to contribute to both these issues, offering answers to issues around the ecological, but also political feasibility of UBI, while discussing important methodological challenges from experimenting with basic income. Given these twofold aims, the volume is divided into two parts: In Part I, we explore the political feasibility of UBI as well as its ecological and moral dimensions. In Part II, we address some of its main methodological challenges.

Part I: Ecological and Moral Dimensions of Basic Income

The first part, entitled *Ecological and Moral Dimensions of Basic Income*, features contributions from three authors—James P. Mulvale, Thiago Souza, and Michael W. Howard—who engage with the fundamental question of whether we can call UBI green.

In the first chapter, James P. Mulvale aims to discuss the green argument for basic income, considering the normative reasons for UBI, alongside the evidence-based ones. The chapter claims that a post-growth economy that endorses UBI requires that both minds and hearts are changed, and hence that both the normative and evidence-based arguments are taken into consideration in the political debate around a green UBI.

Thiago Monteiro de Souza also takes up the question of a green UBI. In Chap. 3, he analyses two well-known UBI policies—the Alaska's Permanent Fund Dividend in the United States and Maricá's Citizen Basic Income in Brazil. He tries to address whether UBI should be read as an environmental or ecological policy, by discussing its benefits in promoting economic growth and development, but also by considering the arguments of green republicans. Using the evidence from both experiments allows him to show both the merits and limitations that Basic Income can have in promoting an ecological agenda.

Finally, in Chap. 4, Michael W. Howard discusses what he takes to be the two types of arguments connecting UBI and an ecological agenda. The first, the 'minimalist' version, argues for UBI funded through a carbon dividend. The second argument, which he calls the strong or 'maximalist' ecological argument, claims that a full BI funded from sources in addition to carbon pricing can or will have positive ecological effects. His chapter focuses on the maximalist argument, evaluating its premises, including that a BI will facilitate a post-growth economy by freeing people to spend more time in less carbon-intensive activity, by facilitating work-time reduction and work sharing, and by reducing inequality.

Part II: Political Feasibility and Global Perspectives

The second part of this edited volume, entitled *Political Feasibility and Global Perspectives*, features the additional four chapters of the book. For the most part, they provide insights on methodological issues that are cornerstones of any UBI discussion around pilot or policy adoption.

In Chap. 5, Sara Bizarro warns us of how intended and unintended consequences play a crucial role in political strategizing for UBI. She requests that we go beyond the efficacy of the policy on stated intended goals and consider unintended consequences from the onset. In her chapter, she claims that the stated intended goals of policy-makers can often occlude other goals, namely unintended and hence presumed-to-be-out-of-responsibility outcomes. The latter can be detrimental to the lives of many individuals, to the point that a policy should have been modified or not adopted, but can also be used to either justify or reject a policy later on, closing the debate on what—if revised—could be a sound policy option.

In Chap. 6, Evelyn Forget claims that qualitative analysis that uses storytelling and storylistening requires being attentive to several voices, often from marginalized populations. In the chapter, Forget demonstrates how basic income researchers can advance an iterative narrative methodology that allows researchers to understand how particular criticisms of basic income can persist even in the face of empirical evidence to the contrary and, perhaps more importantly, open up new research questions and new policy formulations that address important but unarticulated considerations.

Pedro Goulart and Carla Costa argue in Chap. 7 that critical socio-economic indicators can help us predict whether a UBI pilot will be successfully implemented, leaving open the question of whether success implies replication or good results (i.e. defined based on the questions asked). Their analysis is centred on the assumptions that existing literature on the pros and cons of UBI is focused on concerns with the efficiency of targeted welfare programmes, the cost and financial feasibility of a UBI, and the policy's potential to encourage workers' large-scale exit from the labour market. Hence, we need to look at the context of a country to determine whether welfare programmes are efficient or not; whether labour markets and workers' conditions are more or less prone to generate massive exits when a cash transfer is implemented; and whether the country's financial health will be able to accommodate an ambitious programme such as a large-scale cash transfer.

Finally, in Chap. 8, Soomi Lee focuses on the cost and related concerns with funding of a basic income, highlighting that any UBI proposal needs to be considered alongside the tax and welfare-state context where it will be implemented. Her chapter argues that the most desirable proposals (especially in the United States) will likely follow the 'targeting with universalism' approach, where a means-tested guaranteed income is adopted alongside other social programmes. Besides claiming that this will probably be the most fiscally sound proposal, Lee argues that those wishing to implement a UBI should be mindful of political feasibility issues, alongside financial ones. The former requires considering how support for UBI tends to be lower in countries with robust safety nets. While we can plausibly speculate that this is also due to the fact that in such countries citizens believe poverty and insecurity are adequately covered, Lee offers another explanation, namely that in such countries citizens might fear that UBI will replace existing programmes.

On How to Read This Volume

This edited volume's two-part structure can feel challenging to navigate, as if two distinct sets of claims, arguments, and proposals are put forth in the seven chapters comprising the book. There are certainly more commonalities found in the chapters within each section; hence, the readers might consider reading each part separately, given their research interests.

However, we also encourage readers to take the findings of the volume together. We believe this can show the lessons, tensions, and limitations that run through the entire volume, while highlighting possible new research pathways.

References

Birnbaum, S. (2012). *Basic income reconsidered: Social justice, liberalism, and the demands of equality*. Palgrave Macmillan.

Langridge, N., Buchs, M., & Howard, N. (2023). An ecological basic income? Examining the ecological credentials of basic income through a review of selected pilot interventions. *Basic Income Studies, 18*(1), 47–87. https://doi.org/10.1515/bis-2021-0044

Merrill, R., Bizarro, S., Marcelo, G., & Pinto, J. (2019). *Rendimento Básico Incondicional: Uma defesa da liberdade*. O Saber da Filosofia.

Noguera, Y., Vanderborght, & De Wispelaere, J. (Eds.). (2013). *Basic income: An anthology of contemporary research* (pp. 297–306). Blackwell.

Pinto, J. (2020). *Green republicanism: Non-domination for an ecologically sustainable planet* (Ph.D.). Universidade do Minho, Braga. https://repositorium.sdum.uminho.pt/handle/1822/76484

Van Parijs, P. (1991). Why surfers should be fed: The liberal case for an unconditional basic income. *Philosophy & Public Affairs, 20*(2), 101–131.

Van Parijs, P. (1995). *Real freedom for all.* Oxford University Press.
Van Parijs, P. (2013). A green case for basic income? In *Basic income: An anthology of contemporary research* (pp. 269–274).
Van Parijs, P., & Vanderborght, Y. (2017). *Basic income: A radical proposal for a free society and a sane economy.* Harvard University Press.
Widerquist, K. (2013). *Independence, propertylessness, and basic income: A theory of freedom as the power to say no.* Palgrave Macmillan.
Widerquist, K. (2017). The cost of basic income: Back-of-the-envelope calculations. *Basic Income Studies, 12*(2). https://doi.org/10.1515/bis-2017-0016
White, S. (2003). *The civic minimum: On the rights and obligations of economic citizenship.* Oxford University Press.
Zelleke, A. (2005). Basic income in the United States: Redefining citizenship in the liberal state. In K. Widerquist, M. A. Lewis, & S. Pressman (Eds.), *The ethics and economics of the basic income guarantee* (pp. 109–121). Ashgate.
Zelleke, A. (2011). Feminist Political Theory and the Argument for an Unconditional Basic Income. *Policy and Politics, 39*(1), 27–42.

PART I

Ecological and Moral Dimensions of Basic Income

CHAPTER 2

The Moral-Ecological Case for Basic Income: Changing Minds and Hearts

James P. Mulvale

Introduction

There are many rationales for why a universal basic income[1] (UBI) is a desirable and feasible policy. They include the reduction or elimination of poverty, economic security for all workers in a precarious labour market,

[1] In this chapter, I am using 'universal basic income' as a term that encompasses both the ***universal demogrant*** model ***and*** the ***basic income guarantee*** model. In the demogrant model, everyone receives a regular (for example, monthly) amount of money from the government that is enough by itself to sustain a modest but adequate standard of living. In the basic income guarantee model, benefits go only to those whose income falls below a threshold of adequacy. Those who are below this threshold (as determined by a simple and non-stigmatizing income test) receive a basic income benefit sufficient to bring them up this amount. Of course a range of details would have to be determined in real world implementation of either approach (e.g. Would a demogrant to those with high income be subject to income tax?

J. P. Mulvale (✉)
University of Manitoba, Winnipeg, MB, Canada
e-mail: james.mulvale@umanitoba.ca

R. Merrill, C. Neves (eds.), *Determining the Value of Universal Basic Income*, Exploring the Basic Income Guarantee,
https://doi.org/10.1007/978-3-032-04004-6_2

lower economic inequality, amelioration of other forms of social inequality (such as those related to gender, racialization, or disability), and augmentation of the freedom of individuals to pursue human flourishing and the good life as they see it. This chapter will focus on another imperative for UBI, one related to the environment. The argument is that UBI is necessary if societies are to achieve a radical social-ecological transition to a steady-state or post-growth economy, especially in highly developed economies prone to overconsumption and a large ecological footprint. Such a fundamental shift is seen as necessary if we are to adequately address the environmental and climate emergency and to achieve a social order that is both ecologically sustainable and socially just.

Implementation of such a radical transition will require winning over both the 'minds' and 'hearts' of average people in society and political leaders. Winning over minds to the moral-ecological case for socio-ecological transition and UBI will involve using practical reason that draws on evidence from research, policy analysis, and first-hand voices of people who have benefited from UBI in pilots and demonstration projects. Winning over hearts to the moral-ecological case for UBI will involve mobilizing people's emotions and moral sensitivities to support and work for UBI as a new paradigm of universal economic security. The latter goal of winning over hearts needs to be inextricably linked to the former goal of winning over minds, if moral-ecological rationales for UBI are to have their maximum impact in real-world political struggles and social movements.

Changing Minds

One fundamental aspect of convincing people about the necessity of UBI and radical socio-ecological transition is the problematization of indiscriminate and open-ended economic growth; such growth is a primary driver of both social inequality and environmental degradation. Drawing on a large and growing body of research and writing on ecological economics, a convincing case for the necessity of ending overall economic growth on our finite planet can be made. Overall degrowth on a global basis is necessary if we are to avert (or at least minimize) the worst effects

How would the income test in the guarantee model ensure prompt and accurate delivery of benefits? etc.) These details are very important but are beyond the scope of this conceptual paper.

of the environmental emergency on our warming planet, including resource depletion, species extinction, pollution of our air, water and soil, and waste proliferation from plastics and other non-biodegradable products of industrial economies.

A founding figure in ecological economics was Herman Daly, who championed the notion of 'steady-state economics' for 'a full world'. Victor (2022, p. 278) summarizes Daly's perspective this way:

> Rich economies ... can and should develop without growing, especially since there were already strong indications that growth had become uneconomic in the sense that the costs of growth were exceeding its benefits. In economies with high income and wealth ... redistribution rather than growth is the answer to poverty. ... [T]he excessive use by advanced economies of the Earth's capacity to support life – human and non-human – [is] depriving those living in poorer countries and future generations everywhere of the opportunity to enjoy a good life based on sufficiency. All countries ... should seek qualitative development, but only poor ones should pursue quantitative economic growth while every effort is made by all to stay within planetary boundaries for resources and ecological systems.

A similar perspective has been advanced by Kate Raworth (2018) using the metaphor of 'doughnut economics'. From this perspective, production and distribution must stay in the ring of the economic doughnut, neither failing to provide what everyone needs (falling into the hole of the doughnut) nor exceeding environmental limits (falling off the doughnut on the outside and exacerbating the environmental emergency).

Some thinkers have gone a step beyond the steady-state ideas of Daly and Raworth and called for degrowth as an antidote to ever-increasing economic expansion in our finite and stressed environment. Hickel (2021) (drawing on Kallis and Latouche) defines degrowth in this way:

> Degrowth is a planned reduction of energy and resource throughput designed to bring the economy back into balance with the living world in a way that reduces inequality and improves human well-being.

In macroeconomic terms, degrowth also means the abandonment of forms of production that threaten the biosphere (e.g. fossil fuel production; indiscriminate resource extraction; industrial agriculture, logging, and other extractive activities in global carbon sinks such as Amazonia; etc.).

Hickel (2021) stresses that degrowth is **not** equivalent to economic recession or the forced lowering of essential consumption of necessary goods, such as good-quality food, adequate and affordable housing, and public goods such as health care, education, and public transportation. Degrowth *does* mean the curtailment of unnecessary and luxury consumption (think gas-guzzling private automobiles, the construction and habitation of monster homes, diets with a lot of beef, dairy, and imported produce, etc.). Such excess consumption is the norm among most of the population of wealthy countries, and also among the wealthy elites of medium- and low-income countries.

In ecological terms, economic degrowth can help to create the conditions for the mitigation of global warming, the curbing of habitat destruction and species extinction, and the abatement of pollution and waste accumulation. In social terms, degrowth—that is linked to more fundamentally just patterns of redistribution of income and wealth within and among nations—can help to create the conditions for slower, more humane, and more sociable patterns of living, in which modest levels of consumption ensure the material needs of all and, at the same time, ensure everyone more discretionary time. More control over our time will enable us to freely allocate energy to the activities that matter most to us—family and friends, leisure, personal development, and socially necessary and useful work both in the paid labour market and in our homes, families, and communities.

Changing Hearts

The evidence drawn from ecological economics outlined above offers a convincing *intellectual* argument based on research evidence and practical reasoning for the absolute necessity of a radical socio-ecological transition that includes UBI.

But intellectual arguments on their own (especially ones for a broad, transformative change like the one under discussion here) are unlikely to capture the public imagination or affect political decision-making. What is needed, additionally, is deep and resilient moral and emotional commitment at both individual and collective levels to bring about change for the better. Such commitment must be shaped and sustained by rational arguments, practical reasoning, and empirical evidence. But this commitment also requires a deep moral commitment rooted in human emotion and relationships with other people (perhaps we should dare to say 'love' in this regard). These moral-emotive ties to others extend to those with whom we are personally close, such as family and friends. But we must also form moral-emotive ties with others in the human communities to which we belong, and with the flora and fauna that share the earth with us.

In fact, this emotional commitment to our fellow creatures and to transformative social-ecological change can be construed as *moral courage*. Such courage is required if we are to confront the 'polycrisis' that we currently face—a rapidly warming planet, gross economic inequalities, hot wars in different parts of the world, and the growing power of authoritarian political figures and movements on the right. In this context, it is more difficult to convince others with purely rational arguments. This is especially true given the growth of epistemological nihilism in our 'post-truth' era, when science, professional journalism, and cultural guideposts for moral and civil treatment of others are flouted and questioned by the forces of reaction and right-wing populism.

* * *

Given the rationale and general line of argument as set out above, the remainder of this chapter is divided into four sections:

i) An outline of evidence for the ecological or 'green' case for UBI.
ii) An overview of general moral arguments made for the implementation of UBI.
iii) A presentation of moral arguments for UBI specifically focused on the ecological imperative (that is, the 'moral-ecological' justification for UBI).
iv) Some strategic and practical ideas on how such a moral-ecological case for UBI and broader social-ecological transition can be advanced with the public and with political leaders.

(i) *The Ecological or 'Green' Case for UBI*

Arguments for UBI grounded in ecological/environmental rationales go back many years. Fitzpatrick (1999, 201) drew on the work of Robertson, Gorz, and Offe to call for a 'Green policy package' that 'should include not only BI but also land and energy taxes, working-time reductions and the expansion of informal exchanges in the third sector'. Goodin (2013, 283–84) posits a 'post-productivist' social welfare regime of 'welfare without work', which stands in sharp contrast with welfare regimes that are—in the classic Esping-Andersen typology—liberal ('work, not welfare'), corporatist/conservative ('welfare *through* work'), or social democratic ('welfare and work'). In this post-productivist political economy, paid work in the labour market would not disappear. However, automation harnessed for social (not profit-seeking) ends, boldly redistributive tax measures, and an adequate and dependable UBI would enable a shorter work week and increased individual autonomy over the use of one's time.

In 2009, the journal *Basic Income Studies* published a themed issue (Vol. 4, No. 2) on 'Basic Income, Sustainability and Post-Productivism'. The editor of this issue, Simon Birnbaum (2009, 2), summarizes a key argument of those who see UBI as a necessary component in a green economy.

> The availability of a universal, work-independent source of basic security and the creating of new forms of meaningful activity and integration beyond the employment contract may remove one of the most important driving forces behind environmentally destructive forms of growth. When we do not need a full-time job to survive and gain social recognition, we no longer need to embrace unsustainable engines of growth in order to achieve full employment at any cost.

In a similar vein, Andersson's (2009, 1) contribution to this special issue makes 'a case on equity grounds for linking a BI to ecological taxes and degrowth in the overconsuming societies, but to use BI as a tool for improving production in poverty struck regions'.

It is important to stress that implementation of UBI will not in and of itself bring about a social-ecological transition to a post-growth, sustainable economy and just society. I have argued elsewhere (Mulvale, 2019) that UBI must be part of a broad set of policy initiatives and shifts that include decommodification of essential human needs such as housing and health care, robust public services, carbon-free public transportation, ecological land use and taxation, and green job creation and labour market policies. The breadth and complexity of such a shift is politically daunting and technically challenging. But as the planet heats up, nature is assaulted, species are extinguished, and millions of people are displaced and impoverished, ways must be found to effectively address the challenge of the climate emergency.

Langridge et al. (2023) made an empirical inquiry into whether or not seven UBI pilots in various parts of the world exhibited characteristics of an 'ecological BI' that would support a post-growth economy focused on meeting fundamental human needs rather than economic growth. As a counterpoint to post-growth, they also looked at pilots considering the 'green growth' model that is often touted as a sufficient response to the environmental crisis (UNEP, 2011; de Mello & Dutz, 2014). Langridge et al. (2023, 79) concluded that 'the pilots they examined align[ed] more with green growth than post-growth positions', that '[e]cological considerations were not and [sic] integral part of the design and operation of these pilots', and that the pilots included 'little analysis of BI's impact on material or ecological footprints'. On a more optimistic note, Langridge et al. (2023, 79) hold out the hope that a UBI paid at 'a level of sufficiency' has the potential to increase human needs satisfaction in a post-growth economic context, along with bringing about 'improvements in economic, social, and gender equality'.

One real-world example of a de facto green basic income has been examined by MacNeill and Drummond (2025). The Bolsa Verde (BV) was delivered in the Brazilian Amazon during the period from 2011 to 2017. It provided a cash payment to very low-income inhabitants of this region to discourage them from engaging in environmentally damaging deforestation activities in their scramble to secure a livelihood. The delivery of the BV piggybacked on the existing much more extensive Bolsa Familia programme (an income-tested basic income for the Brazil's very poor). For this reason, the environmental and poverty alleviation benefits of the BV were somewhat hard to disentangle from each other. Nonetheless, MacNeill and Drummond (2025, 147) conclude that

> there is hope for those who would advocate Basic income as an environmentally beneficial social program. The ... [Bolsa Verde Program] may have been the world's only actually-implemented largescale Green Basic Income project, and ... it was successful in achieving its stated goals of poverty alleviation and reduction of deforestation. As such, it may offer a valuable model not only for ongoing efforts to preserve the Amazonian biome, but in other social contexts as well.

Additionally, MacNeill and Drummond (2025, 141) indicate that the positive outcomes 'were achieved without undermining collective community institutions that could have positive anti-poverty and environmental protection benefits of their own'. Critics of UBI sometimes worry that, as a highly individuated benefit, it will erode community ties and mutuality among recipients. This might be a particular worry in the case of Indigenous peoples on traditional territories earning their livelihoods from the land. At least in this study, such a worry appeared to be unfounded.

(ii) *Moral Arguments for UBI*

There is a wide range of moral arguments for basic income that have been advanced over the last three decades and more. In this section, the focus is on general ('non-ecological') moral arguments for UBI. In the next section, the focus will be on moral arguments related specifically to the *ecological* rationale for UBI.

General moral arguments for UBI that are not explicitly ecological have focused on these challenges:

- The need to alleviate human suffering and exclusion related to living in *poverty*, economic vulnerability, and labour market precarity;
- The imperative to achieve greater economic and social *equality* within societies and on a global basis;
- Increasing human *freedom* to pursue one's goals related to human fulfilment and flourishing; the flip side of this goal is to ensure non-domination of individuals by others, whether such forces of domination are at play within the family, the workplace, the community, or the broader nation-state and its various components.

These three arguments are grounded in moral standards and imperatives that relate to broader conceptions of *justice* as theorized in philosophy, political studies, sociology, and economics. The final bullet point above is also related to libertarian theory (about human freedom) and to feminist, anti-racist, decolonial, and republican political theories (that value non-domination).

Before delving into some of the moral implications for UBI in regard to theories of justice, freedom, and non-domination, it is worthwhile to flag a moral *objection* to UBI that was the focus of much discussion and debate in academic literature and at conferences in the late 1980s and throughout the 1990s. This was the moral objection to alleged 'free riders' in a hypothetical, full-fledged basic income scheme. Non-labour market participants (like the famous 'Malibu surfer' who was assumed to be devoting all of his time and energy to the pursuit of hedonistic pleasure) would have a livelihood at a subsistence level. But the surfer's UBI would be financed by 'hard working' members of society who had to show up at their job every day and pay taxes on their wages or salaries in order to finance UBI. Such a hypothetical scenario could be judged to be fundamentally unfair and immoral in that the carefree surfer is exploiting the strenuous efforts of the hard workers.

These two caricatures (the surfer with zero obligations or cares, and the worker whose primary motivation is the avoidance of economic privation) are simplistic and largely misleading social stereotypes. The motivations and moral decision-making that adhere in real life—to people both in and outside of the paid labour market—are more complicated and multi-layered. Nonetheless, this moral objection is one that merits a response that can morally justify UBI as a new paradigm of universal economic security.

Offe (1992, 65–67) identifies four challenges that, if overcome, can lead to a broad consensus on a 'non-productivist' social policy that is universal, effective, and generous. To attain this goal, he argues that we must

- Overcome the coding of people as us/them based on who they are and what they do.
- Realistically assess the actual availability of resources and life chances for people who struggle or are excluded.
- Be aware oneself of the potential need for help at some point in the future.
- Be cognizant of 'second-order, indirect and long-term collective consequences of social policies' aside from how they might help a particular individual in a specific place and time. They may help us to build a fairer and more just society that benefits everybody.

A policy regime with the above characteristics would reflect a high degree of 'moral universalism'. Reaching such a social consensus is no easy task, and there are many discouraging signs that people and politicians often exhibit attitudes and behaviour that are the antithesis of Offe's desiderata outlined above. But at least in conceptual terms, his framework gives us practical moral guideposts to reframe and navigate apparent social policy dilemmas and conundrums such as that of the surfer/hard worker.

Such a framework can thereby help us move closer to justice and equality as moral and practical goals in social welfare.

In moving beyond responding to objections and thinking about positive moral arguments for UBI, it is instructive to revisit the edited collection by Widerquist and Lewis (2005) on 'The Ethics and Economics of the Basic Income Guarantee'. In the introductory chapter, Lewis et al. (2005) refer to a number of ethical reasons for implementing UBI that are explored in subsequent parts of the book. These reasons include fair sharing of the bounty and resources of the nation among all citizens; the elimination of destitution and poverty; underwriting fair wages and decent working conditions in the labour market; supporting social altruism and cooperation; and enabling individuals to make free choices in regard to their participation in the market economy and their pursuit of a good life as they see it.

Widerquist and Lewis (2005) did not specifically address ecological arguments for UBI, but it did introduce an array of ethical reasons for implementing it. Different contributors to the book also addressed the primary moral objection to UBI as discussed above—the argument that giving people money unconditionally will weaken work incentives and create 'free riders'. It can be added on this question that subsequent research has shown that those who receive some form of basic guaranteed income mostly stay engaged with the labour market (Forget, 2018, 85–91; Widerquist, 2024, 123), and that there may be very good, morally justifiable reasons to exit paid employment for at least periods in one's life course (Forget, 2018, 91–94).

It is not difficult to find ethical arguments for basic income in publications and forums aimed at broad popular audiences. For instance, in the mass circulation magazine *The Atlantic*, Yuan (2018) points out that basic income can address poverty as a violation of human rights. In *Psychology Today*, Thagard (2019) argues that basic income is ethically justified by its contribution to vital human needs. There are also right-of-centre defenders of basic income on moral grounds. From a neoliberal vantage point, Zwolinski (2020) makes a moral case for basic income as a defence of individual liberty and property rights. The Seven Pillars Institute (n.d.) promotes ethical standards and the application of moral principles in the financial services sector and gives basic income at least conditional support. None of these sources specifically reference ecological rationales, but a green case for basic income might be logically inferred from some of their extant arguments.

Another sector making moral arguments in favour of UBI has been faith communities. To use Canadian examples, at least four Protestant churches have come out strongly in favour of UBI. The United Church of Canada has been advocating for basic income (then called 'guaranteed annual income') dating back to 1972 (Mulvale, 2001, p. 104–05). When Canada was in the full grip of the Covid-19 pandemic in May 2020, a joint letter signed by 44 bishops of the Evangelical Lutheran Church in Canada and the Anglican Church of Canada[2] called upon the Prime Minister and the federal government to implement a 'Guaranteed Basic Income' immediately. The signatories said they were 'compelled by our shared faith convictions and moral obligation to care for the human condition of all'. Another denomination that has spoken out for UBI is the Unitarian-Universalist Church. In August 2020 the Canadian Unitarian Council 'issued a statement and a call to action to our members to press the Government of Canada to include a Guaranteed Income program as part of the COVID recovery plan'.[3] The Catholic Church—or at least Pope Francis at the Vatican in his role as moral guide for the entire body of the Catholic faithful—has supported UBI (Pentin, 2021) as part of his broader body of teaching on social justice and 'integral ecology'. Support for UBI among other bishops and Catholic lay organizations has been less evident, although scholars who analyse economic questions through the prism of Catholic Social Teaching have come out in favour of UBI (e.g. Clark, 2002; Ward, 2020).

(iii) *Moral-Ecological Rationales for UBI*

In this section, the focus will be on moral arguments for UBI that can be constructed specifically around the *ecological* rationale for this new paradigm of economic security. To some extent, these moral arguments overlap with or can be drawn from 'non-ecological' moral arguments for UBI as outlined in section (ii) above. Connections can be made in both sets of argument to broader standards of justice, equality, and freedom. But it is also my contention that moral-ecological arguments in support of UBI are underdeveloped. If they were to be more fully articulated and widely promulgated, these arguments could play an important role in winning over

[2] See https://www.anglicanlutheran.ca/statements/a-public-letter-on-guaranteed-basic-income/

[3] See https://cuc.ca/economic-justice/

both minds and hearts to a radical commitment (at both individual and collective levels) to a sustainable economy and a just society that includes UBI.

There are two general sources in what follows for moral-ecological justifications for UBI and broader social-ecological transition. These sources are:

1. Indigenous knowledge and teachings
2. Thinkers and ideas in Western moral philosophy

In the latter category, I will focus on ideas advanced by four thinkers that provide valuable entry points for moral-ecologic justifications for UBI:

- The work of Alasdair MacIntyre as a useful general framework in moral philosophy
- A radical-egalitarian-communitarian case for UBI that is made by Bill Jordan (who posits the environment as an 'indivisible' public good)
- A discussion of reciprocity and UBI advanced by Catarina Neves
- The concept of intergenerational justice as set out by Juliana Uhuru Bidadanure

Moral-Ecological Rationales for UBI Drawing on Indigenous Moral Teachings

One constituency that must play a key role in the transformation to sustainable and just societies are Indigenous peoples. Indigenous philosophies and values honour Mother Earth and all forms of life therein and point the way to ecological justice and sustainable societies (Nelson, 2008; McGregor, 2004; Hart, 2002). But the history of Canada has been steeped in colonization and racism, as first French and then British imperial powers arrived in the north part of Turtle Island. These colonizers appropriated Indigenous land to extract its natural resources and populate it with white settlers, thereby enriching themselves as imperial metropoles. Colonialism persists today in the poverty and economic marginalization of Indigenous peoples in their own homelands, and in the sequelae of Euro-Canadian attempts at cultural erasure such as Indian Residential Schools and the Sixties Scoop in child welfare. Carlson-Manathara and Hiller (2024) emphasize that white people and politicians must fully commit to decolonization, but also that Indigenous peoples must be agents and leaders in environmental struggles over land, resources, and climate change. They point to Indigenous knowledges and Indigenous sovereignty that have 'the potential to shift settler values, thoughts, and ways of being … away from those based on extractivism and greed and towards those based on life and relationship' (p. 53).

So there is a clear and compelling connection between Indigenous knowledges and moral teachings and the preservation and protection of the natural world. When it comes to the specific question of if and how the UBI model of economic security fits with Indigenous worldviews, however, things get more complicated. Indigenous communities have powerful negative experiences over many decades with income support delivered as social assistance by colonialist governments. These programmes were means-tested, stigmatizing, intrusive, and controlling. Social assistance, especially on First Nations reserves and in isolated northern communities, was used to exercise colonialist control and to enforce poverty (Shewell, 2004). So Indigenous people and leaders might be understandably reticent about a new model of income support that is being touted as an improvement on (but also a replacement for) social assistance.

On a more conceptual level, Nixon (2023) points to tensions and consistencies between the UBI concept and an Anishinaabe worldview. UBI (or at least a fulsome version of it) is intended to advance individual autonomy and freedom and to be neutral about different (and possibly conflicting) conceptions of 'the good life' across a diverse population. On the other hand, Anishinaabe teachings stress relationality among humans and with other species, ethical codes focused on the welfare of the entire community and Mother Earth, and a conception of the good life grounded in spiritual beliefs and practices.

Nixon (2023) points to this conceptual dissonance, but also recognizes the potential benefits of a UBI model as a practical tool in facilitating Indigenous cultural and economic resurgence. Nixon sees the potential for UBI to 'reduce the prevalence of arbitrary domination within Canadian society, and increase the relative economic and political power of Indigenous folks' (p. 135). She also sees UBI as a support that will 'promote the wellbeing of Indigenous communities [through] the revitalization of rooted worldviews, legalities, and law' (p. 136).

A provision in Treaties is financial compensation to Indigenous peoples for sharing their land with European traders and settlers. In many of the historical Treaties this compensation took the form of Annuities paid to individual members and leaders of First Nations who entered into Treaty relationships with the Crown. For instance, in the case of Treaty 4 on the Canadian prairies an Annuity of $5 per person per year is paid by the Crown to every member of the Nations who are Treaty signatories (the Chief and Headmen were paid larger amounts, $25 and $15 per year respectively). These Treaty Annuities were not insignificant amounts of money at the time of Treaty signing, but these payments have never been adjusted in the intervening 150 years. This failure by the Crown to increase annuity amounts is being challenged legally in different parts of Canada. For instance, the 33 Nations who are signatories to Treaty 4 have launched a class-action lawsuit against the federal government to correct this injustice (D'Souza Butts, 2024). The 21 Nations who were signatories to the Robinson Huron Treaty in Ontario in 1850 launched a similar lawsuit in 2014. After nine years of litigation and negotiation the First Nations in the Robinson Huron Treaty were awarded $10 billion as a collective annuity in light of increasing resource revenues for the governments of Ontario and Canada since the signing of the Treaty (Canada, 2023). A Winnipeg-based group called Modernized Annuities Working Group[4] has developed a general template for how Indigenous Nations and the Crown can restructure Annuity payments in ways that correct historical injustices and reflect twenty-first-century economic circumstances.

Given the above developments in refashioning Indigenous-Crown Treaties in Canada, positive scenarios can be envisaged in which Indigenous peoples have the practical means to choose to pursue livelihoods that align more closely with their spiritual and moral teachings on environmental stewardship. On the collective level, Indigenous Nations could say no to resource extraction proposals from the corporate sector that would harm the land and the humans and other species who live on it; alternatively, they could chart their own course for community economic development based on respect for Mother Earth and caring for everyone in the community. On the individual and family level, Indigenous people would have support (in the form of a dependable regular cash benefit) that would underwrite their ability to gain at least part of their livelihood on the land through traditional and sustainable practices.

[4] See https://www.mawg.ca/

Moral-Ecological Rationales for UBI Drawing on Western Moral Philosophy

Phronesis[5] *(Alasdair MacIntyre)*

Alasdair MacIntyre (1984) is a moral philosopher who made a conversation-shifting contribution to this field with the publication of *After Virtue* in 1981. His conception of morality develops and enhances Aristotle's classical work on ethics. MacIntyre sees moral systems not as abstract, timeless and universal, but as being rooted in a given polis (political community) and in the particular historical, cultural, and social context that gives rise to an extant moral code, with all of its nuances, variations, and contradictions. MacIntyre emphasizes the potential for human beings to apply *phronesis* (practical reason) to reach just and ethical decisions. He also recognizes that this reasoning process takes place in our complicated and messy world in which conflicting rational claims and diverse and egocentric emotional drives may occlude our moral decision-making.

MacIntyre (as far as I know) did not pronounce on UBI as a specific mechanism to achieve universal economic security for all. But according to Clayton (n.d.) MacIntyre prefers a society in which there are 'only small inequalities of income and wealth, to prevent people from being excluded from the community by their poverty or placing themselves above it on account of their great wealth'. Clayton (n.d.) also points to MacIntyre's contention that capitalism—with its emphasis on individualism, acquisitiveness, and 'free' market mechanisms—can undermine the valuing of community and the common good. Clayton (n.d.) quotes MacIntyre directly in this regard:

> Market relationships can only be sustained by being embedded in certain types of local nonmarket relationship, relationships of uncalculated giving and receiving, if they are to contribute to overall flourishing ....

[5] *The Oxford Companion to Philosophy* defines phronesis as: 'Practical wisdom. In ancient Greek the term ... has connotations of intelligence and soundness of judgement, especially in practical contexts. In Aristotle's ethics it is the complete excellence of the practical intellect, the counterpart of sophia in the theoretical sphere, comprising a true conception of the good life and the deliberative excellence necessary to realize that conception in practice via choice.'

MacIntyre is widely credited with reviving interest in Aristotelian 'virtue ethics' in recent decades. Applying this approach in economics, Clayton contends that

> Markets must be subordinated to the development of the virtues in individuals and the community, rather than the other way around, which is what happens in the world in which we now live.

Thus it would seem that MacIntyre's moral vision for the economy is consonant with assumptions that underlie UBI, and in particular the 'radical-egalitarian-communitarian' rationale for UBI offered by Bill Jordan as discussed below. Extrapolating from MacIntyre's approach, one can discern a set of ethical guideposts that could serve as a moral-ecological justification for UBI:

- We derive our moral meaning and standards from those with whom we are connected and from our culture and history.
- This morality must include justice for all of the earth's human inhabitants and non-human species, which depend on the ecological health of the biosphere for their survival and flourishing.
- We can and must recover ecological ethics from our moral history—frugality, mutual aid, biological efficiency (as opposed to 'efficiency' understood as maximization of output).
- Aristotelian/MacIntyrean virtues (such as courage, justice, moderation) must guide our personal and professional practices if we are to actualize such ecological ethics; being in such an ethical place will improve our chances of effectively addressing the environmental emergency through public policy and behaviour change at the individual and collective levels.

Thus, it can be argued that practical rationality (*phronesis*) is absolutely required, if we are to discern ethical choices and develop smart public policy to ensure planetary ecological health. This enactment of practical rationality—guided by a clear moral compass and strong emotional commitment to the welfare of others—is particularly important in our current 'post-truth' era. We need a broad and strong commitment to *phronesis* to counteract the delegitimization of natural and social sciences and the epistemological nihilism promoted by right-wing authoritarian leaders and social media machines promoting 'alternative truth' and conspiracy theories.

The resonance of MacIntyre's general moral vision with the perspective of faith communities on UBI (as discussed in section (ii) above) can be noted. MacIntyre is considered to be not only an Aristotelian but also a Thomist, in that his thought is influenced by the philosophical and theological work of Thomas Aquinas (who himself was heavily influenced by Aristotle). Faith-based moral arguments for UBI are directly linked to virtues such as compassion for others and a thirst for justice that are also grounded in practical rationality. Such virtues come into play, as discussed above, when certain faith communities advocate for UBI as an imperative based on justice for and compassion towards fellow human beings. Many of these same faiths advocate for protection and care of the environment, although it must be noted that they tend to address economic justice and ecological stewardship in separate pronouncements and documents.[6]

Radical Egalitarian Communitarianism (Bill Jordan)

Bill Jordan (1992) makes an intriguing moral argument for UBI using what could be called a radical-egalitarian-communitarian framework. He is aligned with the broader theoretical and moral commitments to justice, equality, and freedom that underlie the UBI model, but also emphasizes the importance of community and the common good. Specifically, he focuses on the ecology as an indivisible and vital common good, and he sees the common good in general as more important than individual autonomy.

Jordan's perspective was a departure from prevailing debates about UBI in the late 1980s and early 1990s that focused a great deal of attention on the autonomy and freedom of the Malibu surfer. Jordan does not ignore the need for fairness in the labour market (while also seeing jobs as

[6] A notable exception in this regard is the encyclical of Pope Francis, *Laudato Si'*. Francis links the need for ecological action directly to the general imperative for economic justice in Sec. 25: 'Climate change is a global problem with grave implications: environmental, social, economic, political and for the distribution of goods. It represents one of the principal challenges facing humanity in our day. Its worst impact will probably be felt by developing countries in coming decades. Many of the poor live in areas particularly affected by phenomena related to warming, and their means of subsistence are largely dependent on natural reserves and ecosystemic services such as agriculture, fishing and forestry. They have no other financial activities or resources which can enable them to adapt to climate change or to face natural disasters, and their access to social services and protection is very limited.'

'assets' that are held by many but not all potential labour market participants). But he balances a concern for justice in the marketplace with the moral imperative for fairness and inclusion in community life and the collective sharing and enjoyment of common goods. A radical-egalitarian-communitarianism that includes a UBI can, in this view, illuminate a moral path to balancing individual liberty and equality on one hand with protecting the health of the ecology as an indivisible common good on the other hand.

Reciprocity (Catarina Neves)
The ethical imperatives of reciprocity (exchanging forms of assistance and positive social regard between individuals in relationship with one another) is an idea with much relevance to UBI. In moral terms, some early objections to UBI (as discussed in section (ii) above) were that it lacked reciprocity— 'free riders' who shirk work can still receive a UBI financed by employed individuals who pay taxes.

Catarina Neves (2024) takes a more nuanced view and offers an analysis on how UBI can *encourage* what she calls 'positive' reciprocity. This can occur in three ways. First of all, UBI can in fact facilitate labour market participation by enabling people to manage and afford household costs related to paid employment, such as childcare expenses, necessary clothing and equipment for a job, and transportation to the workplace. Secondly, UBI means that individuals can gain control over their time and make judicious decisions 'not only in terms of their "mix" of activities i.e. paid employment, care work, community work, leisure, but also their life projects' (p. 128). Thirdly, the unconditional and non-stigmatizing nature of UBI counters the 'negative-reciprocity attitudes' that adhere to existing means-tested social assistance programmes, and 'enables citizens to be reciprocators through employment, but also by caring for their relatives or friends, engaging in the community, and participating in political processes' (p. 129).

Intergenerational Justice (Juliana Uhuru Bidadanure)
Another useful concept when making an ecological-moral case for basic income is that of intergenerational justice. Bidadanure (2013) argues that UBI is an essential component of intergenerational justice, especially as a corrective to precarity in the labour market that affects young people disproportionately compared to older people. The same intergenerational justice lens can be applied to other aspects of economic security (e.g.

housing affordability) *and* to the existential question of ensuring a habitable and healthy environment for subsequent generations. It is up to those currently living—especially older people who occupy the commanding heights of economic and political decision-making—to minimize environmental damages and ensure a sustainable economy for those who are coming after them. (It should be noted that the imperative of intergenerational climate justice aligns with the Indigenous teaching of looking after the welfare of the next seven generations, part of Indigenous philosophy as discussed above.)

As components of intergenerational justice, Bidadanure (2021) supports UBI, job guarantees, social benefits tailored to youth, and guaranteed participation of young people in political decision-making. Pushing her argument a bit, her call for UBI could underpin other bold measures (such as decommodification of housing) to achieve a sustainable, post-growth economy for younger people and subsequent generations.

(iv) ***Strategies Moving Forward***

In this final section, I will discuss some possible approaches and strategies for winning over public opinion and mobilizing political leaders to advance social-ecological transition, which includes UBI as one necessary component.

One important arena in which minds and hearts must be won over is that of electoral politics. Since the late 1970s Green parties in various countries have shifted the political discourse in ways that have raised popular consciousness of the environment. In terms of electoral success, Greens have not gone beyond being minority partners in government coalitions in certain countries in Western Europe. But Green parties have played an important role in raising awareness of and support for UBI (Van Parijs & Vanderborght, 2017, pp. 200-01).

It is a reasonable assumption that voters' concerns about the ecological health of the planet will continue and grow in the years ahead, particularly among young people, as they are the people who will be inhabiting the planet and voting in elections for the longest period of time to come. With support from newer voters and young people who will soon be voting, Green politicians (in concert with their fellow travellers in other parties) could be in a position to advance a radical agenda for a sustainable economy and guaranteed economic support for all. As limits to growth are reached and exceeded on our finite planet, transformative green policy initiatives may gain traction, with redistribution of wealth seen as the preferable alternative to unending economic growth and 'survival of the fittest' in the marketplace.

Green parties have helped to make possible political conversations about the need for social-ecological transition to post-growth supported by UBI. But what about social democrats? I have argued elsewhere (Mulvale, 2024) that social democratic parties must commit to UBI and post-growth economic justice if they are to remain politically relevant in the twenty-first century. This new vision for the democratic left must embrace a new and expanded understanding of 'social reproduction'—how we support everyone in society and especially the vulnerable, how we nurture the next generation, and what we must do to restore and safeguard the continuing health of the planet.

Social democrats have had a longstanding focus on gender equality issues in the labour market, including access to employment for women, pay and employment equity, and publicly funded childcare. In fact, the democratic left has scored significant victories on these issues. But now it is time to reformulate our understanding of employment and the production/social reproduction nexus based on ecological sustainability, economic justice, and full political participation for people of all classes, genders and sexual identities, and family forms. Kathi Weeks (2020) provides some helpful theoretical and programmatic guideposts in this regard. A reimagined vision of employment and production/social reproduction could provoke new conversations on the democratic left on questions such as job sharing, work-time reduction, convivial activities that reshape families and communities, and productive activity outside the capitalist labour market. UBI would be a necessary component to enable and support all these innovative aspects of social reproduction carried out in a just and sustainable manner.

Such a renewed social democratic vision of security, equality, and sustainability may be our last best hope of countering the rise over the last several years of right-wing authoritarianism. This threatening movement with a global reach promulgates white supremacy, xenophobia, and market fundamentalism and ignores environmental destruction and the climate crisis. As a countervailing movement, reimagined social democracy focused on social *and* climate justice could capture the public imagination in ways that earlier social democrats did at points in time during the twentieth century. The democratic left could map out a radical new vision of universal economic security for everyone that includes preserving the planet for the good of all. Such bold thinking and action are required, if we are to take an effective stand against the authoritarian right's anthropocentrism and mobilization of anxiety about economic insecurity to amass power for itself. A new left agenda for ecological action and economic justice has the potential to counter the drift towards climate catastrophe and social fascism. Such a progressive agenda could counter the right-authoritarian suppression of critical thinking and social dissent and the accelerating oppression of women, people who are racialized, newcomers, 2SLGBTQIA+ individuals and communities, and others who are marginalized based on some other aspect of their personal identity.

A daunting strategic question is how to advance public support for UBI and a social-ecological transition in this current highly polarized political climate that is rife with toxic disinformation and attacks on critical thinking and fact-based journalism. There is no easy answer here. But a constructive suggestion has been made by environmental journalist Mitchell Beer (2024). He notes a worrying trend that '[s]upport for climate action is slipping as affordability issues seize public attention and populist politicians pounce'. As a constructive response, Beer (2024) recommends carefully constructed community dialogue as a means to expand both understanding and action on environmental and ecological justice. He makes this observation:

> When people get a chance to meet informally, confront the climate emergency and the affordable crisis in the same conversation, and compare notes on how the two issues intersect to harm their communities and their lives, mutual trust grows and polarization… depolarizes. Often, those conversations produce some very smart thinking on what a local response to climate change, affordability, and a list of other intersecting issues would look like.

Profound social-ecological transformation must be based on 'big ideas' such as the ones discussed in this chapter. But convincing and motivating individuals and groups to support bold moves towards ecological and economic security in a post-growth society will also require marrying big ideas to stories of the real-life experiences of people—in this case, those who have participated in UBI pilots or similar programmes providing relatively unconditional cash transfers.

There has been voluminous evidence collected from and about these participants in UBI pilot studies and demonstration projects (e.g. Basic Income Canada Network, 2019; Forget, 2011; Marinescu, 2017; Gibson et al., 2018). The consistent findings across these studies are that UBI recipients have benefited not just by escaping the travails of living in poverty. They have also enjoyed improved physical and mental health, better nutrition, greater housing stability, more discretion over their use of time, and more choice about how to engage in paid and unpaid work. Such specific outcomes in personal and family life improve overall quality of life and can pave the way to greener choices in activities and patterns of consumption. With basic economic security guaranteed, human fulfilment can be about personal self-determination, more fulfilling family and social relationships, and a sense of accomplishment in attaining our goals. Such a way of life can provide an attractive alternative to scrambling in a precarious labour market to earn (often not enough) money to consume (often unnecessary) goods and services that promise but do not deliver human fulfilment, and that also leave an outsized ecological footprint.

Various ideas and perspectives that could ground moral-ecological choices have been examined in this chapter—Indigenous worldviews, a strong commitment to the common good, a broad understanding of human reciprocity, giving people control over their time and daily lives, the clarion call of intergenerational justice, rethinking social reproduction and how we support it, and direct and evocative evidence from those with lived experience of how UBI can improve lives. All of these can be starting points in strengthening our messaging about social-ecological transition and UBI to both broad public audiences and political decision-makers.

For broad public audiences, these messages must be expressed in non-specialized and emotionally resonate language that speaks directly and powerfully to people's sense of 'doing the right thing'. For politicians and public officials, heavy stress will need to be placed on evidence, but we should still assume that political decision-makers possess 'moral good will' and want to make the right ethical choices based on convincing evidence. A shorthand way to think about a general messaging strategy might run something like this: in messaging for the broader public our arguments should consist of 20% evidence and 80% moral suasion; and in messaging politicians and government officials our arguments should consist of 80% evidence and 20% moral suasion,

Both the basic income movement and the environmental movement have advanced their causes with vigour and effect for several decades. We are currently confronting a global polycrisis—gross economic inequality, ecological devastation, hot wars in different parts of the world, and the decline of democratic freedoms. It is imperative that these environmentalists and UBI advocates engage in dialogue and joint effort to achieve both universal economic security and a social-ecological transition. If we do not make progress in this regard, our future is not guaranteed, given the limited (and highly stressed) carrying capacity of our planet.

It has been argued here that progress towards the overarching and mutually reinforcing goals of ecological sustainability and economic justice can best be achieved through practical rationality to connect the ***mind*** (informed by evidence from natural and social sciences) and the ***heart*** (using compelling moral arguments that motivate action). It is time to undertake this challenge with the knowledge and tools at our disposal.

References

Basic Income Canada Network. (2019). *Signposts to success: Report of a BICN survey of Ontario basic income recipients.* BICN. https://basicincomecanada.org/wp-content/uploads/2021/04/BICN-Signposts-to-Success.pdf

Beer, M. (2024, June 2). With polarization running wild, let's restart the climate conversation from the ground up. When we address them hand in hand, the two problems can help solve each other. *The Energy Mix.* https://open.substack.com/pub/energymixweekender/p/with-polarization-running-wild-lets?r=1rxmtd&utm_campaign=post&utm_medium=web

Bidadanure, J. (2013). The precariat, intergenerational justice and universal basic income. *Global Discourse, 3*(3–4), 554–560. https://doi.org/10.1080/23269995.2014.898531

Bidadanure, J. (2021). *Justice across ages: Treating young and old as equals.* Oxford University Press.

Canada. (2023, June 17). *Robinson Huron Treaty Leadership, Ontario and Canada announce proposed settlement and next steps in Treaty annuities court case.* https://www.canada.ca/en/crown-indigenous-relations-northern-affairs/news/2023/06/robinson-huron-treaty-leadership-ontario-and-canada-announce-proposed-settlement-and-next-steps-in-treaty-annuities-court-case.html

Carlson-Manathara, L., & Hiller, C. (2024). Indigenous sovereignty is climate action: Centring indigenous lands and jurisdiction in social work education towards climate justice. In S. Hillock (Ed.), *Greening social work education* (pp. 45–64). University of Toronto Press.

Clark, C. M. A. (2002). *The basic income guarantee: Ensuring progress and prosperity in the 21st century.* Liffey Press in association with CORI Justice Commission.

Clayton, T. (n.d.). Political philosophy of Alasdair MacIntyre. In *Internet Encyclopedia of Philosophy.* https://iep.utm.edu/p-macint/

D'Souza Butts, S. (2024, Feb. 13). Treaty 4 takes legal action against feds for annuity payments. *CTV News Regina.* https://regina.ctvnews.ca/treaty-4-takes-legal-action-against-feds-for-annuity-payments-1.6767781

de Mello, L., & Dutz, M. A. (2014). *Promoting inclusive growth. Challenges and policies.* OECD and the World Bank.

Fitzpatrick, T. (with Campling, J.). (1999). *Freedom and security: An introduction to the basic income debate.* St.Martin's Press.

Forget, E. L. (2011). The town with no poverty: The health effects of a Canadian guaranteed annual income field experiment. *Canadian Public Policy, 37*, 3.

Forget, E. (2018). *Basic income for Canadians: The key to a healthier, happier, more secure life for all.* James Lorimer & Co.

Gibson, M., Hearty, W., & Craig. P. (2018). *Universal basic income: A scoping review of evidence on impacts and study characteristics.* What Works Scotland. [LINK].

Goodin, R. E. (2013) [2001]. A post-productivist welfare regime. In K. Widerquist, J. A. Noguera, Y. Vanderborght, & J. De Wispelaere (Eds.), *Basic income: An anthology of contemporary research* (pp. 283–88). Wiley Blackwell.

Hart, M. A. (2002). *Seeking Mino-Pimatisiwin: An aboriginal approach to helping.* Fernwood Publishing.

Hickel, J. (2021). What does degrowth mean? A few points of clarification. *Globalizations, 18*(7), 1105–1111. https://doi.org/10.1080/14747731.2020.1812222

Jordan, B. (1992). Basic income and the common good. In P. Van Parijs (Ed.), *Arguing for basic income: Ethical foundations for a radical reform* (pp. 155–177). Verso.

Langridge, N., Buchs, M., & Howard, N. (2023). An ecological basic income? Examining the ecological credentials of basic income through a review of selected pilot interventions. *Basic Income Studies, 18*(1), 47–87. https://doi.org/10.1515/bis-2021-0044

Lewis, M. A., Pressman, S., & Widerquist, K. (2005). An introduction to the basic income guarantee. In K. Widerquist, S. Pressman, & M. A. Lewis (Eds.), *The ethics and economics of the basic income guarantee* (pp. 1–10). Routledge.

MacIntyre, A. (1984). *After virtue: A study in moral theory* (2nd ed.). University on Notre Dame Press.

MacNeill, T. & Drummond, C. (2025). Green Basic Income: Evaluating the Bolsa Verde Project in the Brazilian Amazon. *Basic Income Studies, 20*(1), 125–149. https://doi-org.uml.idm.oclc.org/10.1515/bis-2023-0031

Marinescu, I. (2017). *No strings attached: The behavioral effects of U.S. unconditional cash transfer programs.* Roosevelt Institute.

McGregor, D. (2004). Traditional ecological knowledge and sustainable development: Towards coexistance. In M. Blaser, H. A. Feit, & G. McRae (Eds.), *In the way of development: Indigenous peoples, life projects and globalization* (pp. 72–91). International Development Research Centre.

Mulvale, J. P. (2001). *Reimagining Social Welfare: Beyond the Keynesian Welfare State*. University of Toronto Press.

Mulvale, J. P. (2019). Social-ecological transformation and the necessity of universal basic income. *Social Alternatives, 38*(2), 39–46.

Mulvale, J. (2024, Spring). Basic income for a new model of Canadian social democracy. *Perspectives* (1). Broadbent Institute.

Nelson, M. K. (Ed.). (2008). *Original instructions: Indigenous teachings for a sustainable future*. Bear & Company.

Neves, C. (2024). How unconditional basic income encourages reciprocity. *Análise Social, 59*(250), 110–132. https://doi.org/10.31447/2021127

Nixon, S. (2023). Basic income and Anishinaabe worldview: Exploring tensions and compatibilities. *Basic Income Studies, 18*(1), 123–136. https://doi.org/10.1515/bis-2021-0042

Offe, C. (1992). A non-productivist design for social policies. In P. Van Parijs (Ed.), *Arguing for basic income: Ethical foundations for a radical reform* (pp. 61–78). Verso.

Pentin, E. (2021, February 17). *Is Pope Francis sympathetic to the universal basic income concept?* National Catholic Register.

Raworth, K. (2018). *Doughnut economics: Seven ways to think like a 21st-century economist*. Chelsea Green Publishing Company.

Seven Pillars Institute. (n.d.). *Universal Basic Income Series*. https://sevenpillarsinstitute.org/ethics-of-universal-basic-income/

Shewell, H. (2004). Enough to keep them alive. In *Indian welfare in Canada, 1873–1965*. University of Toronto Press.

Thagard, P. (2019, March 26). The ethics of basic income. Psychology Today Canada . Retrieved June 8, 2024,from https://www.psychologytoday.com/ca/blog/hot-thought/201903/the-ethics-basic-income.

UN Environment Programme (UNEP). (2011). *Towards a green economy. Pathways to sustainable development and poverty eradication*. UNEP.

Van Parijs, P., & Vanderborght, Y. (2017). *Basic income: A radical proposal for a free society and a sane economy*. Harvard University Press.

Victor, P. A. (2022). *Herman Daly's economics for a full world: His life and ideas*. Routledge.

Ward, K. (2020). Universal basic income and work in Catholic social thought. *American Journal of Economics and Sociology, 79*(4), 1271–1306. https://doi.org/10.1111/ajes.12353

Weeks, K. (2020). Anti/Postwork feminist politics and a case for basic income. TripleC: Communication, capitalism & critique. *Open Access Journal for a Global Sustainable Information Society*, 575–594. https://doi.org/10.31269/triplec.v18i2.1174

Widerquist, K. (2024). *Universal basic income*. MIT Press.
Widerquist, K., & Lewis, M. (2005). *The ethics and economics of the basic income guarantee*. Routledge.
Yuan, K. (2018, August 22). A moral case for giving people money: "Poverty is a human-rights issue." *The Atlantic*. https://www.theatlantic.com/membership/archive/2018/08/a-moral-case-for-giving-people-money/568207/
Zwolinski, M. (2020, July/August). A moral case for universal basic income; a neoliberal argument for UBI based on individual freedom and property rights. *The Critic*. https://thecritic.co.uk/issues/july-august-2020/money-for-nothing-2/

CHAPTER 3

The Environmental Value of Unconditional Basic Income Policies

Thiago Monteiro de Souza

Introduction[1]

The following years will be decisive for humankind regarding environmental issues. The climate crisis is already bringing about severe consequences, endangering lives all over the world. The biggest challenge of the present human society is mitigating and overcoming our "actually existing unsustainability" (Barry, 2012, p. 259). This context, therefore, urges for a thorough political, social, and academic debate.

The Unconditional Basic Income proposal (hereinafter UBI) has been the subject of social, political, and economic discussions for hundreds of years, and this article considers UBI a viable policy to face the

[1] List of figures: 1—Pillars of the framework (page 12); 2—Framework built for application (page 15); 3—Result of the framework application (page 28). List of Tables: 1—Comparative Analysis of Alaska and Maricá Across Six Pillars (page 27).

T. M. de Souza (✉)
University of Minho, Braga, Portugal

R. Merrill, C. Neves (eds.), *Determining the Value of Universal Basic Income*, Exploring the Basic Income Guarantee,
https://doi.org/10.1007/978-3-032-04004-6_3

environmental crisis, as discussed throughout the literature review. This study follows the concept of UBI given by Van Parijs (2004, p. 8), who defines it as "an income paid by a political community to all its members on an individual and periodic basis without means test or work requirement".

There are ongoing UBI pilots and policies around the world nowadays.[2] Many of them are temporary tests that aim to analyse the potential impacts of the Basic Income, but there are a few long-lasting policies. For their longevity and stability, two of the most prominent examples that are brought up here are the Alaska Permanent Fund and the Citizen Basic Income of Maricá in Rio de Janeiro, Brazil.

The central objective of this research is to analyse how these two Basic Income policies impact the green transitional perspective according to Dobson's (2007) concepts of environmentalism and ecologism. In other words, the aim is to understand the main environmental effects, either positive or negative, of the selected UBI policies. By means of such debate, the article intends to defend, via empirical analysis, that the Unconditional Basic Income can be a strong policy in the current reality of environmental urgency, possibly stimulating both environmental and ecological paths of transition.

To achieve this objective, the paper is divided into three sections. Firstly, the article approaches the green transitional perspectives of the UBI (Block, 1990; Offe, 1992; Merrill et al., 2019; Standing, 2020; Pinto, 2020). The effects of UBI on productivism[3] and sustainable development are critical in the present debate. This research argues that Basic Income can enhance labour conditions, foster a just green economic transition,[4] foment less pollutant and circular economies, and provide citizens with socioeconomic dignity. Under this context, the article also reflects on degrowth and post-productivism horizons as viable alternatives to face the current environmental emergency.

[2] Finland, the Netherlands, and Spain have received experiments that are often analysed in the UBI literature but are not perfect UBI examples since they are means-tested, being closer to the Negative Income Tax (Merrill et al., 2022).

[3] The meaning of *productivism* adopted is the one according to which work (especially paid work) is a central pillar of society, and full employment is a political goal (Widerquist et al., 2013, p. 260).

[4] *Just green transitioning* means a series of measures that ensure greening the economy in a way that is as fair and inclusive as possible to everyone concerned, creating decent work opportunities and leaving no one behind (ILO, 2015).

The following section then focuses on devising a framework through which the selected UBI policies will be viewed and discussed. The literature inspires and supports the formulation of this framework and thus brings up desirable policy effects in the environmental and ecological spectra, both based on Dobson's definition of environmentalism and ecologism.[5] The first classification refers to a "managerial approach to environmental problems, secure in the belief that they can be solved without fundamental changes in present values or patterns of production and consumption"; the latter is connected to "radical changes in our relationship with the non-human natural world, and our mode of social and political life" (Merrill et al., 2019, p. 229).

The framework consists of six pillars, namely: (i) the form of funding of the UBI, (ii) the policy rationale (i.e., the governmental objectives that guided the policy's implementation), (iii) the impact on the productivist perspective (work and consumerism) at the individual and collective levels, (iv) other public policies that accompanied the UBI with a more green transitional-oriented focus, (v) the concern for economic freedom and democratic inclusion combined with other public policies, (vi) the circular-regionalist focus. All these pillars will demonstrate whether the UBI policies under analysis are environmental, ecological, or none of them, meaning that they do not have a green transitional tendency.

Subsequently, each UBI policy (Alaska and Maricá) will be addressed separately in light of this framework. In this segment, empirical research focused on these two policies is brought up (e.g., Widerquist & Howard, 2012; Jones & Marinescu, 2018; Waltenberg & Katz, 2023). The analysed cases show environmental alignment according to Dobson's (2007) concept of environmentalism, since both of them are policies that adapt their developing economy toward a more sustainable path and do not propose to be revolutionary in terms of human-nature relations. Nevertheless, in comparison to Alaska, Maricá's case is a more robust Basic Income policy from the framework's perspective.

Such analysis, therefore, proposes to apply philosophical normative thoughts of the literature to the selected empirical cases, which is carried

[5] Another classification that could be used in the present article is the one offered by Neumayer (2013) of weak and strong sustainability. However, since the literature that addresses the green perspectives of a UBI policy (namely Merrill et al., 2019; Pinto, 2020) is based on Dobson's definitions of ecologism and environmentalism, the present research opted for these terms to formulate the analytical prism.

out by means of the suggested framework. That is, the normative theoretical foundation and the framework will enable the connection of theory and empirical data to better understand the UBI cases' ecological/environmental value. By doing that, this article aims to stimulate the debate towards solutions that may help society face some of the most urgent current world problems, namely environmental ones.

2. UBI as an Environmental or Ecological Policy

This section is designed for normative debates that will serve as the foundation for the central analysis of this work. Namely, the main topics discussed here are Green Republicanism[6] and Productivism and how they both relate to the Basic Income theory and environmental urgency. These two topics were chosen for their fundamental roles in the philosophical, economic, and social discussions that orbit the green transition debate, as it is recognized through the literature that addresses green perspectives of UBI (e.g., Merrill et al., 2019; Pinto, 2020; Langridge, 2024). First, the relevance of post-productivist[7] and degrowth agendas is addressed. The degrowth debate adds depth to post-productivism by highlighting the limitations of both agendas in addressing the environmental crisis. These limitations support the idea of a reformational or environmental basic income, which could create opportunities for a certain level of green growth within the context of the global green transition. Afterward, Green Republican theories are also discussed, and their importance is justified. These two debates pave the way for the literature defending a Green UBI. The degrowth discussion also connects to the dichotomic relation between productivism and Green Republicanism.

Originally, the main idea of the UBI was to address socioeconomic and political-philosophical issues concerning inequality and redistribution (Widerquist et al., 2013). Recently, it has become the subject of ecological

[6] *Green Republicanism* refers to Republican perspectives that encompass environmental worries and advocate for a sustainable society. Pinto (2020) defines the term as post-productivist and non-neutral concerning the common good.

[7] *Post-productivism* refers to societal efforts that move beyond the traditional emphasis on productivity. It suggests that work, especially paid employment, should no longer be a central focus of society. Consequently, the goal of achieving full employment is seen as both unattainable and undesirable (Widerquist et al., 2013, p. 260). *Non-productivist* activities include occupations that are not measured by their contribution to the country's GDP, such as caregiving or volunteer work.

debates on the urgency of the green transition (Pinto, 2020). Nevertheless, the association between Environmentalism and Basic Income is complex. In order for the Basic Income proposal to promote both environmental sustainability and economic security, authors argue for a post-productivist approach (e.g., Van Parijs, 2013; Merrill et al., 2019; Pinto, 2020). Still, it is pivotal to better understand the meanings surrounding post-productivism and Basic Income, which serve as the foundation for analysing the selected UBI policies (see section Setting and Analytical Framwork).

At first glance, Basic Income can be easily associated with an increase in consumer power through which citizens can achieve socioeconomic security; consequently, UBI might increase deforestation and pollution. However, the way labour and consumerism function within society is likely to be profoundly transformed because of structural changes produced by a UBI policy (Merrill et al., 2019). As a result, the productivist manner around which economies currently organize themselves could also be transformed. Concretely, the higher the value of the Basic Income is, the more powerful it can be toward a post-productivist path, since it allows people to spend less time working and more time performing non-productivist activities. As Standing (2020) explains, implementing a UBI would give new value to several taken-for-granted activities, such as caregiving. It would also allow people to turn down undervalued jobs and focus on long-term careers that are not economically feasible today. This panorama shift brought about by a UBI can profoundly transform the economy and mainstream consumerism, since it allows long-term plans via economic security. Thus, it is an opportunity to value many non-productivist activities and stimulate individual/small entrepreneurs, enabling a degrowth agenda.

Still, UBI will most likely not be self-sufficient to foster such non-productivist activities, requiring a broader framework of policies that stimulate such a transition in the labour-economic structure (Pinto, 2020).

The degrowth agenda focuses on abandoning the idea of constant productivist growth as synonymous with economic success. As D'Alisa et al. (2014) put it, the concept of degrowth is justified on three fundamental pillars: (i) growth is unfair and unequal in terms of the distribution of benefits; (ii) growth is ecologically unsustainable; and (iii) growth will never be enough. Besides, the authors suggest that individual and institutional interactions would be fundamentally transformed through a degrowth agenda. Work and consumption will undergo significant changes, promoting a stronger sense of ecological sustainability in human societies.

Nevertheless, Pinto (2020) is uncertain about the feasibility and promise of degrowth policies in the struggle against climate change and recognizes the need for greater empirical evidence. Authors such as Giljum et al. (2014) and Nørgård and Xue (2016) are sceptical that the present society can achieve significant GDP-decoupling growth to prevent climate disasters. Degrowth can be accepted as an agenda but should not be considered the salvation of society against global warming (Pinto, 2020). Degrowth policies are indeed favourable, but short-term measures are indispensable, such as Basic Income, green taxation, and green growth policies. As a matter of fact, degrowth policies are much more feasible in the short term for the Global North than for the Global South due to the transnational concentration of capital. It is not enough to push for degrowth and green transitional agendas while not advocating for a redistribution of wealth, both from the national and transnational perspectives.

In this sense, it is unreasonable to separate the green transition and environmental sustainability debate from that on global socioeconomic inequality (Souza, 2024a). A green economy, coupled with policies that address poverty and inequality at both national and international levels, is essential. A UBI can help society move in both directions: green transitioning and overcoming poverty/inequality.

If degrowth is accepted as a plausible long-term agenda, short- and mid-term actions are pivotal in the struggle against global warming. A Basic Income, alongside other policies, can foster green growth and then gradually stimulate society to post-productivist and degrowth paths, decentralizing paid labour and enabling non-productivist activities.

As for the labour aspects of Basic Income theory, philosophers argue that the UBI offers transformative horizons. Offe (1992) defends the idea that the Basic Income proposal reduces pressures for full employment and productivism. According to the author, UBI's post-productivist tendency opens the possibility for public policies that can align more with environmental and sustainable agendas. In line with Offe, Block (1990) recognizes the possibility created by the UBI for beneficiaries to invest in their ventures, which can even strengthen causes such as feminism and environmentalism, since people would have greater capacity (and time) to engage in political activism.

The advent of a UBI would also intensely stimulate automation. Unworthy job positions, or “Bullshit Jobs”, as Graeber (2018) puts it,[8] would considerably decrease if people no longer needed to submit themselves to precarious working conditions. Due to the Basic Income, employees would have much greater autonomy to negotiate with their employers, which in turn would improve labour conditions. This conjuncture, allied with technological advances, can pave the way for a less exploitative labour market.

Despite its potential, there is no guarantee that recipients of a UBI would behave in a more environmentally friendly way. This uncertainty is one reason why many environmentalists and ecologists are sceptical about a green Basic Income policy. While UBI alone cannot be immediately deemed as a green transitional policy, it does have several meeting points with both environmentalists and ecologists (Van Parijs, 2013). A crucial factor in determining whether a UBI policy can be considered green is the context in which it is implemented, including aspects such as the level of financial support provided, other public policies introduced alongside it, and the funding mechanisms used.

Imagining a post-productivist approach to UBI poses potential funding challenges. If this approach indeed encourages individuals to step away from the productivist sphere, it could lead to economic scarcity, making it difficult to fund UBI and other public policies. While this concern may seem logical, it contradicts post-productivist and degrowth goals. In a scenario where mass consumption is no longer prioritized, this “scarcity” issue would not be a significant problem. Suppose society achieves high levels of socioeconomic welfare funded via strong progressive taxation and maintains a sustainable relationship with natural ecosystems. In that case, there may be a decreasing need for expensive public policies aimed at socioeconomic and environmental justice. Even though such views might seem utopic, they are part of post-productivist and degrowth agendas.

In a similar vein, a society that produces less to meet its needs might not require an ever-increasing UBI payment and could even potentially cease the need for a UBI altogether if the principles of Dobson’s ecologism are realized. Although this discussion is speculative, it hints at future debates on the path of a green transition. What is particularly intriguing is

[8] Graeber (2018) points out five categories of meaningless jobs: flunkies (e.g., receptionists), goons (e.g., lobbyists), duct tapers (e.g., programmers that repair minor tech issues), box tickers (e.g., survey administrators), and taskmasters (e.g., leadership professionals).

the possibility that a genuinely ecological (degrowth and post-productivist) Basic Income could lead to a reality where UBI is no longer necessary, positioning it as a transitional policy.

When compared to the traditional Welfare State (Esping-Andersen, 1990), UBI presents alternative methods for addressing inequality and socioeconomic exclusion by providing individuals with the freedom to determine their own needs. In many situations, allowing people to decide how to spend their money is more effective. Moreover, a UBI does not prevent essential public services from being provided by the state. Instead, it represents a reform of the means-tested social assistance programmes of the traditional Welfare State rather than its dismantlement. Still, implementing a basic income policy would require either new tax revenues or the reallocation of existing public funds.

Alternatively, the UBI can also present a green growth alignment. Some research results indicate that implementing a Basic Income can successfully elevate employment rates (cf. Section 3). A UBI can take different paths depending on the conditions that surround its application. From an environmental standpoint, such a productivist UBI should be accompanied by a series of green growth policies, alleviating negative effects such as pollution and deforestation. This so-called environmental basic income (Dobson, 2007) promotes sustainable development, distancing itself from the ecological one, which is aligned with degrowth and post-productivism. Advocates of environmentalism argue that green growth models are a better way to address both economic and environmental injustice agendas (Souza, 2024a).

Another critical aspect of UBI is the means through which it will be funded. A potent strategy to address ecologically harmful consumption is through taxation (Boyce, 2016). Increasing tariffs on fossil fuels can effectively finance social and environmental policies, discourage unsustainable consumption, and stimulate the use of green alternative fuels (Casal, 2012). However, relying on this form of funding may pose challenges if the long-term goal is to eliminate carbon consumption entirely. Thus, while this taxation can be a temporary solution during the transition to a greener society, it highlights a tension between short-term and long-term funding strategies.

Another relevant point of the UBI is its capacity to stimulate localism and circular economies. Regionalist commerce tends to rise significantly by giving small entrepreneurs economic security and enabling them to implement long-term plans (Merrill et al., 2019). This localist perspective, combined with the possibility of several non-paid activities, has significant environmental consequences for sustainability, since circular economies tend to be more sustainable from an environmental perspective (Standing, 2020), demanding less resource consumption through the supply chain.[9]

In discussing localist and circular economies, it is important to consider their ecological implications. Short supply chains can help create a stronger connection between individuals and the surrounding environment. As Naess (1985) points out, one of the major environmental challenges humanity faces is its disconnection from nature and the "ecological Self". This disconnection has been worsened by the rise of globalized supply chains, which further deepen the connection gap identified by Naess.

While it cannot be claimed that simply regionalizing economies and supply chains will solve these issues, nor that globalization is inherently problematic, fostering smaller supply chains and promoting regional justice can be effective strategies. These approaches can help address regional inequality, mitigate the impact of unsustainable supply chains, and reconnect human society with natural ecosystems.

The theoretical discussion concerning Green Republicanism is also relevant in the present debate because it is one of the normative foundations for a green UBI (Pinto, 2020). The concept of Republicanism is not necessarily associated with environmentalism. Admitting that republican ideals and debates must encompass the ecological dimension, Audier (2015) was one of the first authors to address republicanism from an environmental perspective. However, these assumptions are accompanied by the necessity to review a series of republican concepts, especially those concerning individual freedom and its limits.

In recent years, republican theorists have been advocating for a third understanding of freedom as non-domination. As Philipp Pettit (1997) points out, this republican understanding of freedom advocates that a subject is free to the extent that, in the relevant set of nearby possible worlds, no one can arbitrarily interfere with one's actions. In this sense, only an understanding of freedom as non-domination would comprehend such non-arbitrarily interference.

[9] As there is a tendency for localist and circular economies to be less environmentally harmful, this is not an absolute truth, meaning that there are cases in which short supply chains are profoundly pollutant (Kiss et al., 2019).

Nevertheless, Pettit acknowledges the insufficiency of his conception of freedom due to the need for environmental sustainability.[10] The philosopher connects this type of Republican freedom to environmentalism by stating that any assault on the environment should be considered an attack on the human undominated choice and, thus, a constraint on Republican freedom as non-domination (Pettit, 1997, p. 137). In other words, Pettit's undominated freedom relies on a sustainable environment.

On the other hand, some thinkers believe that Pettit's approach (1997, 2012), encompassing sustainability as a republican necessity, is not enough to tackle the existing climate and environmental crisis. Cannavó (2016), for example, argues that more structural and fundamental changes are needed in society and that republicanism falls short of ecological concerns. Audier (2015) considers the productivist-ecologist dichotomy by defending the idea that republican thinking needs to distance itself from productivism and the exploitation of nature. Hence, freedom as non-domination would not only be extended to individuals but also to nature and non-human actors, putting an end to the exploitation of nature to benefit humans and solidifying flora and fauna as democratic actors with fundamental rights. Both those authors (Cannavó, 2016; Audier, 2015) partially agree with Pettit (1997, 2012) but delve deeper into the understanding of nature as a republican actor entitled to non-domination freedom and reassert the interdependency between humans and nature.

One of the main causes of environmental and socioeconomic oppression is the human tendency to accumulate natural resources (Bookchin, 1990). The solution to this problem is to reform human society into one that interacts with nature in a more circular way. This alternative reality aligns with the concept of freedom as non-domination (Pettit, 2012). A circular relationship between humans and non-human actors would involve constant interaction and mutual flourishing. This circularity argument emphasizes the importance of mutual interference within human society and between humans and non-human actors without allowing for domination. The crucial point is to recognize the interdependence of humans with each other and with the environment around them.

[10] This republican critique of arbitrariness is thoroughly debated by Fremaux (2018), who raises a discussion that concerns economic liberalism and market democracies. This is a topic that needs to be addressed, and that bears clear relation to the present article. However, as far as the republican debate is concerned, this article, due to its scope, focuses on demonstrating that the Liberal Republican line of thought is not enough to satisfy freedom as non-domination, which consequently leads to Green Republicanism.

Concomitantly, globalized productivism has led society in recent decades to a deep aggravation of inequality and unsustainable consumption (Fremaux, 2018). This goes against green Republican ideals and represents an attack on human freedom and environmental actors. The increase in inequality and unsustainable consumption also undermines democratic practice since it restricts individual and communitarian citizenship (Gourevitch, 2015). White (2008) points out that limiting leisure and activities outside the productivist sphere weakens democratic and republican practices.

Van Parijs (2013) addresses these Republican challenges by advocating for a post-productivist system that emphasizes leisure and communitarian activities. In this alternative conjuncture, roles that entail communitarian value to society—such as certain types of volunteer work—would be more viable than in the current productivist framework. According to the author, it is essential to break away from the existing paradigm of interconnected production, consumerism, and economic growth.

Therefore, both radical changes in human consumer habits and a post-productivist agenda are necessary in order to reach a fair (Green) Republican relationship between humankind and nature. Pinto (2020) defines Green Republicanism as post-productivist and non-neutral concerning the common good, aiming to promote conviviality and an ecologically sound sense of sustainability (Dobson, 2007). Still, as new forms of public services, social contributions, and taxation schemes are needed, reforms in welfare state regimes are indispensable to reach such objectives. In this sense, a basic income policy can act strongly in accordance with this green republican orientation.

As for a more practical debate, there is no guarantee that a Basic Income will live up to Green Republicanism and post-productivist ideals. A UBI can align with two different approaches when considering a green Basic Income: the environmental and the ecological. Both are based on Dobson's (2007) definitions of *environmentalism* and *ecologism*.

An *environmental* BI focuses on adjusting society to achieve a more sustainable economy. As it turns out, no profound changes affect the social structures. In practical terms, this *environmental* path means, for instance, green growth agendas that encourage reliance on renewable fuel. This type of BI is one of many policies that help adjust society so that humanity does not run out of natural resources. An ecological BI would fundamentally depart from capitalism by moving towards a non-growth or even degrowth economy, profoundly transforming the relationship between humankind and nature. This is the model that aims at the decrease in consumerism and productivist labour.

Merrill et al. (2019) generally consider existing UBI policies to be environmental ones. The authors do not perceive any radical changes in the economy or in human society's relationship with nature. Nevertheless, the possibility that such an alternative could be influenced by a set of coordinated policies that stimulate a more radical (ecological) sense of sustainability should be considered.[11]

Having sketched some of UBI's features that can justify it as ecological or environmental, I will now propose a framework to analyse the empirical UBI cases (see Empirical Case Analysis).

3. Setting an Analytical Framework

Considering the selected UBI policies (Alaska and Maricá), this section describes the framework, consisting of six different lenses demonstrating how each policy performs from the environmental/ecological perspective. These lenses are listed as follows: (i) the form of funding of the UBI, (ii) the policy's rationale (i.e., the objectives that guided the government in implementing the Basic Income), (iii) the impact on the productivist perspective (work and consumerism) at the individual and collective levels, (iv) other public policies that accompanied the UBI with a more green-oriented focus, (v) the concern for economic freedom and democratic inclusion (republicanism) combined with other public policies, (vi) the circular-regionalist focus. All these lenses will demonstrate whether the UBI policies under analysis are environmental, ecological, or none of them, meaning that they do not have a green transitional tendency. Each of these pillars is based on the first section (Fig. 3.1).

Firstly, one central aspect of the UBI regarding green transition is how it will be funded. A powerful way to tackle ecologically irresponsible consumption is through taxation (Casal, 2012; Boyce, 2016; Merrill et al., 2019). However, this type of taxation would only be a temporary solution to a green-transitional society. In other words, it is plausible to defend taxation on polluting fuels to fund public policies in the short term, but it is not a long-term solution. To be long-term and ecological, a Basic Income policy needs to be financed independently from fuel taxation or

[11] These policies can encompass fields like education, housing, transportation, consumerism, and health, to name a few, decommodifying key areas of society.

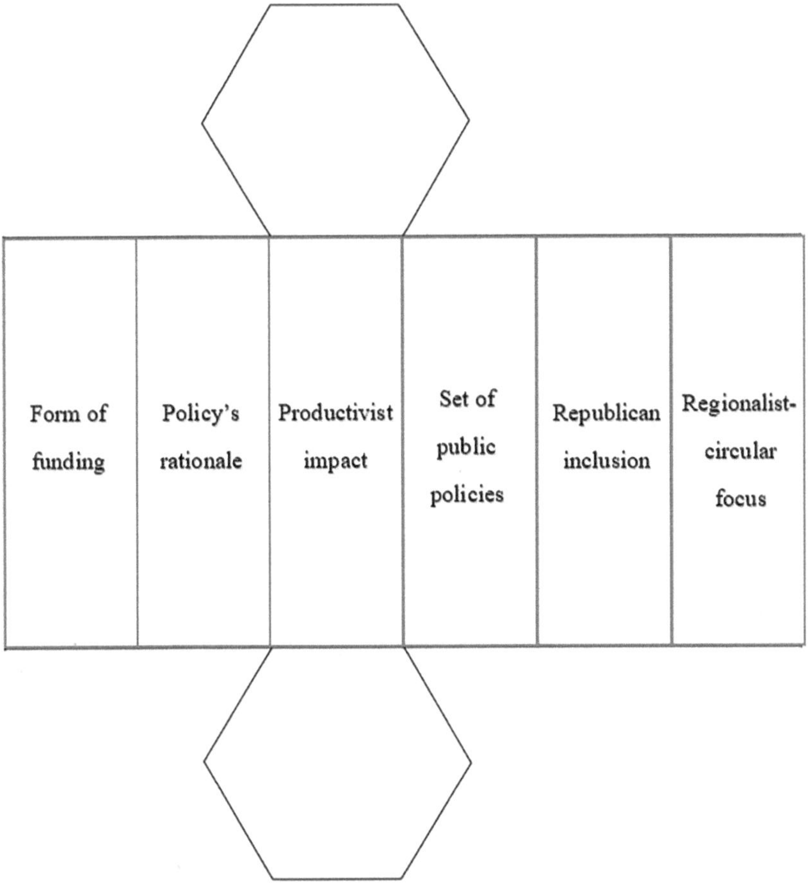

Fig. 3.1 Pillars of the framework (The prism's metaphor consists of the pillars (each one relating to one point of analysis) forming together an object through which beams of light (representing each of the policies in Fig. 3.2) will pass, thus aligning with the environmental or ecological spectra)

planned to gain independence from fuel taxes in the future (Souza, 2024b), which sheds light on the **first** pillar of the framework: **the funding of the UBI**.

As for the second aspect under analysis, it is crucial to mention that the rationale behind the UBI implementation must be considered, since it is a policy subjected to political spectrum shifts (Purdy & Van Trier, 1988), which may or may not be part of a green agenda. Therefore, the main objective of this analytical aspect is to discuss to what extent the government should be held accountable for the effects of the implemented policy/policies. This justifies the **second** pillar of the framework: **the BI policy rationale** (i.e., the objectives that guided the government in implementing the Basic Income).

The implementation of Basic Income can potentially increase consumer power, leading to greater socioeconomic security for citizens. However, this may also increase deforestation and pollution (cf. section 2). With the environmental impact of economic globalization and the correlation between consumption and pollution in mind (Meadows et al., 1972), it is clear that a UBI policy can have significant effects on labour and consumption (Merrill et al., 2019). Consequently, the current productivist approach to organizing economies could undergo transformation. A UBI can thus act in convergence with degrowth and post-productivist agendas or a green-growth-oriented one, which relates to the **third** pillar of the framework: **the impact on the growth and productivist perspective (work and consumption) at the individual and collective levels**.

When examining the impact of UBI, it is essential to consider how it is connected to other public policies. The effects of UBI can be enhanced by complementary policies that work in tandem with it. Although UBI is a robust policy, it cannot solve all problems on its own. Therefore, when it comes to issues like socioeconomic justice and green transition, it is vital to have a set of public policies that can work symbiotically with UBI to achieve a more equitable and sustainable society. This leads up to the **fourth** pillar of the framework: policy aggregation (**other public policies that accompany the UBI with a more ecological or environmental orientation**).

From a green republican perspective (Pinto, 2020), building up a healthy and balanced society is vital to guarantee that all citizens have individual freedom (and non-humans as well). In the green republican view[12], *freedom* needs to imply non-domination and encourage human and ecological flourishing (Souza, 2024a). Accordingly, it is indispensable that all individuals are provided with basic needs to participate more equally in a democratic society, fostering non-dominative relations among citizens while giving margin for republican interference between them. As it turns out, mechanisms that allow popular participation in politics, such as assemblies and social services (Pinto, 2020), are also necessary, and the state could build such republican mechanisms via a set of policies that include a UBI. This interfaces with the **fifth** pillar of the framework (**the concern for economic freedom and republican inclusion**) and also relates to the fourth aspect by supporting the State as a propulsor of Green Republicanism toward degrowth and post-productivism.

Moreover, stimulating localism and circular economies is also relevant to the UBI. Localist commerce will rise significantly by conceding small entrepreneurs economic security and enabling them to implement long-term plans (Merrill et al., 2019). This localist perspective, combined with the possibility of several non-paid activities (Standing, 2020), has significant environmental consequences for sustainability (cf. section 1). In addition, promoting socioeconomic justice also strengthens the economies of poorer communities. This can be a robust measure to oppose regionalist/global inequalities but not necessarily a viable path for sustainable development, which links to the **sixth** pillar of the framework: **the circular-regionalist focus**.

Finally, the framework's application will tell us **whether each UBI policy under analysis is *environmental* or *ecological*.** As the environmental UBI proposes adaptations of human society to a sustainable reality, the ecological kind advocates for more profound transformations. It is pivotal to remark that this classification will be used in a spectral form, which means that each analysed policy may be deemed closer to an *ecological* UBI than others, even if they are classified as *environmental*, for example.

After explaining each aspect of the analytical framework, the present article applies each analytical pillar to the selected UBI policies (Fig. 3.2).

[12] The Green Republican perspective (Pinto, 2020) is the one adopted in the present article.

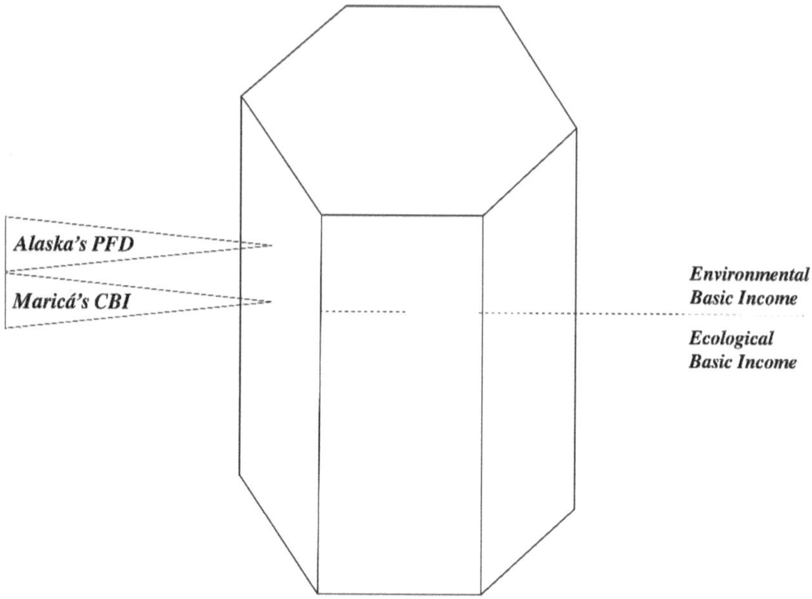

Fig. 3.2 Framework built for application (As stated in Fig. 3.1 (cf. footnote 6), the prism poses as an object through which the beams of light (the policies in question) cross. After this prism application, each beam of light (policy) falls onto the ecological or environmental spectrum)

4. Empirical Case Analysis

Firstly, it is important to justify the Basic Income policies selected for the present analysis. The choices of Alaska and Maricá were made due to the following aspects: they are (i) unconditional,[13] (ii) public-funded and state-organized, and aim to be (iii) long-lasting. Other policies/pilots were not considered for not being public-funded (as the GiveDirectly programme), for being limited temporary tests (as the ones in Finland, Berlin, and Barcelona), or for being recently implemented (as the one in Gyeonggi, South Korea), which would hinder long-term result analysis.

[13] In the case of Maricá, there are some conditionalities regarding how the money is spent, especially in the fact that the currency can only be spent in the municipality's limits. Besides, the beneficiary needs to be enrolled in the government's social register to be eligible. In this sense, Maricá's government treats the CBI as unconditional and non-universal, understanding that there are no conditionalities for the beneficiaries, but only a part of the population is encompassed by the programme.

Still, considering Van Parijs' (2004, p. 8) definition of Unconditional Basic Income[14], it is vital to point out the limitations of each UBI policy under analysis. One significant limitation of both Alaska and Maricá cases is that the payments cannot cover all the recipients' basic expenses.[15] Even though this limitation goes beyond Van Parijs' definition, it is a commonly accepted characteristic of the UBI throughout the literature (Torry, 2019). Besides, Alaska's payment is not a stable income; the transfer is influenced by the economic context, which also goes against the concept of the UBI. Besides these two reservations, Alaska's policy satisfies other essential pillars of a Basic Income, namely unconditionality, periodicity (on a yearly basis), universality, individuality, and cash payment.

In the Maricá case, the policy has other limitations. Even though the payment is not conditioned on any obligations from the recipients, nearly half of the municipality's population is eligible for the Basic Income, as the beneficiaries need to be enrolled in a social registry. Therefore, it is not a universal basic income. It is also insufficient to cover an individual's expenses. Nevertheless, it is a monthly payment in cash (a digital currency that only circulates in Maricá) that does not decrease. It is paid to individuals by the city hall, without conditionalities, and regardless of the beneficiary's work situation.

4.1. Alaska's Case

The first case under analysis is the most famous UBI example: the Alaska Permanent Fund (APF hereinafter). Though it is not considered a Basic Income policy for some authors (Goldsmith, 2012, pp. 49–50), it is a permanent, unconditional, and universal cash transfer with several meeting points with the UBI theory (Merrill et al., 2022).

From the discovery of oil reserves in 1967 in Alaska, the local government voted in 1976 to distribute a portion of the new revenues to a public investment fund called the Alaska Permanent Fund. A few years later, in 1982, an annual payment of a part of the fund revenue, called the Permanent Fund Dividend (PFD hereinafter), was instituted and given to each Alaska citizen. The payment amount is constantly changing; if the

[14] "An income a political community pays to all its members individually and periodically without means test or work requirement" (Van Parijs, 2004, p. 8).

[15] In terms of comparison, Alaska's PFD for the year 2023 ($1,312.00) represents 1.8% of the state's GDP per capita in the same year. In the case of Maricá, the transfer for the year 2023 (13 installments of 200 Mumbucas) represents 1.2% of the city's GDP per capita in the same year.

annual revenue of oil extraction rises, the payment also rises. The transfer in 2022 amounted to $3,284 to each individual.

This scheme, called the Alaska model, is defined by three fundamental elements; "(1) resource-based revenue, (2) which is put into an SWF or some other permanent endowment, (3) the returns of which are distributed as a cash payment to all citizens or all residents" (Widerquist & Howard, 2012, p. 4).

Moving onto the framework application, the **first pillar** refers to the funding of the Basic Income policy. The Alaska Permanent Fund and the Permanent Fund Dividend are based on petroleum exploitation (Widerquist & Howard, 2012). A part of the UBI literature defends carbon fuel taxation to fund Basic Income schemes (see Merrill et al., 2019; Howard et al., 2019). However, in order for consumption taxation to support a more sustainable path for society, carbon fuel taxation must aim to discourage the use and exploration of such fuels. In the case of Alaska, there is no such ecological-oriented taxation.

Alaska's dependence on oil revenues to fund the cash transfer policy does not drive the city toward a more sustainable reality (environmental BI), nor does it enable a profound transformation of the relationship between the local population and nature (ecological BI). The dependence on petroleum extraction indicates an even more severe exploitation of non-sustainable resources.

Moving onto the **second pillar** of the proposed framework, which regards Alaska's government rationale, there is a more complex conjuncture than that brought up in the first pillar:

> For Hammond and the small group of Alaska legislators, aides, and ordinary citizens who worked with him when he was governor to achieve a resource-based investment dividend, the shared core idea was neither charity, nor leveling, nor an attempt to build an income floor. <u>Their shared commitment was to the notion of collective ownership and the fundamental fairness of sharing the returns in equal proportion to their equal ownership</u>. (Erickson & Groh, 2012, pp. 26) (emphasis mine)

The government's fundamental concern was to share the revenues from petroleum exploitation among Alaska's population. This represents an effort to avoid an increase in socioeconomic inequality levels (Goldsmith, 2012). Such logic also relates to the Basic Income case of Maricá, in which the government aimed to democratize the rich revenues from fossil fuel exploitation (Dektar et al., 2020). In fact, an increase in inequality due to petroleum exploitation is commonly seen in countries with large oil reserves.

Besides, as far as the Alaska government is concerned, the BI literature highlights no ecological or environmental concern in introducing the PFD (Widerquist & Howard, 2012). Once again, the concerns and objectives were fundamentally socioeconomic and thus implied granting a fair share of oil profits and consumer power to citizens so they could achieve a better quality of life.

Regarding productivism and labour effects, the third pillar of the analytical framework, the PFD, did not bring about a decrease in employment rates (Jones & Marinescu, 2018). As a matter of fact, the authors suggest that, due to macroeconomic effects, employment rates were pushed up by the PFD. The logic of such a consequence is explained by the increased consumption of Alaska's population, especially among low earners, which in turn increases labour demand and employment (Gilbert et al., 2019). However, this effect on labour is not deemed significant, although there is a small positive effect of the PFD regarding the working hours of part-time workers (Jones & Marinescu, 2018).

Such outcomes suggest that there was an economic impact on the security of Alaska citizens. The increase in consumption indicates more access to essential goods and financial freedom. From the productivist perspective, the scenario brought up by the PFD represents an accentuation of productivism. The PFD had no post-productivist tendency when it came to increasing labour and consumption. The bet made by the government was on the productivist path as the solution to poverty and inequality in Alaska, which means social dignity via consumption power. Laboural effects resulted from such a scenario and hence reinforced productivist tendencies in Alaska. In this sense, the PFD can be deemed as a promoter of productivism.

Regarding the **fourth pillar** (other public policies that accompanied the PFD), the literature points out that the "Alaska model" is a product of the combination of (i) resource tax, (ii) fund, and (iii) dividend. The embryo of the PFD—a policy that bears close resemblance to a Basic Income—was the creation of the Alaska Permanent Fund and the agreement that a portion of the oil revenues would be destined for the Fund. Those political decisions were the pillars of the periodic payment to citizens.

On the other hand, the Alaska government did not create a set of policies to act symbiotically with the PFD. Such fact will heavily influence an analysis of the PFD, as pointed out by Casassas and De Wispelaere (2012, p. 178): "An economic floor really only promotes republican freedom in conjunction with a wider set of social policies, including in-kind benefits such as access to health care and education, family policies, regulations pertaining to pension provision, employment directives, and so on."

The inexistence of other policies imposes limitations on the PFD's effects in Alaska. It affects several perspectives, including the (Green) Republican, which is precisely the central element of the **fifth pillar** of the framework: how the Basic Income affects republican ideals, such as economic freedom and democratic inclusion.

Casassas and De Wispelaere (2012) thoroughly address the Republican perspectives on the Alaska PFD. The authors praise the "economic floor" that the PFD brings about and through which citizens gain purchasing power and improve living conditions. Both academics use the Rawlsian basic liberties perspective to distinguish the "economic floor" and the "worth of the economic floor", according to which only a broad set of policies can guarantee that the economic floor will be protective of the citizens' basic needs.

Considering the liberal welfare regime in Alaska, each beneficiary will be impacted differently by the PFD transfer. If the dividend is transferred in a "protective policy context", the republican freedom is strongly enhanced. Any fetishism that proposes a high/expansive dividend as the sole public policy is not a guarantor of republican freedom. It is vital to have a wide range of state policies that work alongside the Basic Income to build true republican freedom and even to empower the dividend amount. Alaska's PFD does not function that way, as the authors propose. Besides, the republican perspectives are strongly limited due to the apolitical culture of individual entitlement and the lack of democratic practice (or control) regarding the PFD (Casassas & De Wispelaere, 2012).

Moving onto the **sixth analytical pillar** of the framework, we approach regionalism and circular economies in Alaska. Despite the non-existence of extensive literature on the specific debate on regionalism and circular economies in the PFD context, one of the main effects of this policy was the strengthening of small and individual entrepreneurs. Such an effect creates new jobs and stimulates cash transfers within the city limits. Nevertheless, there is no control over the money transferred by the PFD or where it will be spent. The only rule is that the dividend is paid to Alaska citizens; it says nothing about where the beneficiaries will spend it. In this sense, the literature (Erickson & Groh, 2012) suggests that Alaska has strengthened its regional economy; however, it cannot be said that a circular economy has been stimulated.

Applying the framework shows that the APF was a policy with little connection to environmental goals. In this sense, we get to the following points: (i) Even though it is funded by oil extraction, the APF does not discourage oil consumption, and the policy is heavily dependent on this resource exploration; (ii) the prime objective of the government was to share royalties in land exploitation, without an ecological/environmental agenda behind it; (iii) there has been a significant effect on individual consumption, but labour and productivist perspectives were not significantly affected by the dividend; (iv) there is no set of public policies that accompanied the PFD to enhance the possible effects of the policy; (v) Republican freedom was not significantly affected either, though it is viable to suggest that, with greater consumption power, there was an increase in individual liberties; (vi) Alaska's economy was strengthened by the PFD, with the stimulation of small and individual entrepreneurs, but it is not possible to say that it strengthened a circular and less pollutant economy.

Thus, regarding whether the policy is *environmental* or *ecological*, the present article deems the PFD to be a weak basic environmental **income policy**. The only environmentally positive points were enhancing individual freedom, sharing common resources, and strengthening the regional economy. However, even in those three aspects, there was no significant environmental impact. The policy did not aim to have such an outcome, which justifies the classification as a **weak environmental basic income policy**.

4.2. Maricá Case

The second case of analysis is the Basic Income policy implemented in Maricá, a municipality located in Rio de Janeiro State, Brazil. At the beginning of the twenty-first century, Maricá was one of the many cities in Rio and Brazil that suffered from inequality, poverty, and lack of public services (Souza, 2022).

The former mayor, Washington Quaquá, implemented the Citizen Basic Income in Maricá in 2013. From the profits of the oil reserves discovered on the city shore, Quaquá and his successor (Fabiano Horta) could implement a whole range of public services and increase the city's welfare protection.

Before the implementation of the Basic Income programme, the first act of the city hall was to pass Law 2.448 of 2013, creating the Municipal Programme of Solidary Economy, Fight Against Poverty, and Economic and Social Development of Maricá.[16] This programme was the foundation of all social policies that would emerge in the city in the following years. It is fundamental to comprehend the city's Basic Income as a part of this set of public policies. Shortly afterward, the *Mumbuca* bank was created to centralize the financing of the programme and issue the digital currency (also called *Mumbuca*) through which the payment would be made. This currency equals the value of the official Brazilian counterpart, the Real (BRL), but it is only accepted within Maricá city limits.

In December 2013, the first payment of 85 *Mumbucas* was made to 14,000 households. In order to be eligible for the benefit, the families needed to be enrolled in the "Brazilian Unified Register"[17] of social assistance; that is, the household needed to earn up to three minimum wages as their total monthly income. Additionally, the beneficiaries needed to be residents of Maricá for at least three years (Souza, 2022).

The *Mumbuca* payment was gradually enhanced. In 2019, it eventually became a payment made to individuals, no longer households, covering a quarter (25%) of the city's estimated population. Three years later, in 2022, the transfer amount reached M$ 200 (two hundred *Mumbucas*). By 2024, the transfer is planned to reach 230 Mumbucas and will cover almost half of the city's population.

Besides the *Mumbuca* payment, the former mayor, Washington Quaqua, and his successor, Fabiano Horta, introduced the following benefits: (i) scholarships and savings accounts for public school students; (ii) financial support for studies in private higher education institutions; (iii) free public transport system within the city limits; (iv) a basic income of 300 *Mumbucas* per month for Indigenous residents; (v) "Feiras Livres Solidárias" (loosely translated as Free Solidary Fairs) and "Hortas Comunitárias" (loosely translated as Communal Vegetable Garden); (vi) the *Mumbuca Futuro* Programme for students;[18] (vii) the construction of

[16] Loosely translated from "Programa Municipal de Economia Solidária, Combate à Pobreza e Desenvolvimento Econômico e Social de Maricá".

[17] The Unified Register of the Federal Government is a database that contains information on Brazilian social policies, including the list of the beneficiaries (see https://www.gov.br/cidadania/pt-br/acoes-e-programas/cadastro-unico).

[18] The *Mumbuca Futuro* is directed at young students enrolled in public schools so that they can learn and develop critical thinking with regard to financing and labor and engage in socioeconomic debates. The students that take part in the programme have to attend a series of extra classes in order to qualify for an extra benefit of 50 *Mumbucas*. In the event that they

an Industrial Park and a university campus (Dektar et al., 2020); (viii) carbon credit schemes that foster the reduction of carbon fuel emissions.

Analysing the Maricá Citizen's Basic Income (hereinafter CBI) policy under the scope of the proposed framework, it is possible to point out complex findings. The **first pillar** refers to the funding of the Basic Income policy. The development of the CBI was enabled by the exploration of oil reserves on the city shore (Waltenberg & Katz, 2023). Maricá would not have been able to implement such a wide range of public services without the oil royalties. Other municipalities in the state of Rio de Janeiro aim to implement a basic income similar to Maricá. However, this process is significantly more challenging due to the lack of resources.

In 2017, the government of Maricá created a sovereign wealth fund inspired by the Alaska Permanent Fund, which aims to perpetuate all the social policies created over the last years. The city hall promoted such a move, hoping to make Basic Income and other public policies independent from oil funding in the long term. However, this is still a possibility for the future, as the CBI's funding mechanism does not discourage oil consumption and does not demonstrate environmental or ecological alignment.

As for the **second pillar** of the framework, the local government's rationale, it is possible to find the guiding principles of the city hall in the law that instituted the Basic Income and other public policies from the Solidary Economy Programme. Law 2.448[19] of 2013 created the *Municipal Programme of Solidary Economy, Fight Against Poverty and Economic and Social Development of Maricá*.[20] This law serves as the legal foundation for the public programme that created the city's Basic Income and other public policies.

Article 12 of the law lists the guiding objectives for the municipality's policy:

> Section II - Objectives - Art. 12: The Municipal Public Policy on Solidary Economy has the following objectives: (i) provide access to the generation of work and income from the perspective of Solidary Economy; (ii) contrib-

are approved during the school year, they get an additional 1.200 *Mumbucas*, so they can also learn how to manage their money.

[19] Available on: https://www.marica.rj.gov.br/wp-content/uploads/2013/07/jom-383.pdf

[20] Loosely translated from "Programa Municipal de Economia Solidária, Combate à Pobreza e Desenvolvimento Econômico e Social de Maricá".

ute to the improvement of the quality of life by creating sources of income; (iii) encourage the creation of productive chains in Solidary Economy; (iv) support solidary economic enterprises in aspects related to fair and solidary trade; (v) provide access to Solidary Economy actions through decentralized and territorialized physical structures; (vi) support popular and solidary cooperativism; (vii) promote the intersectorality and multidisciplinarity of the actions of the Municipal Government; (viii) support Solidary Finance instruments, community banks, social currencies, solidary funds, and cooperative credit, by promoting access to financial and banking services based on the Solidary Economy. (Maricá, 2013)[21]

Based on the previous excerpt, it is possible to affirm that the rationale that paved the way for the CBI of Maricá was mostly related to socioeconomic matters and not environmental concerns. Nevertheless, it is worth highlighting that the city hall of Maricá constantly brings up sustainable development in Law 2.448 when sustainability is associated with the CBI policy (Maricá, 2013; Alves, 2022).

The **third pillar** of the analytical framework refers to the impact on the productivist perspective—work and consumption—at the individual and collective levels. In this context, Maricá's Basic Income and its coordinated set of policies foment individual entrepreneurs and increase the beneficiaries' consumption power. Consequently, this policy does not promote a post-productivist approach but rather emphasizes a green productivist alignment.

Regarding consumption and pollution, Maricá's CBI shows complex findings. Whereas consumption was strongly stimulated in the city, sanitation, recycling, and life quality have improved significantly since the implementation of the Basic Income and other public policies (Dektar et al., 2020). Even though consumption levels rose, it is not possible to say that pollution levels followed suit, and the improvement of sanitation services is a relevant aspect of Maricá's conjuncture.

In concomitance, the fact that the CBI is neither considered a universal policy nor a payment that is sufficient for the beneficiary to exit the labour market could be seen as productivist tendencies. Maricá's government aims for an increase in employment rates. However, it is pivotal to understand the Brazilian context in which Maricá is situated. Like most Brazilian

[21] Loosely translated from Portuguese to English. As an author of the present article, I take full responsibility for the loose translation from the original Portuguese of this excerpt to English.

cities, Maricá was one more case that presented high inequality and poverty rates (Dektar et al., 2020). Oil exploration heavily impacted the city's revenue, which enabled public policies to confront its socioeconomic problems. Due to such conjuncture, it is reasonable that Maricá started its Basic Income policy targeting poorer segments of the population and gradually increasing both the number of beneficiaries and the amount of the cash transfer. For a political community to walk toward post-productivism, it is indispensable to correct historical socioeconomic inequities and thus justify gradual Basic Income implementations in more unequal countries, which means beginning on a non-universal basis so as to increase cash transfers slowly. As a matter of fact, the Maricá government has gradually increased the transfer amount and the number of beneficiaries since 2013. Still, the policy currently aims for green productivism, being environmental in this aspect.[22]

The **fourth pillar** of the analytical prism refers to other public policies that accompanied the UBI with a more green-oriented focus. The policies that can be more easily connected to ecological orientation are the "Mumbuca Indígena" (loosely translated as Indigenous Mumbuca), the "Feiras Livres Solidárias" (loosely translated as Free Solidary Fairs), the carbon credit schemes, the free public transportation (which is planned to be carbon neutral in the near future) within the city limits, and "Hortas Comunitárias" (loosely translated as Communal Vegetable Garden), which consist of public aid to family farming activities and small businesses. Such policies can be deemed ecologically oriented to promote a circular and less pollutant economy. The city's public transportation is also worth highlighting since it is free of charge for the city's residents and is partly fuelled with clean energy. Besides, considering that ecological efforts also encompass socioeconomic dignity, policies that promote education (such as the *Mumbuca Futuro*), public health, sanitation, and work (such as entrepreneurial incentives and the construction of industrial parks) can be understood as ecologically valuable.

The Mumbuca Futuro, specifically, is a programme directed at young students enrolled in public schools to learn and develop critical thinking regarding finance and labour and to engage in socioeconomic debates. The students who take part in the programme have to attend a series of

[22] It is worth highlighting that there are more restrictive financial regulations in the Brazilian federative scheme than in the American one, and this is taken in consideration. All in all, Alaska has much more freedom to manage its UBI policy than Maricá.

extra classes in order to qualify for an extra benefit of 50 Mumbucas. If approved during the school year, they get an additional 1,200 Mumbucas to learn how to manage their money. As it is a long-term project, it is still too early to see the results. However, it can be deemed a thriving, innovative, and exciting policy that raises awareness of economic and environmental debates (Souza, 2022).

The **fifth pillar** of the analytical prism refers to Republican freedom and democratic inclusion. The present work has already made clear that Maricá's Basic Income is part of a broad set of public policies. Still, what is most relevant about the fifth pillar is how the CBI and the other policies affect Republican freedom and democratic inclusion.

The Solidary Economy of Maricá aims at the socioeconomic inclusion of its citizens in two manners: (i) the increase of consumption power as a result of the BI cash transfer and work-stimulating policies, and (ii) the decommodification of certain fundamental needs, such as transportation, education, sanitation, and health services.[23]

Maricá's government has been able to fight poverty and exclusion within the city limits (Silva et al., 2020; Pereira et al., 2020). The residents' consumption power has significantly increased as a result of the Basic Income and the fomentation of the economy. Concomitantly, public services have provided the residents with fundamental needs. Therefore, Maricá has been able to enhance republican freedom and democratic inclusion by granting fundamental rights to the citizens.

As for the circular-regionalist focus (**sixth analytical pillar**), Maricá has also acted positively in this sense. Since the Basic Income is transferred through a digital currency (*Mumbuca*), which is only accepted within the city limits, the money from the Basic Income does not exit the city economy. Besides, due to the stimulation of small/individual entrepreneurs, the "Feiras Livres Solidárias" (loosely translated as Free Solidary Fairs) and "Hortas Comunitárias" (loosely translated as Communal Vegetable Garden) programmes, a more circular economy is promoted. So, even though the city economy cannot yet be deemed circular, it may be argued that Maricá has been promoting its regional commerce and small-scale production toward circularity.

After taking all of these pillars of the proposed analytical framework into consideration and evaluating the Citizen Basic Income of Maricá as

[23] The city hall inaugurated the new municipal hospital in 2020, called Dr. Ernesto Che Guevara.

either environmental or ecological, it is possible to say that it qualifies as a strong environmental BI. Maricá has shown substantial developments concerning socioeconomic inclusion, republicanism, circularity, common ownership of resources (via oil royalties funding of public services), and the decommodification of some fundamental needs. However, this Basic Income programme has not moved toward post-productivism or made a profound change in the relationship between humans and nature. In other words, the city still maintains the productivist model of economic success but aims to be sustainable, which fits the environmental concept of Basic Income.

The framework application shows that the CBI was a policy with strong connections to environmental goals. In this sense, we get to the following points: (i) Despite being funded by oil exploration, it cannot be said that it is a taxation that discourages oil consumption.[24] The policy is still heavily dependent on this funding despite the creation of the Sovereign Wealth Fund, which is an effort to make the Basic Income independent from oil profits; (ii) the prime objective of Maricá's city hall was to share oil royalties to promote sustainable socioeconomic development, which goes in line with the environmental BI; (iii) the consumption power of the beneficiaries was strengthened and small entrepreneurs were heavily stimulated, which represents a productivist orientation in the Maricá case that aims at green-growth horizons; (iv) there is a broad set of public policies (some with environmental orientation and others with ecological) that accompanied the CBI in order to enhance the possible effects of the policy, namely education, health system, sanitation, and public transportation; (v) Republican freedom was significantly affected by the increase on consumerism power (through which citizens accessed basic goods) and the enhancement of public basic services with an environmental orientation of sustainability; (vi) Maricá's economy was strengthened by the CBI. Small and individual entrepreneurs were stimulated, and a circular economy was fomented, but significant results on sustainability are still needed.

Based on this analysis and discussion, the present article deems the CBI to be an **environmental basic income policy** with a stronger tendency toward environmentalism than the PFD. The environmentally positive significant aspects were as follows: the governmental objective of

[24] It is important to note that the legal framework in Brazil restricts municipalities' taxation independence, making it impossible for Maricá to create its own environmental taxation that discourages oil consumption.

sustainable growth, the enhancement in individual freedom, the sharing of common resources, the offer of a comprehensive set of basic public policies through the Basic Income, and the strengthening of the regional economy. The only pillar of the analytical prism that suggests the Maricá BI did not show an environmental orientation was the first one: the form of funding. It is also relevant to point out that the policy did not have a post-productivist tendency, even though it is possible to point out some ecological aspects in the city's ecosystem of policies. However, due to the efforts of the city to promote sustainable productivism, this aspect of the policy is in line with Dobson's (2007) concept of environmentalism (Fig. 3.3 and Table 3.1).

Analysing the policies of both Maricá and Alaska, it becomes clear that Maricá places a greater emphasis on achieving sustainability and promoting socioeconomic inclusion. Alaska's policy is centred around the

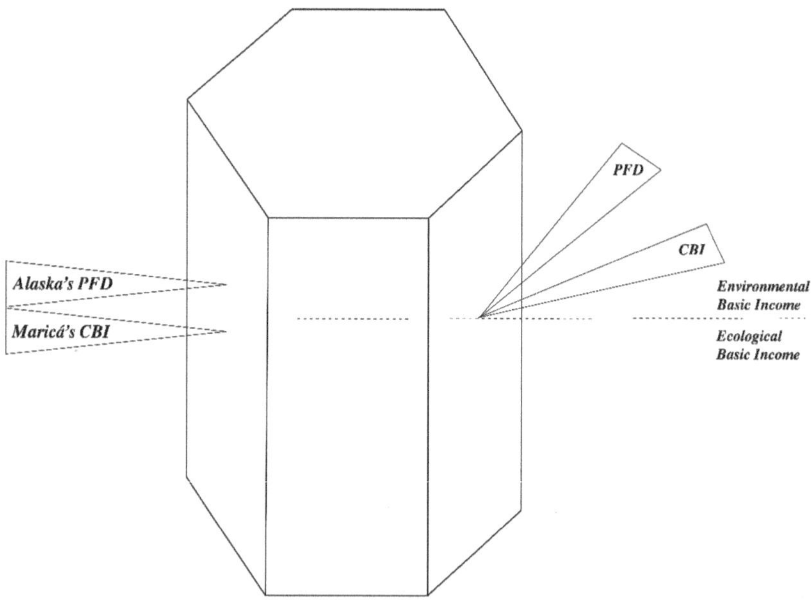

Fig. 3.3 Result of the framework application (After this prism application, both beams of light (policy) fall onto the environmental spectrum. Maricá's case shows a stronger environmental alignment and is closer to the Ecological spectrum)

Table 3.1 Comparative analysis of Alaska and Maricá across six pillars

Pillar	*Alaska's PFD*	*Maricá's CBI*	*Key insights*
Funding	Oil-dependent and transition strategy based on the APF	Oil-dependent and transition strategy based on the Sovereign Fund	Both cases rely on oil revenue, with no direct discouragement of consumption or exploitation
Policy Rationale	Focus on equitable revenue sharing	Emphasis on socioeconomic inclusion and sustainability	Maricá integrates sustainability goals more explicitly
Productivist Impact	Slightly reinforces productivism through increased consumption	Encourages consumption but with green-growth-oriented policies	Neither case embraces post-productivism
Other Policies	Minimal integration with other green initiatives	Includes transport, carbon credit, local agriculture, and education programmes	Maricá's policies are more synergistic and comprehensive
Republican Freedom	Promotes individual freedom via increased consumption power	Promotes individual freedom via increased consumption power and public services	Both policies enhance freedom by providing economic security, but Maricá includes public services
Circular-Regional Focus	Indirect effects on the local economy	Strengthens local economy via Mumbuca currency	Alaska's effects are indirect, while Maricá actively fosters regional economic activities

environmental aspect of shared ownership of resources but does not actively promote inclusion and sustainability as Maricá does.

It is important to highlight the discrepancy between existing literature and practical case studies. While normative discussions often support more radical frameworks, such as post-productivist and degrowth agendas, actual implementations of Unconditional Basic Income policies tend to align more closely with green growth perspectives. Nevertheless, these empirical policies may still offer opportunities for a more transformative approach as they develop in the future.

Furthermore, as discussed in the literature review, Dobson's ecological path can be initiated from a short-term environmental standpoint. Therefore, the gap between philosophical discussions and practical realities should be viewed as an opportunity for the future of green transitional policies. This relationship between the normative and empirical realms represents one of the central contributions of this work.

5. Final Remarks

The comparison between Alaska's PFD and Maricá's CBI highlights both the potential and limitations of UBI policies as tools for environmental and ecological transitions. Alaska's approach, though rooted in the principle of shared resource ownership, exhibits weak environmental alignment due to its dependence on fossil fuels and a lack of complementary green policies. By contrast, Maricá's policy framework demonstrates a stronger orientation toward sustainability, incorporating public transport, carbon credit schemes, and localized green growth initiatives.

The theoretical lens provided by Dobson's (2007) concepts of environmentalism and ecologism clarifies these distinctions. Alaska's PFD aligns with environmentalism's managerial approach, adapting the existing economic structure to accommodate sustainability without challenging core productivist values. Maricá, while still operating within a productivist framework, goes further by offering green-growth initiatives and introducing elements of ecological thinking through policies like communal vegetable gardens and educational programmes aimed at fostering ecological awareness.

This analysis also underscores the tension between normative aspirations and empirical realities. For instance, while post-productivist ideals envision a society less dependent on labour and consumption, Maricá's approach currently emphasizes green growth as a pathway to equity and sustainability. Similarly, Alaska's reliance on oil undermines its potential as a green transitional policy despite its success in redistributing wealth.

Looking ahead, the lessons from these cases suggest pathways for developing a "strong ecological UBI". This would require:

(i) Innovative Funding Mechanisms: Introduce carbon taxation and other progressive environmental levies to discourage unsustainable practices while financing UBI. Explore non-resource-dependent revenues, such as wealth or land taxes, for broader adaptability.
(ii) Decommodification of Services: Expand access to universal public goods, such as healthcare, education, and transport, reducing dependence on consumption-driven economies.

(iii) Integration with Green Policies: Align UBI with renewable energy initiatives, circular economy models, and sustainable urban planning to amplify its ecological impact.
(iv) Facilitating the Transition to a Post-Work Society: By decoupling economic security from formal employment, UBI can create space for non-productivist lifestyles. This shift allows individuals to engage in caregiving, community-building, and other undervalued activities. Policies must address transitional challenges, such as reskilling workers and redefining the societal value of non-market contributions.

Additionally, UBI policies could play a transformative role in achieving the United Nations' Sustainable Development Goals (SDGs). Specifically, they could directly address SDG 1 (No Poverty) by providing a social safety net, SDG 8 (Decent Work and Economic Growth) by reducing labour exploitation, and SDG 13 (Climate Action) through green funding and reduced overconsumption.

By bridging the gap between theoretical ideals and practical applications, this work advocates for iterative UBI frameworks that evolve toward ecological sustainability while addressing immediate socioeconomic challenges. Our discussion does not aim to be conclusive or restrictive but rather to offer a new perspective through the proposed framework. By doing so, we hope to encourage readers to consider Basic Income policies in association with the environmental literature that surrounds the topic. Our research is aimed at promoting continuous discussions about the UBI towards a more free, just, and sustainable society.

References

Alves, C. (2022). *Aspectos ecológicos de uma Renda Básica: O caso de Maricá. Tese de Mestrado*. Programa de Pós-Graduação em Ciências Econômicas. UFF.

Audier, S. (2015). *Les théories de la république*. La Découverte.

Barry, J. (2012). *The politics of actually existing unsustainability: Human flourishing in a climate changed, carbon constrained world*. Oxford University Press.

Block, F. L. (1990). *Postindustrial possibilities: A critique of economic discourse*. University of California Press.

Bookchin, M. (1990). *The philosophy of social ecology: Essays on dialectical naturalism*. Black Rose Books.

Boyce, J. K. (2016). The challenge of forging sustainable climate policy. *Scholars' Strategy Network Forum on Building Democratic Support for Equitable Carbon*

Pricing. Accessed July 20, 2023, from https://scholars.org/page/challenge-forging-sustainable-climate-policy
Cannavò, P. (2016). Environmental political theory and republicanism. In T. Gabrielson et al. (Eds.), *The Oxford handbook of environmental political theory* (pp. 72–88). Oxford University Press.
Casal, P. (2012). Progressive environmental taxation: A defence. *Political Studies, 60*(2), 419–433.
Casassas, D., & De Wispelaere, J. (2012). The Alaska model: A republican perspective. In K. Widerquist & M. W. Howard (Eds.), *Alaska's permanent fund dividend: Examining its suitability as a model* (pp. 169–188). Palgrave Macmillan.
D'Alisa, G., Demaria, F., & Kallis, G. (2014). *Degrowth: A vocabulary for a new era*. Taylor & Francis.
Dektar, M., Freitas, F., Katz, P., & Mendes, R. (2020). *Informações sobre políticas socioeconômicas de Maricá e sua avaliação/Information on Maricá's socioeconomic policies and their evaluation*. Technical report.
Dobson, A. (2007). *Green political thought* (4th ed.). Routledge.
Erickson, G., & Groh, C. (2012). Permanent perhaps: Challenges to the model in Alaska in its first 30 years. In *Alaska's permanent fund dividend: Examining its suitability as a model* (pp. 99–114). Palgrave Macmillan US.
Esping-Andersen, G. (1990). *The three worlds of welfare capitalism*. Princeton University Press.
Fremaux, A. (2018). *Towards a critical theory of the anthropocene and a life-affirming politics* (PhD). Queen's University, Belfast, UK. https://www.academia.edu/36936310/PhD_Thesis_Towards_a_Critical_Theory_of_the_Anthropocene_and_a_Life_affirming_Politics_A_Post_Anthropocentric_Post_Growth_Post_neo_Liberal_Green_Republican_Analysis
Gilbert, R., Huws, U., & Yi, G. (2019). Employment market effects of basic income. In *The Palgrave international handbook of basic income* (pp. 47–72). Springer International Publishing. https://doi.org/10.1007/978-3-030-23614-4_4
Giljum, S., Dittrich, M., Lieber, M., & Lutter, S. (2014). Global patterns of material flows and their socioeconomic and environmental implications: A MFA study on all countries world-wide from 1980 to 2009. *Resources, 3*(1), 319–339.
Goldsmith, S. (2012). The economic and social impacts of the permanent fund dividend on Alaska. In K. Widerquist & M. W. Howard (Eds.), *Alaska's permanent fund dividend: Examining its suitability as a model* (pp. 49–63). Palgrave Macmillan.
Gourevitch, A. (2015). *From slavery to the cooperative commonwealth: Labour and republican liberty in the nineteenth century*. Cambridge University Press.
Graeber, D. (2018). *Bullshit jobs: A theory*. Penguin Random House UK, 347 pp.

Howard, M. W., Pinto, J., & Schachtschneider, U. (2019). *Ecological effects of basic income* (pp. 111–132). The Palgrave international handbook of Basic Income.

ILO. (2015). *Guidelines for a just transition towards environmentally sustainable economies and societies for all.* https://www.ilo.org/wcmsp5/groups/public/—-ed_emp/—-emp_ent/documents/publication/wcms_432859.pdf

Jones, D., & Marinescu, I. (2018). The labour market impacts of universal and permanent cash transfers: Evidence from the Alaska Permanent Fund. *American Economic Journal: Economic Policy, 14*(2), 315–340.

Kiss, K., Ruszkai, C., & Takács-György, K. (2019). Examination of short supply chains based on circular economy and sustainability aspects. *Resources, 8*(4), 161. https://doi.org/10.3390/resources8040161

Langridge, N. (2024). Unconditional basic income and a degrowth transition: Adding empirical rigour to radical visions. *Futures, 159*, 103375. https://doi.org/10.1016/j.futures.2024.103375

Meadows, D. H., Meadows, D. L., Randers, J., & Behrens, W. W. (1972). *The limits to growth: A report for the Club of Rome's project on the predicament of mankind.* Universe Books.

Merrill, R., Bizarro, S., Marcelo, G., & Pinto, J. (2019). *Rendimento Básico Incondicional: Uma defesa da liberdade.* O Saber da Filosofia.

Merrill, R., Neves, C., & Laín, B. (2022). *Basic income experiments: A critical examination of their goals, contexts, and methods.* Springer Nature.

Município de Maricá. (2013). Lei no 2.448, de 26 de junho de 2013. *Institui o Programa Municipal de Economia Solidária, Combate à Pobreza e Desenvolvimento Econômico e Social de Maricá.* Jornal Oficial de Maricá (JOM), v. 5, n. 383, 8 Jul. 2013b. Accessed July 20, 2023, from https://www.marica.rj.gov.br/wp-content/uploads/2013/07/jom-383.pdf

Naess, A. (1985). Self-realization: An ecological approach to being in the world. *Inquiry: An Interdisciplinary Journal of Philosophy, 28*(1–4), 277–292.

Neumayer, E. (2013). *Weak versus strong sustainability: Exploring the limits of two opposing paradigms.* Edward Elgar Publishing Limited.

Nørgård, J., & Xue, J. (2016). Between green growth and degrowth: Decoupling, rebound effects and the politics for long-term sustainability. In T. Santarius, H. J. Walnum, & C. Aall (Eds.), *Rethinking climate and energy policies: New perspectives on the rebound phenomenon* (pp. 267–284). Springer International Publishing.

Offe, C. (1992). A non-productivist design for social policies. In P. Van Parijs (Ed.), *Arguing for basic income* (pp. 61–80). Verso Books.

Pereira, A., Siqueira, D., Senra, L., & Costa, N. (2020). As políticas públicas de economia solidária no município de Maricá/RJ. IPEA – Instituto De Pesquisa Econômica Aplicada. *Brasil em desenvolvimento: Estado, planejamento e políticas públicas.* Ipea. https://doi.org/10.38116/bmt70/economiasolidaria3

Pettit, P. (1997). *Republicanism: A theory of freedom and government*. Oxford University Press.

Pettit, P. (2012). *On the people's terms: A republican theory and model of democracy*. Cambridge University Press.

Pinto, J. (2020). *Green republicanism: Non-domination for an ecologically sustainable planet* (Ph.D.). Universidade do Minho, Braga. https://repositorium.sdum.uminho.pt/handle/1822/76484

Purdy, D., & Van Trier, W. (1988). Political feasibility of the transition to a basic income society. *Basic income and problems of implementation: Proceedings of these international conference on basic income* (pp. 45–64).

Silva, J., Silva, R., Freitas, F., & Waltenberg, F. (2020). Políticas socioeconômicas de reação à crise da Covid-19 no município de Maricá, Rio de Janeiro. *Boletim Mercado de Trabalho: Conjuntura e Análise IPEA, 26*(69), 149–159.

Souza, T. (2022). Maricá citizen's basic income: An overview of the pilot. In *Proceedings of the 2021 FRIBIS Annual Conference published: Financial Issues of a Universal Basic Income* (UBI) (pp. 155–169).

Souza, T. M. (2024a). The unconditional basic income proposal as a means to promote ecological and socioeconomic justice. *Brazilian Political Science Review, 19*(1), e0002. https://doi.org/10.1590/1981-3821202500010002

Souza, T. (2024b). Fundaments of an ecological unconditional basic income. *Ethics, Politics & Society, 7*(1). https://doi.org/10.21814/eps.7.1.4941

Standing, G. (2020). *Battling eight giants: Basic income now*. Bloomsbury Publishing.

Torry, M. (2019). *The Palgrave international handbook of basic income*. Palgrave Macmillan.

Van Parijs, P. (2004). Basic income: A simple and powerful idea for the twenty-first century. *Politics and Society, 32*(1), 7–39.

Van Parijs, P. (2013). A green case for basic income? In: *Basic income: An anthology of contemporary research* (pp. 269–274).

Waltenberg, F., & Katz, P. (2023). *Renda Básica e Economia Solidária: o exemplo de Maricá*. Cortez Editora.

White, S. (2008). Markets, time and citizenship. In S. White & D. Leighton (Eds.), *Building a citizen society: The emerging politics of republican democracy* (pp. 124–136). Lawrence and Wishart.

Widerquist, K., & Howard, M. (Eds.). (2012). *Alaska's permanent fund dividend: Examining its suitability as a model*. Springer.

Widerquist, K., Noguera, J., Vandeborght, Y., & Wispelaere, J. (2013). *Basic income: An anthology of contemporary research*. Wiley.

CHAPTER 4

Is the Strong Ecological Argument for Basic Income a Strong Argument for Basic Income?

Michael W. Howard

Introduction

Ecological interest in basic income has been around for a few decades (Howard et al., 2023), but there is still little empirical research on ecological consequences of a BI (MacNeill & Vibert, 2019). There is some evidence from Indonesia that cash transfers aimed at alleviating poverty can reduce deforestation (Ferraro & Simorangkir, 2020) but also evidence from Sierra Leone of increased land clearance in the short run from unconditional payments (Wilebore et al., 2019). There is growing interest in "conservation basic income", because of "mounting criticisms surrounding market-based instruments for conservation" (Sheehan & Martin--Ortega, 2023; Fletcher & Buscher, 2020). But there is insufficient empirical research to draw clear conclusions. There is some evidence from recent basic income pilot projects that in some ways BI could support ecological goals, but the question of the relationship between BI and

M. W. Howard (✉)
University of Maine, Orono, ME, USA
e-mail: mhoward@maine.edu

R. Merrill, C. Neves (eds.), *Determining the Value of Universal Basic Income*, Exploring the Basic Income Guarantee,
https://doi.org/10.1007/978-3-032-04004-6_4

ecology has not been at the centre of this research (Langridge et al., 2023). In what follows, I will distinguish a minimalist argument for a partial BI, funded from carbon pricing, from a maximalist argument for a full BI, and explore whether BI itself, independent of carbon pricing, might help or hinder ecological goals. I will focus on climate change but note that climate change is only one of several ecological crises (Rees, 2023). A more thorough exploration of BI and ecology would encompass other dimensions of human overshoot of planetary boundaries (Rockström et al., 2009).

Minimalist Argument: Carbon Dividends as Partial Basic Income

Carbon dividends are per capita cash payments distributed periodically to everyone from the revenue from carbon pricing. Carbon pricing is essential for meeting internationally agreed-upon climate mitigation goals. Raising the price of carbon will motivate consumers to buy less carbon--intensive goods and services, and to shift demand towards renewables. Imposing a carbon tax at the wells and mine heads will internalize the environmental costs of fossil fuels throughout the economy. Tariffs on carbon-intensive imports will prevent their under-pricing more renewable alternatives, and motivate importing countries to adopt their own carbon pricing. Similar effects will result from a carbon cap, with an auction of permits. The cost of the permits like the cost of a carbon tax will be passed along to consumers and depress demand for fossil fuels. The advantage of a cap and auction is the assurance that carbon emissions will be steadily reduced in accordance with internationally agreed-upon quotas (Boyce, 2019; Howard, 2012, 2016, 2017).

Carbon pricing alone is insufficient for reaching climate goals (Stiglitz et al., 2017, 3), given the small remaining carbon budget and the urgency of a rapid transition away from fossil fuels. Investments in infrastructure, such as an efficient energy grid, charging stations for electric vehicles, high-speed rail, forest and land management, and subsidies for energy efficiency, will also be needed. But carbon pricing can be thought of as a safety net that captures all the emissions not explicitly targeted by such policies (Boyce, 2019).

Using most of the proceeds for dividends is crucial for rectifying the otherwise unjust effects of a regressive tax, and for making a steadily rising carbon price politically feasible. Even modest carbon pricing introduced without attention to the inequities risks a political backlash (Chrisafis, 2018). Thus, the minimalist ecological argument for BI is a strong argument. However, carbon pricing can yield at most a partial BI, insufficient for basic needs, although a wider scheme of ecological taxation of all natural resources and socially created goods like seignorage might come closer (Flomenhoft, 2012; Barnes, 2014). Moreover, the ecological purpose and framing of carbon dividends are sufficiently different from arguments for BI having to do with automation or poverty elimination that a transition from a carbon dividend to a full BI is not very likely (see Zelleke for an analogous point about Alaska's Permanent Fund Dividend).

Although carbon dividends fall short of a full BI in high-income countries, there is a way that global carbon pricing could support a meaningful low BI in low-income countries. A very small BI can have dramatic effects on extreme poverty.

Consider the evidence from the Indian BI pilot. Each adult received 200 rupees/month, about US$3.75/month or $45/year, about 30% of subsistence (and half that amount for children). The results of this experiment included improvements in medication, education spending, school attendance, infrastructure, more economic activity, savings, and more (Standing, 2013; Standing et al., 2015).

If all of India's carbon dioxide emissions (2.7 billion tons) were taxed at $20 per ton and distributed as a per capita dividend, the dividend would be (not counting reduced emissions) $38/person/year and rising (to perhaps $300+). Over time, the tax is ratcheted up, but emissions decline; dividends will rise, then decline, but the precise peak of the dividend is difficult to predict. Now consider a global carbon tax starting at $20/ton on CO_2 emissions. This would yield an annual dividend globally starting at $96 per person (about twice the dividend of the Indian pilot BI) and rising over time. It would be greater in India than a dividend from a national carbon tax (author's calculations, using data from Wikipedia, 2024a, 2024b). If all greenhouse gases are included in the carbon tax, the dollar figures are significantly higher (a global dividend of $135, and a national Indian dividend of $55; Wikipedia, 2024c).

If the revenue from carbon pricing were distributed equally per capita globally, extreme poverty could be substantially reduced or eliminated worldwide. However, using the revenue in this way would weaken support for carbon pricing at a national level in high- income countries because there would be less revenue to compensate middle- and low-income households for their rising carbon prices, and this in turn would weaken support for the policy of a steadily rising carbon price. Perhaps a compromise could be devised according to which a percentage of each national carbon tax would be directed to an international fund to augment the carbon dividends going to low-income countries. Other variations for developing countries under the rubric of a temporary basic income are considered by Molina and Ortiz-Juarez (2020).

Maximalist Argument: A Full Basic Income as an Ecological Policy

I shall consider two maximalist arguments, one concerning inequality, the other concerning consequences for behaviour in the labour market and in consumption.

Inequality

The first maximalist argument for a full BI is as follows:

1. Carbon emissions are unequally distributed in correlation with unequal distribution of income and wealth.
2. If carbon emissions are to be reduced sufficiently, then wealth and income should be distributed more equally.
3. BI is one policy for reducing income and/or wealth inequality.
4. BI is superior to other policies for reducing income and/or wealth Inequality in at least some respects.

Therefore, if carbon emissions are to be reduced sufficiently, BI should be among the policies adopted for reducing income and wealth inequality.

The third premise affords only weak support for a BI. Premise 4, if it can be supported, strengthens the argument.

Inequality of Income, Wealth, and Emissions

Globally, the richest 10% receive 52% of world income, while the poorest 50% receive only 8% of world income; wealth is even more unequally distributed, 76% and 2% respectively. Carbon emissions correspond with income inequality. The top 10% of emitters are responsible for 48% of global emissions, while the bottom 50% are responsible for 12% of global emissions (Chancel et al., 2022).

Because of the small remaining carbon budget to keep global temperature from rising above 1.5 or two degrees centigrade, and therefore the limited time in which to make a transition to a carbon-neutral economy, reducing inequality of income and wealth must be part of climate change policy.

> According to the latest IPCC report, there are 300 billion tonnes of CO_2 left to be emitted if we are to stay below 1.5 °C (with an 83% confidence rating) and 900 billion tonnes of CO_2 left to stay below 2 °C (with the same level of confidence). At current global emissions rates, the 1.5 °C budget will be depleted in six years and 2 °C budget in 18 years. (Chancel et al., 2022)

Most of the emissions reductions must come from substituting renewable energy for energy from fossil fuels. This will require major investments in high-income countries and also large financial and technological transfers to middle- and low-income countries. While it is likely that the 1.5 °C budget will be exceeded, it is nevertheless urgent to adhere as closely to this goal as possible (Di Liberto, 2024; McKay et al., 2022).

To understand the case for transfers, we need to take note of what should count as a national fair share of global carbon emission reduction. The United Nations Framework Convention on Climate Change calls for greenhouse gas stabilization by nations "on the basis of equity in accordance with their common but differentiated responsibilities and respective capacities" (quoted in Singer, 2008). A reasonable interpretation of this convention is that national fair shares should combine a polluter pays principle based on responsibility for historical carbon emissions, and an ability to pay principle based on a nation's capacity to pay for the cost of reducing or avoiding carbon emissions without impoverishing significant numbers of its citizens. For elaborations and defences of this "hybrid" account, see Caney (2008) and Howard (2011). [Moellendorf, 2014 argues for an interpretation of the convention that involves only ability to pay. The results in practice are distinct from, but not radically divergent from, an interpretation that gives equal weight to ability to pay and polluter pays, as can be verified with the Climate Equity Reference Calculator.]

Combining these principles in their climate equity reference calculator, Kemp-Benedict et al. (2019) enable us to determine national fair shares of various carbon budgets.

Using the climate equity reference calculator, we find that the United States, although currently responsible for only 14% of CO_2 emissions annually (Plumer, 2019), has a national Fair Share of 29% of necessary global carbon emissions reductions. (In making this calculation, I assume a carbon budget for the IPCC 1.5 °C pathway [+Low energy demand, without reliance on BECCS], a $7500 development threshold as a way of marking ability to pay (those with income below this threshold are not held responsible for the cost of their climate mitigation), and responsibility since 1950 (other settings are available, including going back to the industrial revolution, or only back to 1990 when there was international agreement to take responsibility for carbon emissions).)

This means in practice that the United States needs to reduce its emissions 131% below 1990 emissions by 2030. Barring fanciful negative emissions technologies coming to the rescue in the next five years, it is impossible to reduce carbon emissions below 100%. Hence, this national obligation must be met by a combination of national emission reductions and international transfers to support the cost of emission reductions by other countries beyond their national fair share. For example, the United States might reduce its carbon emissions by 60% by 2030 and assume responsibility for the additional 71% through financial and technological transfers to low- and middle-income countries to accelerate their development on a sustainable path (cf. Reyes et al., 2021). Note that this international obligation concerns mitigation only. Responsibility for adaptation and for loss and damages is in addition (Reyes et al., 2021).

In contrast, India, which is a low-income country currently responsible for about 7% of global CO_2 emissions annually (Plumer, 2019), has a national fair share of only 0.95% because of its low percentage of historical emissions and lower ability to pay, due to large numbers of people still below the $7500 development threshold. India's fair share of emissions, however, would allow for a rise from around 3000 MtCO2e to 4000. However, to keep global temperature rise below 1.5 ° C, emissions in India should fall to under 2000 by 2030. Closing that emissions reduction gap of around 2000 MtCO2e must be the responsibility of countries like the United States, on top of the latter's own domestic emissions reductions.

The cost of this international obligation for climate change mitigation will be in the hundreds of billions of dollars annually, and again this does not include additional obligations for climate change adaptation or for loss and damages. Here is a quick back-of-the-envelope calculation:

Global cost of climate mitigation: 1.5–2% GWP ($94 tr. in 2021) = $1.4–$1.9 tr
US Fair Share, 29% = $406–$551 bn
Half for cash transfers: $203–276 bn annually.

This is in the same ballpark as estimates of $264–529 bn by Stiglitz et al. (2017, quoted in Reyes et al., 2021).

How will wealthy countries like the United States reduce their domestic carbon emissions on this scale, and where will the money come from for international transfers? The first question has a very complicated answer, and I will only say here that it includes substantial investments, including and going beyond the Inflation Reduction Act (Nuccitelli, 2022), and including progressively rising carbon pricing that will need to be paired with carbon dividends to ensure that the policy is not regressive in its income effects and consequently politically infeasible. The second question involves a combination of reallocation of existing budgets and increased revenue through higher taxes. Maybe there is some room for reduction in the military budget, but there is no justification for reducing already meagre budgets for education, health care, and other necessary expenditures of the welfare state.

The burden of emissions reductions by 2030 can and should fall on the affluent. Chancel et al. (2022) explain how:

> First, in rich countries, the bottom 50% is already below the 2030 per capita target ...or very close to it.... It follows that all emissions reductions efforts are to be made by the top half of the distribution. In the US, the top 10% must cut its emissions by close to 90% in order to reach the 2030 per capita target, and the middle 40% by around 50%. The degree of efforts required ... in France is similar.
>
> Second, it appears that in emerging countries, not all groups should increase their emissions levels. While the bottom and middle of the distribution are currently below the 2030 target, the top 10% is significantly above it. Indeed, in China, the top 10% must cut its emissions by more than 70% to meet the sustainable target. The value is also significant in India (−58%).

Chancel et al. propose two tax policies: First, a "10% tax rate on the value of carbon assets owned by global multimillionaires would generate at least $100 bn in a year. This value is non-negligible: it represents about 1.5 times the current estimated annual costs of adaptation to global warming in developing countries (about $70 bn per year in 2020)." While such a measure would raise revenue, its primary purpose is to drive investment away from carbon and towards renewable energy. Second, they propose a 1–3% progressive wealth tax on millionaires.

"It is estimated that 2% of GDP in additional annual investments are required (i.e. about $2,000 bn). As a matter of fact, the very large additional investments in infrastructures required to meet the energy transition challenge needs considerable new sources of financing and these will hardly be met by taxes on highly polluting assets alone." Hence, this wealth tax is required in addition to the carbon assets tax.

These two measures together would generate 1.7% of global income (Chancel et al., 2022, Table 6.8), in the range of the 1.5–2% GWP needed for mitigation. Not only will the taxes generate revenue needed for climate mitigation domestically and internationally, but they will also reduce the income of the wealthy and some of their excessive luxury emissions.

Granting all that I have just presented, it is clear that a successful climate mitigation policy will include strong egalitarian measures. What is less clear is whether such an egalitarian tax policy will support a BI. Much of the revenue generated will need to go directly into new technology. Much of it also must go towards international transfers, and although these may be cash transfers, it is not clear that these cash transfers to low-income countries for the purposes of climate mitigation should be converted into individual unconditional cash transfers to poor people, much less to everyone, in those countries. Universal dividends to ease the impact of carbon pricing on poor and low-income people figure prominently among the options for use of revenue from carbon pricing (Stiglitz et al., 2017: 39), and a case might be made for similar dividends from some of the revenue from other climate change related taxation. However, in all these cases, there are competing arguments for using the revenue in a more targeted way to smooth the transition to a post-carbon economy, for infrastructure, for public goods, for research and development, etc. Thus, the inequality argument needs to be complemented by the second maximalist argument, or by non-ecological arguments for BI.

A second difficulty is whether there is enough revenue available for a BI if all of these climate responsibilities are met. I estimated that the US fair share of climate mitigation will be about $406–$551 bn annually. The net cost of a BI in the United States of $1000/person/month (half that for children), as Karl Widerquist (2017) has shown, is around $539 billion. Unless a case can be made that a substantial part of our climate change goals can be achieved through a BI, it will be necessary to budget around $1 trillion to cover both climate mitigation and a BI. Is it possible to do both?

Feasibility of Egalitarian Policies

One worry is that attempting to raise this amount of additional revenue would require raising marginal tax rates to a self-defeating level. The equalization of income required might so undermine incentives particularly for investment that less revenue could be gathered over time than would be needed from raising the tax rates. There is reason to think that current marginal tax rates are suboptimal in the other direction, at least in the United States, and that marginal tax rates could be raised considerably—as much as 80% on incomes over half a million dollars—without undermining the relevant incentives (Saez & Piketty, 2013; Piketty, 2014, p. 512–513). But what is the upper limit beyond which net revenue declines rather than increases, and will the revenue suffice for both environmental obligations and a BI?

Apart from raising the revenue required for climate mitigation, there are ecological considerations as well as considerations of justice that support higher marginal tax rates in order to reduce very high incomes. Individual carbon footprints tend to rise as income rises. If, as Chancel et al. have argued, the top 10% need to reduce their emissions by 90% by 2030, it may be necessary to reduce their incomes in order to get the desired emissions reductions. Given the small carbon budget that remains, such a reduction of high-income spending would enable the entire population to share this shrinking carbon budget more equally.

This ecological argument dovetails with two considerations regarding justice. First, the value of political liberties is undermined when inequality of wealth, income, and power is so great that the voices and influence of a wealthy elite undercut the voices and influence of most of the rest of the population (Rawls, 1999, 2001; Daniels, 1975). One approach to addressing such political inequality is to try and block the power of money in politics through campaign finance restrictions and other measures (Walzer, 1983). But these may be inadequate to the task of securing equality of status among citizens, and if so, then there's a case to be made for not only an income floor but also a cap on high incomes (Casassas & De Wispelaere, 2012). The value of political liberty is such that its importance trumps the importance of efficiency that might otherwise be expected as a result of incentives resulting in income and wealth inequality.

Second, reciprocity in the shared process of production of commodities and other goods supports something like Rawls's difference principle, according to which inequalities of wealth and income associated with different positions in the society are justified only if they are to the advantage of the least advantaged group. Here also the value of reciprocity is prior in importance to maximizing efficiency. Thus, some loss of efficiency would be warranted if it contributed to the realization of reciprocity (Rawls, 1999, 2001).

Whether theories of justice support a basic income is a topic beyond the scope of this paper. For more on this question, see Van Parijs (1995, 2003), Zelleke (2005), Fukuma (2017), Barry (2005), Murphy and Nagel (2002), Birnbaum (2012), White (2003). Suffice it to say that if such a case can be made convincingly, it would complement the ecological argument.

From Egalitarianism to Basic Income?

Universal BI would involve a substantial redistribution from the wealthy to the poor and disadvantaged. But it is not the only form that redistribution can take. In all modern welfare states, much of the redistribution is in the form of in-kind benefits, most notably education and health care, and targeted, conditional cash benefits. Indeed, most advocates of BI are not opposed to in-kind benefits, but see BI as a more efficient and effective way to structure cash benefits. Cash transfers that are typically means-tested and conditional on various behavioural requirements such as seeking employment are not very effective in reaching their targeted recipients. This is partly due to the complexity of the system, partly due to the stigma attached to being on welfare (Hoynes & Rothstein, 2019). Unconditional cash transfers remove many of these barriers and facilitate delivery without the costly processes of means testing and monitoring of behaviour. Thus, whether or not one is persuaded by principled arguments based on a theory of distributive justice, one may embrace BI as a policy that achieves widely shared social justice goals more effectively than existing policies (Barry, 2005). And BI has certain further advantages at least from the perspective of certain constituencies, such as enabling workers to exit from undesirable jobs and, because of that ability, being able to bargain more effectively for better wages and working conditions, and similarly enabling spouses in abusive relationships to exit without losing their economic security (Zelleke, 2011).

Conceived in this way, the actual net cost of a BI is bound to be lower than Widerquist's back-of-the-envelope calculation, because it would simply replace many of the current cash benefits such as, in the United States, food stamps, TANF, and general assistance, although top-ups will most likely be required for other more generous cash benefits such as unemployment insurance and disability benefits.

In the remainder of this paper, I will explore some specific ecological effects of a BI, and address some problems that have been raised about possible undesirable ecological effects of a BI.

Ecological Effects of Basic Income

The second maximalist argument is as follows:

1. Climate change mitigation will require changes in behaviour and in the labour market, including work time reduction (WTR), work sharing, and behaviour involving less carbon-intensive consumption.
2. A BI can promote WTR, etc.
3. A BI can promote WTR, etc. better than competing policies designed for the same end.

Therefore, climate change mitigation will require a BI.

Premise 2 is relatively weak, because there are competing policies that might achieve the desired ends as well as or better than BI. Thus, premise 3 is needed to make the argument stronger.

We should first note a possible negative ecological effect of BI. Lower-income households tend to spend more of their income than high-income households. So a transfer of income from rich to poor will tend to increase consumption, and thus carbon emissions and environmental footprint, at least above a certain level of extreme poverty. This is supported in several modellings of income transfers, including global transfers (Sager, 2017; Hubacek et al., 2017). This is not necessarily an ecological argument against a full BI because the increase in carbon emissions might be avoided if the BI is accompanied by complementary measures such as education about the need for less consumption of energy and materials, WTR, and a maximum income (Howard et al., 2023). But the positive environmental outcome is then flowing from these complementary measures more than from BI per se.

Ecological BI and Degrowth

An ecological BI is often associated with degrowth (Langridge et al., 2023; Pinto, 2020). This need not be the case, but to the extent that this association is correct, the argument must address problems with degrowth.

Degrowth can take multiple forms. As Malmaeus et al. have shown, the relationship between BI and degrowth varies depending upon the kind of post-growth economy envisioned. They modelled two such post-growth scenarios: a local self-sufficiency scenario and an automation scenario, neither of which involves growth, assuming that staying within planetary boundaries will require a steady-state economy. These scenarios differ in the relative intensity of labour versus capital, and in their effects on overall production possibilities and relative prices of goods and services. In the local self-sufficiency scenario, the purpose of a BI is to counteract poverty and inequality in a way that stimulates the local economy. [In some variations of this scenario, the goal might be to foster activity that is outside the market or state, in the "autonomous" sector (Gorz, 2013).] Thus, more investment goes to labour incomes, and capital intensity is reduced, leading to reduced total output. Consequently, it will be harder to fund a given level of BI in the local self-sufficiency scenario than in the automation scenario. A higher tax rate will be needed to achieve the same real minimum income, and, because more activity may be taking place in the informal sector, revenue may be harder to collect.

In the automation scenario, labour productivity is boosted through capital investment. Because the economy is not growing, unemployment may rise. Rising labour productivity can yield a shorter work week for the employed, with more free time for a meaningful life, but for those disconnected from employment there will be growing inequality and job instability. The purpose of BI in this scenario is to rectify the inequality by promoting voluntary job sharing and sharing of the profits of automation.

Malmaeus et al. conclude that "a full UBI [universal basic income] is a more realistic option in the automation scenario", and "in the labour intensive scenario the need for human labour is relatively high and hence the need for income support from a UBI is less". This conclusion raises some doubt about whether a guiding principle of an ecological BI should be to "facilitate a shift from waged labour to activities in the autonomous sphere" (Langridge et al., 2023). While modelled as alternatives, these scenarios in practice are not mutually exclusive. The modelling merely calls attention to the implications for BI of policies that favour one or the other. As we shall see later, the automation scenario is more favourable for a BI consistent with global climate justice obligations.

Green Growth Versus Degrowth

First, a point of clarification: the term "growth" is ambiguous. It can refer, as is usually intended, to growth of GDP. But it can also refer to growth of energy and material throughput. Historically, these have been closely correlated, with growth of GDP leading to increased energy and material throughput, and in particular carbon emissions. It is growth of energy (especially carbon-based) and material throughput that matters ecologically. But it is possible to decouple growth of GDP from growth of (at least fossil-based) energy and material throughputs. Environmental impact is expressed in the Ehrlich equation:

$$I = P \times A \times T$$

where environmental impact, I, in this context, is CO_2 emissions; P is population; A is affluence, represented as income per person; and T is a technological factor, which in the case of global warming is represented as grams of CO_2 emissions per dollar.

Little can be done to decrease population between now and mid-century because of population momentum (Budolfson & Spears, 2021), although demographic policies should be considered now that will affect carbon emissions and sustainability more generally in the latter half of the century and beyond (Rees, 2023).

Advocates of green growth focus on T, believing that it is possible to reduce carbon emissions on the scale required entirely by decoupling GDP growth from carbon energy. Degrowth "is neither necessary nor sufficient for achieving net-zero carbon emissions. Moreover, such a policy is politically unacceptable and for good reason. The political reaction to insisting on stopping growth may undermine the acceptance of climate policies in general" (Stern & Stiglitz, 2023). They point out that merely stopping growth will simply freeze emissions at currently high levels, and the only way to get to net-zero emissions relying solely on degrowth is to reduce consumption to zero (Stern & Stiglitz, 2023; see also Pollin, 2015; Pollin & Chasman, 2015).

Decoupling is necessary then, for green growth advocates, but also sufficient. What will get us to net-zero carbon emissions is a combination of investments in renewable energy, energy efficiency, and required transfers of capital to low-income countries to ensure development along a sustainable path, thus "breaking the relation between consumption and production on the one hand and destruction of the environment on the other. That will be achieved by consuming and producing in different ways, and many of the technologies needed to do so exist already. We can also change our patterns of consumption towards goods and services that are "greener"—and this too is already happening" (Stern & Stiglitz, 2023). Economic growth will enable the necessary investments and transfers. We might add that if there is some overshoot of the 1.5 to 2°C target, various forms of carbon dioxide capture and removal can presumably bring down atmospheric concentrations. For critical discussion of carbon removal, see Hickel (2020: ch. 3), National Academies (2019: 360), and Shue (2017).

Critics of green growth and advocates of degrowth consider decoupling to be insufficient on its own, given the limited carbon budget and the limited time period in which to make the transition to renewable energy (Parrique et al., 2019; Hickel, 2020; Hickel & Kallis, 2020; Haberl et al., 2020; Jackson, 2009; Victor, 2008). While decoupling is necessary, it is not sufficient and has to be complemented by stopping growth of A, the average income per person globally. Fully decoupling energy use from carbon emissions will be much more manageable along this degrowth path. Of course, reduction in average income per person does not mean that everybody's income must decrease. On the contrary, degrowth advocates seek to reduce both inequality and poverty without reliance on growth, and some also point out that growth has historically been an inefficient method of reducing poverty and inequality (Hickel, 2020; Langridge et al., 2023; Woodward, 2015). So reduction, or stopping the rise, of average income is to be achieved by steep reductions in the incomes and carbon emissions of the wealthy, making room for increases in incomes in lower-income countries and households.

Stern and Stiglitz briefly concede that "To say that investment and growth are essential in the coming two or three decades, it is not, however, a statement that growth should go on forever. Planetary boundaries do impose constraints (Rockström et al., 2009). In the later part of the century and moving into the next, the boundaries may well constrain growth (both in GDP and population) and should already be prominent in thinking about public policy." They do not explain why the problem of planetary boundaries can be deferred until mid-century, when six of nine planetary boundaries are already exceeded (Richardson et al., 2023).

Growth, Degrowth, and Employment

The recent wave of interest in BI dates from the early 1980s, when, particularly in Europe, mature capitalist economies were experiencing declining growth rates and rising unemployment (Van Parijs & Vanderborght, 2017: 6, 28, 96–98, 201–203). Thomas Piketty (2014) has shown how declining growth will result in rising inequality. These concerns with slower growth, unemployment, and rising inequality dovetail with ecological concerns about environmental limits to growth. BI is seen as one way, among a family of egalitarian policies, of reducing inequality and ensuring well-being for those who are less advantaged, without relying on growth.

In the absence of growth, when the productivity of labour rises, so too will unemployment. That is a problem in itself, but it is also a potent threat to ecological policies to limit growth because of political opposition to perceived causes of unemployment. Consequently, those favouring degrowth should support BI as a solution to the problem of unemployment.

Van Parijs (2013) has pointed out that there is a problem with this ecological argument for BI. BI isn't the only policy that can address unemployment. Compulsory WTR would lead to work sharing, thereby reducing unemployment. Wage subsidies would help to keep everyone employed by making viable otherwise inadequately paid jobs. Government investment in renewable energy and infrastructure will, like wage subsidies, result in "green jobs" that otherwise would not exist. (Job guarantees and universal basic services are also sometimes favoured instead of BI, but I will not discuss them further in this paper. Both can be complementary to BI (see Howard, 2005; Buchs, 2021).)

Why should one favour BI over wage subsidies or compulsory WTR? BI shares some similarities with both of these policies. Like WTR, BI "will induce those currently employed to give up part of their current work", opening opportunity for that work to be taken up by others seeking employment. Like a wage subsidy, "Basic Income makes it possible to cut the cost of labour to the employers while maintaining the employees' incomes, and thus makes economically viable a number of jobs which were not productive enough for them to pay a decent wage in the absence of transfers from more productive activities" (Van Parijs, 2013).

If wage subsidies were targeted to employment required for the transition to a zero-carbon economy, they could have an advantage over BI. On the one hand, BI is more likely to result in lower employment than wage subsidies. Less employment and lower incomes could result in lower carbon emissions, which might be a plus for the environment. On the other hand, if production declined, it could undermine an affluent country's capacity to meet its global climate obligations. I discuss this further below in connection with WTR.

Given the uncertainties about the consequences of BI compared to wage subsidies, is there reason prima facie to favour BI over wage subsidies and compulsory WTR? Van Parijs's (2013) answer is unequivocal: BI offers greater freedom (see also Van Parijs & Vanderborght, 2017). Compared with wage subsidies, BI puts the power in the hands of the worker rather than the employer, because BI is not conditional on taking a job. Since most will want more income than would be provided by a BI, some will have more power in bargaining with employers for higher wages and better working conditions. Others will be free to take low-paying but interesting jobs that provide development of skills and social relationships, supplemented by their BI.

Compared with compulsory WTR, BI involves no prohibition against working more than a statutory maximum while at the same time enabling others to work less.

So, the argument for BI from an ecological point of view turns out to be, at least in part, a normative argument with reference to freedom. The ecological consequences of BI on their own appear to afford a rather weak argument because other policies could also, and possibly more effectively, bring about those consequences. Because a maximalist BI's ecological credentials turn on its promoting WTR, I now examine further why WTR is important, and how BI-supported WTR compares with mandatory WTR.

WTR, Work Sharing, and BI

Earlier, I mentioned that redistribution could actually increase carbon emissions because lower-income households spend a higher proportion of their income on energy and, in general, consume more of their income than higher-income households, which tend to save more of their income. However, this redistributive effect can be at least partially reduced by WTR. As Gough (2017) points out, "Trading pay increments for more disposable time limits the rise in consumption and thus emissions."

According to Schor and Jorgenson (2019), "there is a large and significant relationship between annual hours of work and emissions in wealthy countries (Knight et al., 2013; Fitzgerald et al., 2015)". There are also important co-benefits from WTR: "Shorter working hours can also contribute to reduced stress, better physical and mental health, and higher quality of life (Schor, 2010)." Thus, "policies to reduce working hours can be important tools for lowering emissions, while also boosting employment and improving workers' health and well-being (Schor, 2013)".

BI can facilitate mandatory WTR or may achieve the desired effects by facilitating voluntary WTR. Van Parijs and Vanderborght (2017) identify three dilemmas for mandatory WTR.

1. Will WTR involve a reduction in pay or not? If workers cut hours and lose pay as a result, the worst-paid workers will be driven into poverty. If there is no reduction in pay, then the hourly cost of labour will increase. If this is matched by rising productivity, then there will be no hours to redistribute, no work sharing. But if the rise in labour costs is not paid for through rising productivity, there will be a reduced demand for labour and higher unemployment. 2. Will there be an across-the-board reduction in work time, or only for jobs for which there is excess labour supply? Across-the-board WTR will create bottlenecks, and scarce talent will be underused and expensive training wasted, and there will be a decrease in total employment. But if WTR is limited to jobs for which there is excess labour supply, those exempted from WTR will enjoy an unfair privilege. 3. Will WTR apply only to waged workers, or to everyone who works? If applied only to those working for an employer, there will be a proliferation of fake precarious self-employed. But WTR applied to everyone will produce a "nightmarishly expensive and intrusive bureaucracy" in order to ensure fairness. (Van Parijs & Vanderborght, 2017:48–50, my paraphrase).

The authors note that the first dilemma can be solved by coupling WTR with a BI, seizing the first horn of the dilemma (p. 264n48). But the other two dilemmas of mandatory WTR do not appear to be soluble in this way. However, a BI could incentivize voluntary WTR and work sharing. With an unconditional BI, workers in overcrowded labour markets would have resources to exit the labour market or reduce their hours. And workers with special talents or training would be fully utilized, and taxation on their incomes would augment the revenue for the BI scheme. With a BI, wage workers who wish to continue working full time will be free to do so, but others will have more freedom to leave wage work or reduce their hours. Since the WTR would be voluntary, there would be no need for bureaucratic monitoring. And, with a view to supplying desired employment under conditions of slower growth, a BI functions like a wage subsidy, with the important differences noted earlier. Thus, if further evidence proves that BI is effective in bringing about WTR and work sharing, it is a better option than mandatory WTR with a view to reduced overall consumption and more free time. For more on this, see Van Parijs and Vanderborght (2017: 48–50, 28).

WTR and Global Climate Justice
There are two difficulties with WTR and indirectly with a BI designed to incentivize WTR. As Van Parijs (2021) has argued, consistently with the global climate justice principles endorsed in this paper,

> Consuming less in the global North does not mean producing less in the global North, because production in the North must help fund consumption in the South. Anyone who spent any time in less developed countries realizes that it is simply unacceptable for us living in the North to go and tell people in the South: "Sorry, but for the good of our planet, you will have to keep your level of private consumption, public services and infrastructure at a level far lower than the one we have been enjoying for decades." Moreover, even under the most optimistic assumptions, we cannot expect development policies and transnational migration to bring down the level of global inequality to an acceptable level. Consequently, there is no realistic scenario for global justice that can dispense with massive financial transfers from the North to the South.

Thus, the first difficulty for WTR is that it may undermine the ability of the United States, and other affluent countries, to produce enough wealth to meet global obligations for carbon emission reductions. The second difficulty has to do with threats to productivity. As Van Parijs (2021) points out, restriction of fossil fuel use will, other things equal, result in a decrease in labour productivity, so more labour will be needed to produce the same amount of goods. (We are focusing on the threat to productivity from reduction in fossil fuel use, but there are other threats, such as we have experienced during the pandemic.) This entails that more labour will be needed to produce a given level of GDP out of which BI is funded. So a decline in work effort, other things equal, will lead to a lower BI, or threaten its viability altogether. And here is the problem for WTR:

> Faced with the prospect of falling productivity, therefore, we cannot nonchalantly respond that we shall work less and relax, contenting ourselves with a lower level of consumption. If we believe in global justice, the degrowth of Northern consumption should rather be combined with whatever additional efforts are needed to prevent falling productivity to show in falling production. Introducing an unconditional **basic income**, in this context, does not exactly seem the soundest thing to do.

Van Parijs acknowledges a couple of mitigating factors:

1. Automation may more than compensate for productivity losses.
2. BI may enhance productivity, functioning as "venture capital for the people"—if combined with lifelong learning and promotion of local communities. [For some evidence supporting this claim in poor countries, see Banerjee et al. (2019).]

Note that the first accords with Malmaeus et al.'s automation scenario, the second with their local self-sufficiency scenario.

It is clear, then, that the goal of BI is to be compatible with, or even enhance, production, not to promote "*la dolce vita*". Is it politically feasible to ask working people to work more but consume less? Van Parijs responds:

> The younger and future generations in the global North will need to content themselves with less material consumption than what our generation could get away with. To make this fact acceptable to them, indeed to make them embrace their future enthusiastically in spite of this fact, one needs to offer them a realistic utopia, on which hopes for a better life can credibly be hooked. This utopia must be consistent with both global justice and intergenerational justice yet able to outcompete the rival dystopias of neoliberalism, xenophobic nationalism and religious fundamentalism. ... the emancipatory idea of an unconditional basic income must feature at the core of such a realistic utopia.

An emancipatory BI must involve real freedom (Van Parijs, 1995; Van Parijs & Vanderborght, 2017), the "power to say no", as Karl Widerquist (2013) puts it, the freedom to form your own communities for work and living. BI must be high enough to make good on this promise. Is a BI at the poverty line high enough? In the United States, the annual cost of such a BI would be more than $500 bn—not the gross cost but the net cost to net contributors (Widerquist, 2017). I will not attempt to answer this question here (see Calnitsky, 2017, 2018; Gourevitch & Stanczyk, 2018; Howard, 2019), but will only make two comments:

First, even a partial BI can have some emancipatory effect. Alaska's PFD had no overall effect on employment and "increased part-time work by 1.8 percentage points" (Jones & Marinescu, 2022). It enabled some people to work less and others to work more, enhancing the freedom of both. [This, unfortunately, suggests that there is little effect on overall consumption.]

Second, most will still seek work if the BI is set at the poverty line, based on all the evidence from guaranteed income pilot programmes. But the BI could have profound effects on the ability of workers to form their own enterprises or cooperatives, or to bargain from a position of strength to gain a greater share of decision-making and productivity gains, and to take those productivity gains in free time rather than increased consumption. Whether they would more often choose free time is difficult to determine.

Now, to return to Van Parijs's question about WTR, I want to make two points. First, WTR is compatible with sustaining overall work effort. If combined with work sharing, it is possible to have fewer hours worked per person but the same total hours worked when there are more people employed. And, if WTR is achieved through productivity improvements, there need not be any loss in production. Juliet Schor (2025) has shown how a four-day work week can be as productive as a five-day workweek because workers can be more efficient during those four days. And the four-day work week has many environmental, health, and social benefits connected with less commuting, better work-life balance, less consumption of fast food, and so on. If the above-mentioned objections to mandatory WTR are decisive, then BI is the preferred instrument for facilitating voluntary WTR and work sharing.

Second, in order to maintain production while reducing consumption, keep in mind that most of the reduction in consumption must be by the more affluent, who can reduce carbon emissions and spending without great loss to their well-being. As we noted earlier, in a wealthy country like the United States, the top 10% will need to reduce their emissions by about 90%, and the middle 40% by half, and this will be difficult to do without reducing their overall consumption. Redistributive tax policies (and/or transferring wealth to the Commons and sharing it more equitably) are the instruments for reducing luxury consumption. The only constraints on such redistribution are that marginal tax rates not be raised so high that they self-defeatingly undermine incentives and reduce net tax revenue, and that wealth in common be managed at least as efficiently as privately held wealth. There is, of course, much controversy about such constraints, which I will not address here, except to say that there is considerable inefficiency—even plunder—when it comes to the management of global natural resources such as fisheries, and thus room for protecting the Commons (Standing, 2019, 2022).

One final comment pertaining to the relationship between a maximalist BI and degrowth: Given the need for economic growth in the global South, and also the need for continued production in the global North, oriented towards transfers to the global South, it is not clear that there should be degrowth of production in the global North. All parties agree that GDP is a poor measure of social and economic progress (Stiglitz et al., 2009; Jackson, 2009; Hickel, 2020). So perhaps the controversy about GDP growth can be avoided by focusing on the growth of sustainable energy sources, particularly in countries still struggling with extreme poverty, and focusing on reducing luxury emissions, increasing egalitarian distribution of wealth and income nationally and globally, and other measures often associated with degrowth that are worth considering whether the overall economy is growing or not, such as WTR, work sharing, and public investment in healthcare and public transportation.

Conclusion

There are many unanswered questions remaining. I conclude by listing some of the issues for future research.

For Further Empirical Study and Analysis

While it is intuitively plausible that BI can support WTR, more work is needed to estimate how great this effect is likely to be in various contexts, and how compatible it is with sustaining production.

BI clearly allows more freedom than wage subsidies. But if the latter are needed (directly, or indirectly via alternative energy investment), how might BI and wage subsidies be combined?

In this paper, I have said little about the implications of BI for consumption. If the goal of environmental policy is to deter deforestation and other environmental bads, and to encourage sustainable consumption, it would seem that conditional cash payments would be preferable to BI. There is need for more research on conditional versus unconditional cash in relation to sustainable consumption.

Normative Issues

How much does the maximalist case depend on a normative commitment to freedom? If Van Parijs is correct, the ecological case for a basic income should include a normative dimension, specifically a case for real freedom. There are, however, competing conceptions of freedom, such as left libertarianism (Van Parijs, 1995), liberal egalitarianism (Rawls, 1999, 2001; Birnbaum, 2012), independentarianism (Widerquist, 2013); freedom from domination (Pettit, 1997; Casassas & De Wispelaere, 2012), and developmental freedom (Sen, 1999; Haagh, 2019). Which of these is the more philosophically defensible view of freedom, and to what extent they support a basic income, are topics that go beyond the scope of this paper.

Political Economy Considerations

Van Parijs's point about the need to sustain production while decreasing consumption of fossil fuels raises the question of whether such a policy, along with the tax policies recommended in the inequality argument, is made more feasible and attractive with a BI. It is one thing to show that BI can solve certain problems. It is an additional task to demonstrate the possibility of popular support and overcoming institutional barriers and opposition from interested parties (Chrisp & De Wispelaere, 2023).

Acknowledgements I am grateful for comments from the participants at the Workshop on Guaranteed Income Experiments at New Orleans University, February 2024, as well as people who commented on earlier related papers at the Hoover Chair Diaspora Conference, Louvain-la-Neuve, 2022; at the Centre for Ethics, Politics, and Society, University of Minho, Braga, Portugal, 2020; and at several Basic Income Earth Network congresses and North American Basic Income Guarantee conferences.

References

Banerjee, A., Niehaus, P., & Suri, T. (2019). Universal basic income in the developing world. *Annual Review of Economics, 11*, 959–983. https://doi.org/10.1146/annurev-economics-080218-030229

Barnes, P. (2014). *With liberty and dividends for all.* Berrett-Koehler.

Barry, B. (2005). *Why social justice matters.* Polity.

Birnbaum, S. (2012). *Basic income reconsidered: Social justice, liberalism, and the demands of equality.* Palgrave Macmillan.

Boyce, J. K. (2019). *The case for carbon dividends.* Polity.

Buchs, M. (2021). Sustainable welfare: How do universal basic income and universal basic services compare? *Ecological Economics, 189*, 1–9.

Budolfson, M., & Spears, D. (2021). Population ethics and the prospects for fertility policy as climate mitigation policy. *The Journal of Development Studies, 57*(9), 1499–1510. https://doi.org/10.1080/00220388.2021.1915481

Calnitsky, D. (2017). Debating basic income. *Catalyst (Washington, D.C.), 1*(3), 62–91.

Calnitsky, D. (2018). Does basic income assume a can opener? *Catalyst (Washington, D.C.), 2*(3), 137–155.

Caney, S. (2008). Cosmopolitan justice, responsibility, and global climate change. In T. Brooks (Ed.), *The global justice reader* (pp. 689–713). Blackwell Publishing. First published in Leiden Journal of International Law 18 (2005).

Casassas, D., & De Wispelaere, J. (2012). The Alaska model: A republican perspective. In K. Widerquist & M. W. Howard (Eds.), *Alaska's permanent fund dividend: Examining its suitability as a model* (pp. 169–188). Palgrave Macmillan.

Chancel, L., Piketty, T., Saez, E., & Zucman, G. (2022). *World inequality report.* https://wir2022.wid.world/

Chrisafis, A. (2018). Who are the gilets jaunes and what do they want? *The Guardian*, 7 December. https://www.theguardian.com/world/2018/dec/03/who-are-the-gilets-jaunes-and-what-do-they-want

Chrisp, J., & De Wispelaere, J. (2023). A basic income for every crisis? Building blocks of a political economy framework. *Journal of Sociology, 59*(4), 914–930.

Daniels, N. (1975). Equal liberty and unequal worth of liberty. In N. Daniels (Ed.), *Reading Rawls* (pp. 253–281). Basic Books.

Di Liberto, T. (2024). What's in a number? The meaning of the 1.5-C climate threshold. *NOAA*, 9 January, https://www.climate.gov/news-features/features/whats-number-meaning-15-c-climate-threshold

Ferraro, P., & Simorangkir, R. (2020). Conditional cash transfers to alleviate poverty also reduced deforestation in Indonesia. *Science Advances 12*, https://doi.org/10.1126/sciadv.aaz1298

Fitzgerald, J. B., Jorgenson, A. K., & Clark, B. (2015). Energy consumption and working hours: A longitudinal study of developed and developing nations, 1990–2008. *Environmental Sociology, 1*(3), 213–223.

Fletcher, R., & Buscher, B. (2020). Conservation basic income: A non- market mechanism to support convivial conservation. *Biological Conservation, 244*, 108520.

Flomenhoft, G. (2012). Applying the Alaska model in a resource-poor state: The example of Vermont. In K. Widerquist & M. W. Howard (Eds.), *Exporting the Alaska model: Adapting the permanent fund dividend* (pp. 85–107). Palgrave Macmillan.

Fukuma, S. (2017). Meaningful work, worthwhile life, and self-respect: Reexamination of the Rawlsian perspective on basic income in a property-owning democracy. *Basic Income Studies, 12*(1).

Gorz, A. (2013). Beyond the wage-based society. In K. Widerquist, J. A. Noguera, Y. Vanderborght, & J. De Wispelaere (Eds.), *Basic income: An anthology of contemporary research* (pp. 297–306). Blackwell.

Gough, I. (2017). *Heat, greed, and human need: Climate change, capitalism and sustainable wellbeing*. Edward Elgar.

Gourevitch, A., & Stanczyk, L. (2018). The basic income illusion. *Catalyst (Philadelphia, Pa), 1*(4), 151–177.

Haagh, L. (2019). *The case for universal basic income*. Polity.

Haberl, H., Wiedenhofer, D., Virág, D., Kalt, G., Plank, B., Brockway, P., Creutzig, F. et al. (2020). A systematic review of the evidence on decoupling of GDP, resource use and GHG emissions, part II: Synthesizing the insights. *Environmental Research Letters*. https://doi.org/10.1088/1748-9326/ab842a

Hickel, J. (2020). *Less is more: How degrowth will save the world*. Penguin Random House.

Hickel, J., & Kallis, G. (2020). Is green growth possible? *New Political Economy, 25*(4), 469–486. https://doi.org/10.1080/13563467.2019.1598964

Howard, M. W. (2005). Basic income and job guarantees: Alternatives or complements? Symposium: Basic income guarantees and the right to work. *Rutgers Journal of Law and Urban Policy, 2*(1), Fall, 186–95 (also online at: https://rutgerspolicyjournal.org/2005/01/11/volume-2-issue-1/)

Howard, M. W. (2011). Sharing the burdens of climate change: Environmental justice and qualified cosmopolitanism. In P. G. Harris (Ed.), *Ethics and global environmental policy: Cosmopolitan conceptions of climate change* (pp. 108–127). Edward Elgar.

Howard, M. W. (2012). A cap on carbon and a basic income: A defensible combination in the U.S.? In K. Widerquist & M. W. Howard (Eds.), *Exporting the Alaska model: Adapting the Permanent Fund Dividend* (pp. 147–162). Palgrave Macmillan.

Howard, M. W. (2016). *Building support for US climate reforms with universal benefits.* Scholars' Strategy Network Forum on Building Democratic Support for Equitable Carbon Pricing. Accessed January 27, 2019, from https://scholars.org/page/building-support-us-climate-reforms-universal-benefits

Howard, M. W. (2017). A carbon dividend as a step toward a Basic Income in the United States: Prospects and problems. *IPR Blog*, 5 July. Institute for Policy Research, University of Bath. Accessed January 27, 2019, from http://blogs.bath.ac.uk/iprblog/2017/07/05/a-carbon-dividend-as-a-step-toward-a-basic-income-in-the-united-states-prospects-and-problems/

Howard, M. W. (2019). *The left debate on basic income.* USBIG Discussion Paper 356. https://usbig.net/discussion-papers/

Howard, M., Pinto, J., & Schachtschneider, U. (2023). Ecological effects of basic income. In M. Torry (Ed.), *The Palgrave international handbook of basic income* (2nd ed.). Palgrave Macmillan. https://doi.org/10.1007/978-3-031-41001-7_8

Hoynes, H., & Rothstein, J. (2019). Universal basic income in the United States and advanced countries. *Annual Review of Economics, 11*, 929–958.

Hubacek, K., Baiocchi, G., Feng, K., & Patwardhan, A. (2017). Poverty eradication in a carbon constrained world. *Nature Communications, 8*(1), 912.

Jackson, T. (2009). *Prosperity without growth: Economics for a finite planet.* Earthscan.

Jones, D., & Marinescu, I. (2022). The labour market impacts of universal and permanent cash transfers: Evidence from the Alaska Permanent Fund. *American Economic Journal: Economic Policy, 14*(2), 315–340. https://doi.org/10.1257/pol.20190299

Kemp-Benedict, E., Holz, C., Baer, P., Athanaisou, T., & Kartha, S. (2019). *The climate equity reference calculator.* Berkeley and Somerville: Climate Equity Reference Project (EcoEquity and Stockholm Environment Institute), [Online]. Accessed February 13, 2024, from https://calculator.climateequityreference.org

Knight, K., Rosa, E. A., & Schor, J. B. (2013). Reducing growth to achieve environmental sustainability: The role of work hours. In J. Wicks-Lim & R. Pollin (Eds.), *Capitalism on trial – Explorations in the tradition of Thomas E. Weisskopf* (pp. 187–204). Edward Elgar.

Langridge, N., Buchs, M., & Howard, N. (2023). An ecological basic income? Examining the ecological credentials of basic income through a review of selected pilot interventions. *Basic Income Studies, 18*(1), 47–87. https://doi.org/10.1515/bis-2021-0044

MacNeill, T., & Vibert, A. (2019). Universal basic income and the natural environment: Theory and policy. *Basic Income Studies, 14*(1), 1–8.

McKay, D. I. A. et al. (2022). Exceeding 1.5°C global warming could trigger multiple climate tipping points. *Science 377*(6611), 9 September. https://doi.org/10.1126/science.abn7950

Moellendorf, D. (2014). *The moral challenge of dangerous climate change*. Cambridge University Press.

Molina, G. G., & Ortiz-Juarez, E. (2020). *Temporary basic income: Protecting poor and vulnerable people in developing countries*. United Nations Development Programme. https://www.sdg16hub.org/system/files/2021-03/Temporary%2520Basic%2520Income-V4.pdf

Murphy, L., & Nagel, T. (2002). *The myth of ownership: Taxes and justice*. Oxford University Press.

National Academies of Sciences, Engineering, and Medicine. (2019). *Negative emissions technologies and reliable sequestration: A research agenda*. The National Academies Press. https://doi.org/10.17226/25259

Nuccitelli, D. (2022). Experts: Senate-passed bill will yield myriad climate benefits. *Yale Climate Connections*, 8 August. https://yaleclimateconnections.org/2022/08/experts-senate-passed-bill-will-yield-myriad-climate-benefits/

Parrique, T., Barth, J., Briens, F., Kerschner, C., Kraus-Polk, A., Kuokkanen, A., & Spangenberg, J. H. (2019). *Decoupling debunked: Evidence and arguments against green growth as a sole strategy for sustainability*. European Environmental Bureau.

Pettit, P. (1997). *Republicanism: A theory of freedom and government*. Oxford University Press.

Piketty, T. (2014). *Capital in the twenty-first century*. Harvard University Press.

Pinto, J. (2020). Environmentalism, ecologism, and basic income. *Basic Income Studies, 15*(1).

Plumer, B. (2019). Carbon dioxide emissions hit a record in 2019, even as coal fades. *New York Times*, 3 December. https://www.nytimes.com/2019/12/03/climate/carbon-dioxide-emissions.html#

Pollin, R. (2015). Think we can't stabilize the climate while fostering growth? Think again. *The Nation*, 27 October. https://www.thenation.com/article/think-we-cant-st

Pollin, R., & Chasman, D. (2015). *Greening the global economy*. MIT Press.

Rawls, J. (1999). *A theory of justice* (2nd ed.). Harvard University Press.

Rawls, J. (2001). *Justice as fairness: A restatement*. Harvard University Press.

Rees, W. E. (2023). The human eco-predicament: Overshoot and the population conundrum. *Vienna Yearbook of Population Research, 21*, 1–19.

Reyes, O., Orenstein, K., Athanasiou, T., Daniel, T., Holz, C., Kartha, S., Lennon, E., Menotti, V., Stabinsky, D., Stone, K., & Wu, B. (2021). *United States of America fair shares nationally determined contribution*. http://foe.org/wp-content/uploads/2021/04/USA_Fair_Shares_NDC.pdf

Richardson, K., et al. (2023). Earth beyond six of nine planetary boundaries. *Science Advances, 9*(37). https://doi.org/10.1126/sciadv.adh2458

Rockström, J., Steffen, W., Noone, K., Persson, A., Chapin, F. S., Lambin, E. F., Lenton, T. M., Scheffer, M., Folke, C., & Schellnhuber, H. J. (2009). A safe operating space for humanity. *Nature, 461*(7263), 472–475.

Saez, E., & Piketty, T. (2013). Why the 1% should pay tax at 80%. *The Guardian*, 24 October. https://www.theguardian.com/commentisfree/2013/oct/24/1percent-pay-tax-rate-80percent

Sager, L. (2017). *Income inequality and carbon consumption: Evidence from environmental Engel curves.* Grantham Research Institute on Climate Change and the Environment. Working Paper 385. Accessed January 27, 2019, from http://www.lse.ac.uk/GranthamInstitute/publication/income-inequality-and-carbon-consumption-evidence-from-environmental-engel-curves/

Schor, J. B. (2010). *Plenitude: The new economics of true wealth.* Penguin Press.

Schor, J. B. (2013). Why solving climate change requires working less. In A. Coote & J. Franklin (Eds.), *Time on our side: Why we all need a shorter working week* (pp. 3–20). New Economics Foundation.

Schor, J. B., & Jorgenson, A. K. (2019). Is it too late for growth? *Review of Radical Political Economics, 51*(2). https://doi.org/10.1177/0486613419831109

Schor, J. (2025). *Four days a week: The life-changing solution for reducing employee stress, improving well-being and working smarter.* Harper Business.

Sen, A. (1999). *Development as freedom.* Random House.

Sheehan, C., & Martin-Ortega, J. (2023). Is conservation basic income a good idea? A scoping study of the views of conservation professionals on cash giving programs. *Biological Conservation 279.*

Shue, H. (2017). Climate dreaming: Negative emissions, risk transfer, and irreversibility. *Journal of Human Rights and the Environment, 8*(2), 203–216.

Singer, P. (2008). One atmosphere. In T. Brooks (Ed.), *The global justice reader* (pp. 667–688). Blackwell Publishing. First published in P. Singer, *One World: The Ethics of Globalization*, 2nd ed. (New Haven: Yale University Press, 2007): 14–50, 205–208.

Standing, G. (2013). Can basic income cash transfers transform India? *Basic Income News*, 4 February. http://binews.org/2013/02/opinion-can-basic-income-cash-transfers-transform-india/

Standing, G. (2019). *Plunder of the commons.* Pelican Books.

Standing, G. (2022). *The blue commons: Rescuing the economy of the sea.* Pelican Books.

Standing, G., Davala, S., Jhabvala, R., & Kapoor Mehta, S. (2015). *Basic income: A transformative policy for India.* Bloomsbury Academic.

Stern, N., & Stiglitz, J. E. (2023). Climate change and growth. *Industrial and Corporate Change, 32*, 277–303. https://doi.org/10.1093/icc/dtad008

Stiglitz, J., Sen, A., & Fitoussi, J. P. (2009). *Report of the Commission on the Measurement of Economic Performance and Social Progress.* Commission on the Measurement of Economic Performance and Social Progress. http://files.harmonywithnatureun.org/uploads/upload112.pdf

Stiglitz, J., et al. (2017). *Report of the high-level commission on carbon prices.* World Bank. License: Creative Commons Attribution CC BY 3.0 IGO. https://doi.org/10.7916/d8-w2nc-4103

Van Parijs, P. (1995). *Real freedom for all.* Oxford University Press.

Van Parijs, P. (2003). Difference principles. In S. Freeman (Ed.), *The Cambridge companion to Rawls.* Cambridge University Press.

Van Parijs, P. (2013). A green case for basic income? In K. Widerquist, J. A. Noguera, J. De Wispelaere, & Y. Vanderborght (Eds.), *Basic income: An anthology of contemporary research* (pp. 269–274). Wiley.

Van Parijs, P. (2021). Climate change and the Covid-19 pandemic: Crucial pushes or deadly blows for basic income? In D. Rodenhäuser, H. Vetter, B. Held, & H. Diefenbacher (Eds.), *Soziale Sicherungssysteme im Umbruch. Beiträge zur socio-ökologischen Transformation* (pp. 193–211). Metropolis.

Van Parijs, P., & Vanderborght, Y. (2017). *Basic income: A radical proposal for a free society and a sane economy.* Harvard.

Victor, P. A. (2008). *Managing without growth: Slower by design, not disaster.* Edward Elgar.

Walzer, M. (1983). *Spheres of justice.* Basic Books.

White, S. (2003). *The civic minimum: On the rights and obligations of economic citizenship.* Oxford University Press.

Widerquist, K. (2013). *Independence, propertylessness, and basic income: A theory of freedom as the power to say no.* Palgrave Macmillan.

Widerquist, K. (2017). The cost of basic income: Back-of-the-envelope calculations. *Basic Income Studies, 12*(2). https://doi.org/10.1515/bis-2017-0016

Wikipedia. (2024a). *World population.* Accessed February 15, 2024, from https://en.wikipedia.org/wiki/World_population

Wikipedia. (2024b). *List of countries by carbon dioxide emissions.* Accessed February 15, 2024, from https://en.wikipedia.org/wiki/List_of_countries_by_carbon_dioxide_emissions

Wikipedia. (2024c). *List of countries by greenhouse gas emissions.* Accessed February 15, 2024, from https://en.wikipedia.org/wiki/List_of_countries_by_greenhouse_gas_emissions

Wilebore, B., Voors, M., Bulte, E. H., Coomes, D., & Kontoleon, A. (2019). Unconditional transfers and tropical forest conservation: Evidence from a randomized control trial in Sierra Leone. *American Journal of Agricultural Economics, 101*, 894–918.

Woodward, D. (2015). Incrementum ad Absurdum: Global growth, inequality and poverty eradication in a carbon-constrained world. *World Economic Review,*

4, 43–62. Retrieved from http://wer.worldeconomicsassociation.org/files/WEA-WER-4.pdf#page=44

Zelleke, A. (2005). Basic income in the United States: Redefining citizenship in the Liberal State. In K. Widerquist, M. A. Lewis, & S. Pressman (Eds.), *The ethics and economics of the basic income guarantee* (pp. 109–121). Ashgate.

Zelleke, A. (2011). Feminist political theory and the argument for an unconditional basic income. *Policy and Politics, 39*(1), 27–42.

PART II

Political Feasibility and Global Perspectives

CHAPTER 5

Do Side Effects Matter?

Sara Bizarro

Introduction

Social research is often needed when proposing a new public policy. To decide if a policy is to be recommended, we need first to put forward the goals the policy is trying to achieve and then evaluate if it is likely that such a policy will indeed accomplish those goals. In this paper, I argue that beyond evaluating the efficacy of the policy to achieve its intended goals, we also need to ask if there are unintended consequences of the policy, especially if those consequences are antithetical to the expressed goal the policy is trying to achieve. When evaluating a policy, we need to see if it will do what it proposes and if it has any other foreseeable but unintended consequences or results that directly oppose that policy's intended consequences. If this turns out to be the case, then the policy may be problematic.

In Part I of this paper, I will develop a conceptual approach to the problem of intentions. I will draw upon the work of Jeremy Bentham, and I will also discuss the doctrine of double effect. These will be the basis for the conceptual framework that can be used in social research when dealing with both intended and unintended consequences of policies. The

S. Bizarro (✉)
University of New Orleans, New Orleans, LA, USA
e-mail: sbizarro@uno.edu

R. Merrill, C. Neves (eds.), *Determining the Value of Universal Basic Income*, Exploring the Basic Income Guarantee,
https://doi.org/10.1007/978-3-032-04004-6_5

problem of unintended consequences of policy is a longstanding concern of actual social research, and not simply a theoretical concern. I will argue that social policy always needs to address whether it is likely to reach its intended consequences and any possible oblique, unintended side effects, as these can play a crucial role in deciding if the policy is worth implementing. I will put forward many examples of past policies and ways in which unintended consequences undermined those policies.

In Part II, I will apply the conceptual framework to the specific problem of researching Basic Income policies. In order to do this, it is necessary to distinguish between Basic Income policy's intended and unintended consequences. This is particularly problematic in the case of Basic Income. Some have wanted to use Basic Income policies in order to eliminate social security, while others think it is a way to solve problems regarding automation and so on with many other variations. However, one effect seems to be intended by all proponents: to end or significantly reduce poverty. If this is so, research on Basic Income should look into the possibility that it may not reduce poverty. To evaluate this, we need to define poverty and then see if the policy has the potential to create rather than reduce poverty as a side effect of its application. If it turns out that Basic Income has the potential to create and even solidify poverty, then the policy is problematic, and more work is needed to implement it with good results.

Part I

Oblique Intentions and Double Effect

In order to discuss the intended and unintended consequences of public policy, we need to have a conceptual framework to explain what intentions are and what responsibility we have for a consequence that follows from a policy but is not strictly intended. Jeremy Bentham introduced the concept of "oblique intentions" that may be useful in this context. Bentham distinguishes several types of intentions; the main two general types are direct and oblique intentions. Direct intentions are directly linked to the "chain of causes by which the person was determined to do the act" (Bentham, 1789, Chap. 8, VI). On the other hand, oblique intentions are not directly intended but are likely to ensue. Here is how Bentham defines it: "Although the consequence was in contemplation and appeared likely to ensue in case of the act's being performed, yet the prospect of producing such consequence did not constitute a link in the aforesaid chain."

(Bentham, 1789, Chap. 8, VI). According to Bentham, even though the *oblique intention* may not be in the actual causal chain of the particular action, the subject is still responsible for the likely consequences of that action, even if they were not directly intended. An interesting example provided by Bentham is the following: someone saw a stag (male deer) running away, and the King was also riding a horse in that direction: "what he aimed at was to kill the stag; he did not wish to kill the king, at the same time he saw, that if he shot, it was as likely he should kill the king as the stag, yet for all that he shot, and killed the king accordingly. In this case, the incident of his killing the king was intentional, but obliquely so." (Bentham, 1789, Chap. 8, XII, 2). In short, if we say, "I didn't mean to do so and so", if the effect was a likely and foreseeable consequence, the law can still say we could see it coming, and we are responsible. The courts may have to provide further evidence, but if they can show the person (or government or corporation) was aware of the likely consequence, they are liable.[1]

One can question using "intention" to refer to oblique consequences. It can be better described as an effect or a likely consequence rather than an intention. However, in public policy, since I think the supposed "unintended consequences" can sometimes be the true intention of a policy, it may be useful to keep Bentham's definition of oblique intentions rather than a simple unintended consequence. This makes it easier to pinpoint both the distinction and the responsibility associated with it, since if the intention is direct or oblique, in both cases, there is no question that the one who acts is still responsible for the consequences of the action. Still, let us look at a different way to define the idea, the well-known Doctrine of Double Effect.

In Philippa Foot's paper, "The Problem of Abortion and the Doctrine of the Double Effect"[2] (Foot, 1967), she defines the Christian doctrine of

[1] Bentham says: "Lastly, whatever circumstances can be seen to be connected with the consequences of the offense, whether directly in the way of derivation, or obliquely in the way of collateral affinity (to wit, in virtue of its being connected, in the way of derivation, with some of the circumstances with which they stand connected in the same manner) bear a material relation to the offense in the way of evidence, they may accordingly be styled evidentiary circumstances, and may become of use, by being held forth upon occasion as so many proofs, indications, or evidences of its having been committed." (Bentham, 1781, Chap. 7, XXVII)

[2] This is also where Phillippa Foot first introduced the famous Trolley Problem, which will not be addressed in this chapter.

double effect as follows: There is a difference between what someone intends with an action and what someone foresees as a possible consequence of an action. What someone intends comprises both the end and the means to the end. One may regret the means to the end and think there is no better way, but regardless, one still intends both the means and the end. Foot gives as an example when we decide to confine "dangerous lunatics" for the sake of our safety, we may think confining is a regrettable thing but necessary for the end of keeping the lunatic off the streets. A foreseen but not intended action is not part of the means nor the end, but a "side effect", so to speak. The doctrine of the double effect claims that "it is sometimes permissible to bring about by oblique intention what one may not directly intend".

One example presented by Foot of the application of the doctrine of double effect that can lead us to think twice about its usefulness is abortion and how it is discussed within the Christian faith. According to the Christian faith, life is sacred, and we should not put an end to it, and we cannot use ending life as a means to another end either, even if it is to save a life. Therefore, abortion is not acceptable under this framework. However, if a *different* procedure, such as a hysterectomy, is applied and the baby dies as a side effect, the doctrine says this is an unintended consequence, and in that case, it is ok. As Foot says in her paper, Hart thought this example was sufficient to throw out the whole theory—surely you can just change the intentions by a sleight of hand and be off the hook. This is why Bentham wanted to call oblique intentions as *intentions*. One is still responsible for those consequences.

In public policy, we can use a similar framework. If there are foreseeable consequences of a policy that then come to be, we cannot wave responsibility by simply saying that was not the policy's intention. Therefore, when doing a policy experiment, it is crucial to test whether the policy has the results it is meant to have and if there are any *oblique* consequences of the policy. And if there are any, are they good or bad? Should they be considered *oblique*, or can they be veiled as *direct* intentions? In either case, what is our responsibility when implementing these policies? As we will see later, these questions are important for the Basic Income policy debate.

Direct and Oblique Policy Effects

The question of unintended consequences in public policy is quite interesting and has been fascinating to economists for decades.[3] Although there is a lot of serious policy research regarding unintended consequences, there are also abuses of this by people who are against government regulation in general; those critics will say that government regulations have all kinds of unintended consequences that are mostly bad, and they use this to undermine any governmental policy efforts.[4] On the other hand, some policies can be proposed with certain stated intentions, but the real intentions are quite different from the stated ones. In this case, the supposedly unintended consequences are the secretly intended consequences.[5]

Policy does not work in a vacuum, just like in natural ecosystems, when you change one piece, you may have unexpected consequences elsewhere. Furthermore, policies can be proposed in good faith or bad faith. For these reasons, policy implementation is the object of experimentation and criticism before it is enacted. Even admitting that there is some uncertainty involved, we can still argue that by slowly implementing and adjusting different policies, we can improve the total health of a system and at least mitigate some of its worst issues. No one policy will solve every social problem, but a certain set of policies may improve the health of the social system they address.

Before examining Basic Income and the possible direct and oblique effects of that policy, I want to examine other enacted policies with significant *oblique or side effects*. Let us start with healthcare policies in the

[3] Economist Matthew J. Kotchen, for instance, has evaluated what happens when consumers are asked to pay for their "sins of emissions", one example he mentions is when a company in Tennessee introduced a green electricity programme where those who bought in would be giving towards alternative energies, their use of electricity went up by 2.5% (Kotchen, 2018).

[4] See for instance, Professor of Economics Art Cardon's piece in Forbes where he claims that rent control leads to landlords' discrimination when they select their tenants, supposedly because they do not have to worry about profits, and they do not have to simply take the higher bidder or that minimum wage leads to further exclusion of people in the fringes of society (Carden, 2011).

[5] An example of this could be "trickle-down" types of policies, where they are supposed to benefit the economy in general but benefit mostly the rich. The same goes for the "War on Drugs" policies that led to African Americans being incarcerated; it could have been the real intention behind the idea of a "War of Drugs". To prove that these were the intended consequences of the policies, we would need a sort of "backstage" access to policymaking that is quite difficult, if not impossible, to obtain.

United States. Public healthcare programmes in the US aim to reduce the number of uninsured individuals. However, because any partial public health benefit interacts with private insurance, it has often led to more people becoming uninsured than before. One example, Richard L. Bucciarelli (2001) presents is when the State Children's Health Insurance Programme (SCHIP) was implemented in Florida. In this case, low-income families dropped their employer insurance to enroll in SCHIP but later dropped SCHIP because of out-of-pocket costs. Another example by Robert Crittenden (2001) is of a similar kind. Expanding Medicaid has led to more uninsured in King County in Washington because of a decline in employment-based coverage.

In specific healthcare policies, there are also many examples of unintended consequences. Consider, for instance, unintended consequences of health policy aimed at targeting obesity (Brown & Allison, 2013). Here are a few examples from actual policy implementation: taxing sugar and sweetened beverages to decrease intake to reduce weight led to increased consumption of beer, which does not help with weight loss; and alerting patients of their heavyweight status to make them aware as a first step towards addressing the issue may make patients feel stigmatized and depressed, which makes them eat more, and they may avoid future doctors' appointments. These are just a couple of examples of unintended consequences of this type of policy.

There are also interesting results in policies intended to mitigate poverty. In the 1950s and 1960s, in the Dole on Poverty in the US, there was a 1% drop in the official poverty rate for every ten-percentage-point increase in aid. However, after the War on Poverty Act in 1964, in the 11 years after, for every 1% fall, the aid had to be raised by 50%. Economists say that the "relationship between public aid and the poverty rate is subject to the principle of diminishing returns" (Gallaway & Garrett, 2016). So, the more aid money, the less impact it had: "This is a Laffer Curve type relationship, which is to say that while public aid initially decreases poverty, there eventually comes a point at which additional increases in public aid increased poverty".[6]

[6] "The statistical properties of this relationship were explored extensively in the mid-1980s by Gallaway, Vedder, and Foster (1985), as well as Gallaway and Vedder (1985, 1986), using per capita levels as the measure of real public aid. At that time, it was noted that the findings implied the effectiveness of additional real public aid expenditures, as a policy instrument designed to reduce the poverty rate, had been exhausted by the mid-1970s. Indeed, any additional public aid beyond the mid-1970s levels would result in an increase, not a decrease,

Another aspect of the War on Poverty and the welfare system that had "unintended" consequences is the "welfare trap". This is often mentioned in the discussion of basic income, as it is seen as a way out of this trap. The idea here is that even though welfare was intended to "increase incomes at the bottom of the income distribution, reduce poverty, and improve nutrition, health, and human capital" (Bitler & Karoly, 2015), the means-tested programmes end up discouraging work and putting people in a situation where they are trapped in a circle of poverty and social exclusion.

Murky Waters

When unintended consequences of the policy are foreseeable, we can question the *real* intentions of the policymakers. Let us look at welfare and its variations. We can have people living completely on welfare and people who participate in some sort of workfare scenario. As mentioned above, the main intention of these programmes is to reduce poverty. However, in many cases, these policies end up excluding people from the workplace, or encouraging people to have limited involvement in the workforce. This, in turn, can have as a consequence lower unemployment numbers (since people on welfare are not counted as unemployed), but this does not mean that poverty is overcome. In fact, the well-known welfare trap is the idea that people on welfare are trapped in a vicious circle of poverty. This side effect, however, can be one of the original veiled intentions of the policy. It may very well be that Welfare is designed to keep a significant amount of people out of the workforce; it is not designed to help people move out of the poverty level. It is hard to prove that policymakers had that intention in mind when they came up with the policy, but it is possible. A possible first step is to consider that "oblique intentions" have to be part of the stated intentions, and whatever follows from the policy in a predictable way should be taken into consideration as part of the intentions of the policy.

in the poverty rate. The greatest poverty-reducing effect occurs at $1,291 of per capita expenditures on public aid, which produces a 6.07 percentage point reduction in the overall poverty rate. However, as the level of real per capita public aid rises beyond $1,291, the poverty-reducing effect is eroded. At the $1,500 per capita level, the reduction in the poverty rate falls to 5.81 percentage points; at $2,000 per capita, the poverty rate decline is only 3.74 percentage points; at $2,407 of per capita public aid, all of the initial reductions in the poverty rate have disappeared." (Gallaway & Garrett, 2016)

Now let us think about two types of possible welfare policies:[7] programme one is where the participants are not allowed to work, and programme two is where they are allowed (or sometimes forced) to work for low income below a certain threshold before they lose their benefits. Imagine the policymakers claiming that the goal of Programme 1 is to provide people who are not employed with a minimum income so they can survive and fight poverty. Policymakers claim the goal of Programme 2 is to encourage people to work during difficult periods. Hence, they feel socially connected and prepared to enter the job market in the future. Now, let us think about some possible consequences of these policies that are not stated in the overt goals. In Programme 1, we could effectively remove many people from the job market; a large percentage of these people, if they were working, would probably be making a minimum wage. By removing them from the market, we are reducing the pool of people available to work at a minimum wage, and employers may have to pay more to get workers for their entry-level positions. This would be a beneficial side effect of the original policy. On the other hand, the policy leaves people stigmatized and stagnated, a negative side effect of the original policy. These effects are surely in mind when policies are construed, and policymakers have to weigh them when deciding on a policy as much as they have to weigh the original or public intentions of the policy. Let us think about some possible consequences of Programme 2. If welfare recipients are required to work[8] but can only work at a certain rate to keep their benefits, this policy's likely side effect is that more workers are made available to work at low pay in that job market.[9] The pay for entry-level positions will decrease significantly as these workers become available. This would, for many, be considered a negative side effect of the policy, but not for all. It can be a veiled intention of policymakers. Both Programme 1 and Programme 2 have side effects that can be veiled intentions of the policymakers. In both cases, those veiled intentions are somewhat antithetical to the programme, since they both promote one sort of social exclusion or another.

[7] This is a thought experiment, I am not talking about any specific policies.

[8] Work requirements can be argued against in many ways, this is just an illustration. For more on workfare as proposed by Guiliani in the 1990s, for instance, see Deparle (1998).

[9] This is the Walmart scenario where workers want to work a certain limited number of hours at a low pay in order to keep their welfare benefits.

Because there is a strong possibility that social policy can have overt intentions and veiled intentions, ethically sound policymaking *must* look at all possible consequences of a policy. Policymakers cannot simply focus on what a policy is supposed to do or address; they *must* look at the policy's indirect consequences or side effects. If this is not done, we risk having a policy we support used by others for side effects or consequences we do not support. Policy research, therefore, cannot be done ethically simply by looking at specific desired effects of the policy. We must look at possible undesired effects, which must be varied and not picked simply to support our results; they must be genuinely challenging to the main idea of the policy. It can be seen metaphorically this way: use car crash dummies and test different ways the car can crash to see if the policy stands and, if not, what type of security we need to add to the car.

Evaluating Public Policy

Public policies are very often tested in advance and to evaluate any policy, we need to have at hand the intended goals of the proposed policies so that they can be compared with the results of the experiments. These tests work better if two competing policies are at stake. Hausman (2017) calls this idea "restricted consequentialism". The principle of restricted consequentialism is: "A policy is acceptable (other things being equal) if and only if no other alternative results in better consequences and that a policy is required (other things being equal) if and only if its consequences are better than any alternatives." (Hausman, 2017, p. 608). The goods policies are trying to promote may be different and not comparable, but for policies to be comparable and evaluated, there has to be a comparable good; we need to know what counts for better or worse and how to measure it. However, note the "other things being equal" clause. For policies to be compared, they not only need a common value but "other things need to be equal".

Policy evaluation can also be divided into three periods: before the policy is adopted, during the adoption as it is implemented, and after the policy is adopted. The main focus here is on what we can do before adopting a policy, but it is also important to look at the potential of what can happen in the implementation stage and the final stage—if things go wrong in any of these stages, it is useful to have some guidelines that have been created in advance and to be prepared to respond; this work should also be done before the policy is adopted.

Let us start with the stage before implementation, the *policy research stage*. In Social Policy, the commonly accepted way of evaluating policies is by using "randomized controlled experiments or trials" (for short these will be called RCT). These types of experiments include two groups, one to whom the policy is applied and a control group. Philosopher Nancy Cartwright has written extensively on this subject (Cartwright, 2012), arguing that the lessons learned from these experiments are of limited scientific relevance—what works in one setting may not work in another.[10] In short, the "other things being equal" requirement hardly ever transfers from one location to another. These other elements and aspects also require subsidiary evidence. When we design an RCT, we need to consider these subsidiary elements, which should be brought about via a thorough discussion of the intended and unintended consequences of the policy. But here is a serious issue for RCTs: the more elements you bring into an experiment, the more subjects you need for the experiment to bring about significant statistical evidence. So, there is a paradox when using RCTs for social research: if the elements of the experiment are few, their significance is slim; if their elements are many, their cost and scale may be prohibitive for governments to perform.[11]

Besides these well-known issues regarding RCTs, there are always many unexpected behaviours that can occur for a variety of reasons that can be different from site to site and trial to trial. Unintended consequences can happen because of local conditions or unexpected behavioural reactions. For example, when California decided to create a class-size reduction programme in order to improve conditions in the classroom, what ended up happening is that since there was a sudden need for many more teachers, teacher quality decreased (Bohrnstedt & Stecher, 2002). Here, the

[10] Cartwright writes: "Overall, the lesson is simple. It is a long road from an RCT that evidences the fact that a policy works somewhere to the prediction that the policy will work for us. A lot of different kinds of facts requiring evidence of different kinds to support them must be in place before the road is secure, or secure enough for us to bet on it given the costs and benefits of success and failure. That makes policy predictions dicey—but then that is something to expect. Many of the facts we need to establish are sometimes within our grasp or can become so with reasonable effort. Sometimes they aren't and we need to hedge our bets as best we can. But in any case, the more of the road we support, the more likely it is that our inferences will go through." (Cartwright, 2012)

[11] The Manitoba Basic Income experiment was a large scale experiment of this kind: "the Manitoba Basic Annual Income Experiment, or Minincome… was particularly interesting because it included a 'saturation site' in which all residents of the town of Dauphin, Manitoba, were eligible for a poverty-line NIT." (Widerquist, 2024)

unintended consequence arose from a closely related system, not the behaviour derived from the classroom reduction. If there had been an excess of qualified teachers in the area, this would not have been a problem. If much thought is put into the policy, unintended consequences could be foreseeable. However, in the case of changed behaviour of the correlated system, it may be more difficult for the consequence to be identified in the RCT for the policy—since RCTs are usually small, they may not run into issues similar to the decaying quality of teachers.[12]

This type of research on possible unintended consequences is common in many policy proposals. Consider, for instance, the study by Shrubsole, Macmillan, Davies, and May called "100 Unintended Consequences of Policies to Improve the energy efficiency of the UK housing stock" (Shrubsole et al., 2014). In this study, the authors looked at 1600 studies on improving energy efficiency in housing and selected them for relevance, ending with 206 studies. From those, they selected 119 where unintended consequences were highlighted. Here are some examples: regarding "airtightness impacts of a range of measures including, for example, draft proofing, the provision of double glazing, insulation of loft spaces and the filling of cavity walls", there was a wide range of positive and negative impacts. One side effect of airtightness was noise reduction, which was by one study seen as "a more peaceful atmosphere and the accompanying sense of security, which has a positive impact on mental health and psychological well-being" and "Improvements in child development in the spheres of physical, social and emotional health as well as behavioural outcomes are reported". On the other hand: "conversely, it has been emphasized that the 'absence' of sound (e.g. sounds from nature) may lead to negative mental health impacts. For some individuals, this can lead to anxiety from both real and perceived threats and a possible sense of isolation and disconnection, having further impacts on social cohesion. Increased window opening to compensate for lack of natural sounds could increase ventilation heat loss working against GHG emission reduction." (Shrubsole et al., 2014, p. 5). The study goes on to name many other contradictory effects. Airtightness, for instance, promotes water tightness and reduces the dangers of mould, but it also increases dust mites, which may have serious effects on those with asthma. If individuals dry their clothes indoors in such buildings, they can be exposed to microbiological pathogens and infectious diseases. Another effect of this type of building

[12] These examples are intended to be purely illustrative.

to conserve energy is the improvement in heat retention in buildings. In one sense, this is good and can potentially reduce winter mortality, "increased time spent in a more pleasant indoor environment might lead to sedentary behaviour and weight gain and a possible reduction in social cohesion". These effects depend on how individual behaviour will vary after implementing the policy.

The policy also has the potential to impact other external systems. For instance, in historic buildings, efforts to increase energy conservation can have negative effects: the roofs have been known to collapse because they cannot take the weight of the materials. Furthermore, this policy can encourage the demolition of older houses and promote newer construction, increase rents, increase maintenance costs, cause overcrowding, and so on. All these side effects may not be directly related but are indirect consequences of the policy. If we had an RCT of the policy, it would address some of the behavioural experiences mentioned. Still, it could not test the many diverse living situations and areas and the full extent of such a policy. To encourage the maintenance of historical buildings, we may need a co-policy that creates a different, more manageable set of rules for those buildings. We may also need provisions to guarantee that the investment will not make rents prohibitive for most people living there.

The authors of this paper (Shrubsole et al., 2014) then conclude the following: "To explore the issues raised here further, we argue that there is a pressing need for an approach such as 'Participatory Systems Dynamics' (from now on I will refer to these as PSD), which would require the involvement of multiple stakeholders from a variety of disciplines to investigate these issues holistically." (Shrubsole et al., 2014, p. 11). "Furthermore, systematic reviews of the links between aspects of housing and a wide variety of outcomes are also needed. Such reviews must use a holistic framework that includes potential outcomes across various domains, including physical, mental, social, environmental, and economic well-being." (Shrubsole et al., 2014, p. 11). In general, the relevance and range of RCTs are limited, and for most policies, I will argue that PSDs are necessary to have a significant understanding of the policy and its potential impacts, including for Basic Income.

Before analysing Basic Income, let us consider the preparation necessary for the implementation stage. Implementation woes are normally related to bureaucracy and practicality, but this is not what I want to underline here. There are a couple of things that can happen during implementation that we should be aware of: first, we should monitor the subjects' behaviour for any differences from the experimental setting—if such differences occur, they should be addressed and understood immediately. Second, we should closely monitor related systems and their reactions to the new policy. This may not have been possible during the RCT, but it can be done during implementation. Further policies may be necessary to adjust the response of related systems at this point.[13] Some PSD studies can be done in advance, but a research team should be prepared to work on this during implementation.

In sum, when we prepare a new policy, we need to consider how the policy will affect the behaviour of the targeted population and related systems. The scientific methods used to make predictions about this are unreliable; RCT has quite a limited validity, and the more ambitious the policy, the harder it is to create PSD models.

Part II

Basic Income Policy Evaluations

How does all this relate to Basic Income Policy evaluation? Basic Income is a type of policy that presents special difficulties. As we have seen so far, all policies have intended and unintended consequences. These consequences may result from behaviour changes in the policy recipients or in the systems related to the policy. The most common way to test a policy, and the most scientifically credible, is by using RCTs. However, those types of trials typically test the behaviour of policy recipients and not of the related systems. I will argue that RCTs are not helpful for Basic Income policy testing for several reasons. I will also claim that a PSD analysis of the policy will bring to light unintended severe consequences that must be considered. Because of this, I will argue that a Basic Income Policy needs to be placed within a holistic framework to promote the policymakers' intended consequences, especially when the unintended consequences are antithetical to Basic Income's only overreaching goal of eliminating poverty.

[13] "One lesson here, as well as from many of the other case studies, is the difficulty of passing legislation without also creating unintended consequences because so many other dynamics accompany the implementation of a new program or policy. Bucciarelli suggests that the key is to recognize unintended consequences and work on legislation to fix those that may have a particularly negative impact." (Young, 2001)

Why is it so difficult to get concrete lessons from RCTs about basic income policy? As we have seen, philosopher Nancy Cartwright has worked extensively on the limitations of RCTs (Cartwright, 2012); she argues that what works in one context will not work in a different context. Basic Income policy will suffer from this problem as much as any other policy. Another issue is that RCTs are time-constrained; the subjects will be the policy recipients for a limited amount of time, and they know that they are participating in an RCT. It is highly questionable that the subjects' behaviour under an RCT will be similar to that of the full implementation.

Imagine a Public Healthcare trial in the USA and an RCT where a group was selected to have access to healthcare for three years, and the control group did not. We can foresee that the group with access would do as many procedures as possible while the trial lasted. The result of such a trial would be to conclude that with Public Healthcare, people would abuse the system, which would become unsustainable. But of course, the behaviour is related to the limited time of the trial, and we could expect quite a different behaviour with full implementation. These problems are shared by both these policies and Basic Income policy testing, and the subjects' behaviour is bound to be very different during a trial compared to full implementation.

A problem that is specific to Basic Income policy testing, or more severe in the case of Basic Income policy, is the following: Basic Income's great ideological and practical advantage is that it trusts people to make their own choices and allows them to use their money for what they need in their particular circumstances. Most policies are specific and address problems or issues with narrow solutions. Basic Income assumes that this is not the best way to deal with poverty and that each person is the best manager of their lives (or that this is true for most or beneficial for most). However, consider this: if specific policies like the green building policy in the UK have 100 plus unintended consequences, how many different behaviours and different unintended consequences can Basic Income have? Let us focus for now on unintended consequences related to the recipient's behaviour; there could be as many as how many ways there are to use your money. These can be good or bad; I am not trying to say that people will not use their money properly. I am just pointing out that for a study to read the uses people make of money with any statistical significance, its magnitude would have to be enormous. The only way we could have anything of the kind is by doing a saturated study, as it was done in Manitoba in the 70s, and even then, only a few tendencies were identified (such as health benefits). Basic Income's most important strength, flexibility, makes it harder to evaluate as a policy in quantifying individual behaviour, even in a very ambitious study.

What about PSD research? Can we conduct a compelling PSD study to determine how related systems would react to the Basic Income Policy? In a policy as different as Basic Income, it is impossible to create a study that would give us reliable information regarding how the endless related systems would react to BI. How would the labour market react? Would employers be willing to pay more to attract employees, or would they pay less since employees now have a basic income to count on? How would the housing market react? Would rents increase to mirror the money now available to everyone? How would women's roles change in society? Would a BI be liberating, allowing women's work to be compensated, or would it be yet another force pressuring women to stay at home and fulfil their roles as mothers? Would BI stimulate healthier and more sustainable products, allowing for a beneficial environmental consequence, or will it create more demand for junk and use of fossil fuels, creating a larger carbon footprint than before? We could go on and on. Just like with individual behaviour, the behaviour of the related system can be as varied and unexpected. Furthermore, it is impossible to determine its effects before full implementation with any modicum of scientific accuracy.

Even though we cannot run PSD experiments, we can discuss and argue that consequence A is more likely than consequence B, using the effects of already applied similar cash or quasi-cash distribution policies. If we can show that a related system usually reacts in X way to a cash influx, we can argue that BI may reasonably be expected to have that consequence. One of the things already mentioned above is the effect of the Dole on Poverty in the 60s. It was claimed that the "relationship between public aid and the poverty rate is subject to the principle of diminishing returns" (Gallaway & Garrett, 2016). So, the more aid money, the less impact it had, the help had in decreasing poverty.

What Are the Intended Consequences of Basic Income?

Basic Income policies have as many intended consequences as the number of types of proponents they have. Some have advocate for basic income policies to replace Social Security, while others advocate for it as a complement to Social Security. Basic Income can be advocated as a way to achieve

Social Justice; because of the common ownership of the Earth, one can argue that all citizens have a right to be part of the product of the Earth. Others argue that Basic Income is a way to escape the Social Security trap, since often these kinds of programmes may make it unfeasible for the participants to accept the kind of work they would be able to get, which would be of lower or equal pay to the work they will engage in, or worse, when the associated benefits, such as medical care, would also be lost. There are many reasons to argue for Basic Income, but there does not seem to be one unified goal. The only goal that seems to somehow run across all views of Basic Income is that this policy can create at least part of a solution to the problem of poverty.

The Encyclopedia Britannica defines poverty as "the state of one who lacks a usual or socially acceptable amount of money or material possessions. Poverty is said to exist when people lack the means to satisfy their basic needs." Basic needs can be defined in many ways, such as survival or "those reflecting the standard of living of the community". It can be argued that if we are looking for a policy to guarantee only survival needs, it would probably be more effective to provide shelter and food directly (or whatever the survival needs are stated to be in each situation). Basic income, which uses money instead of goods, has a flexibility that policies addressing survival needs only do not. Therefore, if we were to choose the concept of poverty relevant to Basic Income policy from these two, it would be that it would help people achieve the "standard of living of the community" in which they are embedded.

Poverty is not simply a lack of money. As Martin Luther King argued (King, 1968), poverty is related to several aspects, including "lack of education restricting job opportunities; poor housing which stultified home life and suppressed initiative; fragile family relationships which distorted personality development" (King, 1968). Once the elements are identified, he claimed that this suggests "that each of these causes be attacked one by one. Hence a housing program to transform living conditions, improved educational facilities to furnish tools for better job opportunities, and family counselling to create better personal adjustments were designed. In combination these measures were intended to remove the causes of poverty." (King, 1968, p. 170). However, the application of these specific policies is often slow, inefficient, and does not have the intended results.

Martin Luther King Jr. thought that Basic Income was the best way to address all these issues, he wrote:

> I am now convinced that the simplest approach will prove to be the most effective—the solution to poverty is to abolish it directly by a now widely discussed measure: the guaranteed income. Earlier in this century this proposal would have been greeted with ridicule and denunciation as destructive of initiative and responsibility. At that time economic status was considered the measure of the individual's abilities and talents. In the simplistic thinking of that day the absence of worldly goods indicated a want of industrious habits and moral fiber. We have come a long way in our understanding of human motivation and of the blind operation of our economic system. Now we realize that dislocations in the market operation of our economy and the prevalence of discrimination thrust people into idleness and bind them in constant or frequent unemployment against their will. The poor are less often dismissed from our conscience today by being branded as inferior and incompetent. We also know that no matter how dynamically the economy develops and expands it does not eliminate all poverty. (King, 1968, p. 171)

The question we should ask is whether a Basic Income will indeed promote an end to the exclusion that seems to be one of the key factors of poverty or whether it does not. What is the level of income that allows individuals to live a life where their basic needs are met and avoid social exclusion? This depends on many factors. In countries with a robust set of social services, less money may be needed; for instance, free healthcare significantly cuts the costs needed to avoid social exclusion. In countries where such services are unavailable, a higher income is necessary for a person not to be poor. It also depends on customs and attitudes towards certain sets of people; if we give an equal amount of money to all individuals, it does not mean that some suddenly do not face discrimination anymore.

To the question of the amount of Basic Income that would permit true liberation, Martin Luther King argued that: "it must be pegged to the median income of society, not at the lowest levels of income. To guarantee an income at the floor would simply perpetuate welfare standards and freeze into the society poverty conditions. Second, the guaranteed income must be dynamic; it must automatically increase as the total social income grows." (King, 1968, p. 173) Implementing such an income would be a logistic nightmare, even though it is not, in principle, intractable. However, in practice, it is intractable. The amount and logistics necessary to provide adequate Basic Income to respond to the variations of location, expectations, surrounding services, and so on would be incredibly difficult to manage. On the other hand, any Basic Income that is not dynamic, would be a sure-fire way towards social exclusion. A low Basic Income would lead to social exclusion, especially when automation takes over most of the tasks that are necessary for human beings to flourish, and there are no extra jobs to be had to complement the low income. Any low Basic Income is, therefore, antithetical to the stated goal of eliminating poverty, at least when poverty is defined at least partly as exclusion and when eliminating poverty necessarily includes an aspect of integration in society and the possibility of human flourishing. A low Basic Income has the potential *side-effect* of stagnating large groups of the population in pockets of poverty, which is the opposite of what is intended by the policy. A dynamic Basic Income would have a better chance, but it needs to be coupled with other integrative strategies, and the logistic scale of such an endeavour is too grandiose to be able to be scientifically tested in any reliable way. If any conclusion can be taken from all this, it is that *side effects do matter* and should always be thoroughly researched when antithetical to some of the central objectives of the proposed policy. Is a dynamic Basic Income at all possible? That is an open question.

References

Bentham, J. (1789). *An introduction to the principles of morals and legislation*. Pantianos Classics.

Bitler, M. P., & Karoly, L. A. (2015). Intended and Unintended Effects of the War on Poverty: What Research Tells Us and Implications for Policy. *Journal of Policy Analysis and Management,* volume 34, pp. 639–696

Bohrnstedt, G., & Stecher, B. (2002). What we have learned about class size reduction in California. *California Department of Education; CSR Research Consortium*.

Brown, A. W., & Allison, D. B. (2013). *AMA Journal of Ethics 15*, 339–346.

Bucciarelli, R. (2001). Unintended Consequences of Title XXI: State Children's Health Insurance Program Crowd-Out and Adverse Risk Selection. In *Unintended Consequences of Health Policy Programs and Policies: Workshop Summary*. Institute of Medicine (US) Robert Wood Johnson Health Policy Fellowships Program.

Carden, A. (2011). Unintended consequences: Hurting when you think you're helping. *Forbes*.

Cartwright, N. (2012). RCT'S, evidence and predicting policy effectiveness. In H. Kincaid (Ed.), *The Oxford handbook of the philosophy of the social sciences*. Oxford University Press.

Crittenden, R. (2001). A safety net no more? The inadvertent undermining of access for the uninsured. In *Unintended consequences of health policy programs and policies: Workshop summary. Institute of Medicine (US) Robert wood Johnson health policy fellowships program*. National Academies Press (US).
DeParle, J. (1998). What "welfare to work" really means. *The New York Times Magazine*.
Foot, P. (1967). The problem of abortion and the doctrine of the double effect. *Oxford Review*, (5), 5–15.
Gallaway, L. E., & Garrett, D. G. (2016). The Unintended Consequences of the War on Poverty. *Cato Journal*, vol. 36, no. 1, pp. 33–45.
Hausman, D. M. (2017). Evaluating social policy. In H. Kinkade (Ed.), *The Oxford handbook of philosophy of social science* (pp. 607–624). Oxford University Press.
King, M. L., Jr. (1968). *Where do we go from here. Chaos or community?* Beacon Press.
Kotchen, M. J. (2018). Environment, Energy, and Unintended Consequences." NBER Reporter, no. 3, pp. 10–13.
Shrubsole, C., Macmillan, A., Davies, M., & May, N. (2014). 100 Unintended Consequences of Policies to Improve the Energy Efficiency of the UK Housing Stock. *Indoor and Built Environment*, vol. 23, no. 3, pp. 340–352
Widerquist, K. (2024). *Universal basic income*. The MIT Press.
Young, W. B. (2001). *Unintended consequences of health policy programs and policies*. National Academies Press (US).

CHAPTER 6

Sharing Stories: Advancing Narrative Methodology for Basic Income Research

Evelyn L. Forget

Social scientists have long recognized that narratives are integral to policy analysis. Stories help determine how empirical models are used and are equally important to the ways in which model results are disseminated to target audiences. Narratives are collected as part of policy analysis through polls, interviews and focus groups, and those advocating for policy change recognize the importance of framing, language and metaphor (Mair et al., 2019).

The analysis of basic income has participated in these trends. In the United States, for example, a number of cities have conducted or are currently running guaranteed income pilots and demonstration projects, guided by organizations such as the Stanford Basic Income Lab, the Economic Security Project, the Jain Family Institute and Income Movement, among others. Each one of these organizations has an online presence complete with resources that provide advice on language,

E. L. Forget (✉)
University of Manitoba, Winnipeg, MB, Canada
e-mail: Evelyn.Forget@umanitoba.ca

R. Merrill, C. Neves (eds.), *Determining the Value of Universal Basic Income*, Exploring the Basic Income Guarantee,
https://doi.org/10.1007/978-3-032-04004-6_6

framing and metaphor.[1] Virtually every experiment, pilot or demonstration project collects participant "stories" that are subsequently used to provide evidence of the impact of basic income.[2] These stories have been augmented by filmmakers, advocates and journalists keen to disseminate "visual" narratives.[3] Often, but not always, qualitative researchers will take the stories back to their source, seeking "validation" that they have represented the story as the source intended, reflecting a belief that the storyteller is the ultimate authority.

In all these cases, however, less attention has been paid to the ways in which people listen and engage with narratives. Storylistening has been viewed as a passive and automatic process. Claire Craig and Sarah Dillon have attempted to challenge this complacency, setting out a systematic framework of storylistening in policy analysis that articulates four functions that stories can play: creating new points of view; understanding relevant identities; expanding the range of models available; and, supporting new "anticipations" of the future (Craig & Dillon, 2021; Dillon & Craig, 2021). Storylistening, they claim, is less about creating empathy for participants among those who hear stories or avoiding negative responses to particular language, but rather part of the collective and cognitive process of making sense of policy in a complex and uncertain world.

Building on the framework developed by Dillon and Craig, basic income researchers can advance an iterative narrative methodology that allows researchers to understand how particular criticisms of basic income can persist even in the face of empirical evidence to the contrary and, perhaps more importantly, open up new research questions and new policy formulations that address important but unarticulated considerations.

[1] Economic Security Project: https://economicsecurityproject.org/resources/

Stanford Basic Income Lab: https://basicincome.stanford.edu/

Jain Family Institute: https://jainfamilyinstitute.org/toolkit-on-guaranteed-income-in-the-u-s-for-pilots-research/

(see especially "Messaging Basic Income" from the Jain Family)

Income Movement: https://www.incomemovement.org/?gclid=CjwKCAiAkp6tBhB5EiwANTCx1DDGC6auOAm3IuS2NJStuQp4ON_H9kdPKinri6LWRmooW3sxdqouvRoCR2QQAvD_BwE

[2] See, for example, GiveDirectly which has run and is running several experiments in low and middle income countries: https://www.givedirectly.org/ubi/

[3] See a documentary on Ontario's short-lived pilot: https://ahumanpicture.com/

The long-ago Manitoba project: https://www.bigexperience.org/

Jessie Golem's "Humans of Basic Income" portrait series: https://www.jessiegolem.com/humans-of-basic-income

This chapter outlines the Dillon-Craig framework, uses it to show how narrative that goes beyond poll results and focus groups can advance our understanding of basic income by providing a window on new collective identities, and, finally, makes some suggestions to advance the narrative methodology in basic income research.

The Functions of Stories in the Dillon-Craig Framework

The Stanford Basic Income Lab recognizes that narratives can be used to interpret and explain quantitative methods to the public and to provide accessible material for public engagement:

> Qualitative methods can be used to collect rich, in-depth accounts of the changes in recipients' lives. These stories are instrumental to interpreting and conveying the data found in quantitative research and to identifying trends that are not captured by predefined measures. Moreover, qualitative data is easier for the media to package to engage the public at large. (Bidadanure et al., 2018, p. 22)

The articulation of material collected through qualitative methods is an important consideration. How an issue is framed by researchers identifies the target audience to whom they are appealing. Framing reveals who the researchers consider most important and what evidence is most relevant. For example, the Income Movement suggests that researchers avoid terms such as "needy" or "poor", using instead labels such as "citizen's dividend" that foreground the diverse social contributions of those who may not be in the paid workforce.[4] This suggests that a key concern is to remind readers who are not part of the experiment that the recipients of a basic income are not just charity cases, but rather productive members of a community. If participants also share that perception, so much the better.

Dillon and Craig suggest that a broader study of narratives can provide new points of view for policy analysis (Craig & Dillon, 2023, p. 135). Using Artificial Intelligence as an example, they note that the dominant framing is a charismatic portrait of superhuman intelligence, but that this neglects issues such as algorithmic bias that narrative considerations of

[4] https://www.incomemovement.org/?gclid=CjwKCAiAkp6tBhB5EiwANTCx1DDGC6auOAm3IuS2NJStuQp4ON_H9kdPKinri6LWRmooW3sxdqouvRoCR2QQAvD_BwE

human experiences of such systems might reveal. In the case of basic income, the stories of participants in basic income experiments are often collected, but less attention is paid to stories told by those excluded from the experiments whose opinions would certainly influence public acceptability. Whether true or not, stories about "my neighbour who spent the money on drugs and gambling", "my boss's son who just watches television and doesn't even try to work", "that woman whose kids run wild with no supervision" and photos labelled "look what they buy at the supermarket" are well placed on social media. A rigorous analysis of such stories might well prompt new research questions or shift the framing of the debate. However, it is not only the stories of basic income critics that must be collected and analysed. Basic income is a big policy change, and there are many advocates uneasy about some aspects of current modelling who have difficulty formulating their concerns. A few examples will be considered in the next section of this chapter.

A second function of stories, in the Dillon-Craig framework, is to identify and foreground as yet unconsidered collective identities that might lead to new research questions or better methods of communication. Some of the identities that basic income researchers have addressed are generated by the way these researchers frame the debate. For example, the criticism that basic income disincentivizes work is so longstanding that it has become routine to identify "those in the workforce", "those of working age" and "those not in the workforce", and to talk about how basic income would affect each. Other identities are derived from the ways in which policies are currently formulated in high-income countries: how are "women" and the "disabled" affected? Newcomers to the country? The racialized? In each case, not all members of a particular identity would have the same experience, and yet arguments are framed to address these collective identities.

However, identities do not simply exist to be discovered by researchers. They are fictions that evolve over time and, for any actual person or family, can never represent the totality of their lived experience. Pushing narrative beyond the timeworn identities would prompt new research questions, potentially shift the framing of the debate, reformulate policy options and invite public deliberation.

The third function of stories brings us back to empirical and computational models. As Juliana Bidadanure and colleagues recognize, stories help to interpret the quantitative data collected (Bidadanure et al., 2018, p. 22). They also prompt particular questions that models can be used to address, and new ways for models to collectivize and categorize participants. Stories may suggest new causal accounts of the ways that complex systems operate, and occasion new definitions and formulations of key parameters. Examples are offered in the next section of this essay.

Finally, Craig and Dillon suggest that a fourth function of stories is to offer new anticipations of the future (Craig & Dillon, 2021, 2023; Dillon & Craig, 2021). This goes beyond mere forecasting to suggest entirely new ways to organize society to deal with the most pressing policy issues faced today. It is conceivable that basic income would indeed do much more than offer a better income support framework in our existing mixed capitalist economies. It is telling that one of the fictional accounts of basic income is from *Star Trek: First Contact*, in which Captain Picard explains:

> The economics of the future are somewhat different. You see, money doesn't exist in the twenty-fourth century. The acquisition of wealth is no longer the driving force in our lives. We work to better ourselves, and the rest of humanity.

Author Kim Stanley Robinson also asks relevant questions about scarcity in his *Red Mars* trilogy, and James S. A. Corey's *Caliban's War* offers a brilliant discussion of the basic income debate. Narratives, understood broadly enough, push us to reconsider many of the parameters we hold constant in scientific debate.

Whether basic income is just a less bureaucratic, more efficient, arguably more just and certainly less conditional antipoverty policy that could be offered in our current societies at an acceptable cost and with minor disruption, or whether the freedom associated with basic income would require fundamental changes in the way in which we produce and distribute all the goods and services we use to sustain our lives, is a fundamental question at the heart of much of the basic income debate. Certainly storytelling, and especially storylistening, must be at the heart of it.

Some Untold Basic Income Stories and the Storylistening Framework

How might the storylistening framework be operationalized in the service of basic income? The details will be formulated in the next section, but here I would like to demonstrate the ways in which active storylistening can, and has, had an impact on basic income in the Canadian case.

Consider the ways in which some members of the Canadian Indigenous community have responded to basic income policy proposals. In Canada, the impact of any policy on the Indigenous community is a necessary and inevitable aspect of policymaking. However, there is no single pan-Indigenous community. There are many different communities, some of which are delineated geographically, others in terms of status and their relationship with the federal government, and others influenced by many other factors. This description, then, is an exercise in the creation and consolidation of collective identities. To make clear my positionality, I am not Indigenous nor have I ever lived in an isolated community or on reserve. I am a well-educated and well-paid member of the dominant community. These stories represent what I heard, and not necessarily what was said.

One story emerges from the document called *Reclaiming Power and Place: The Final Report of the National Inquiry into Missing and Murdered Indigenous Women and Girls*, which was published in 2019.[5] The Report calls for far-reaching social and political change to address the disproportionate violence experienced by Indigenous women, girls and "2SLGBTQQIA+ people" [two-spirit, lesbian, gay, bisexual, transsexual, queer, questioning, intersex, asexual and others] (National Inquiry into Missing and Murdered Indigenous Women and Girls, 2019). Among the Calls to Justice is 4.5:

> We call upon all governments to establish a guaranteed annual liveable income [basic income] for all Canadians, including Indigenous Peoples, to meet all their social and economic needs. This income must take into account diverse needs, realities, and geographic locations.

The justification for the call is not explicit, but the tone of the entire Report is that the violence experienced by many women, girls and gender nonconforming people results from pervasive and generational deprivation, institutionalized bias (both explicit and implicit), the lack of social services of all types, lack of educational and training opportunities and other inequities. These inequities expose people to dangerous and demeaning work, desperate attempts to compensate for the absence of such basic infrastructure as public transportation by seeking rides with strangers on deserted highways, and the loss of parental supervision and support

[5] https://www.mmiwg-ffada.ca/final-report/

because poverty exposes families to interference by child welfare agencies and because generational trauma imposed by churches, schools and governments has undermined traditional family networks.

One of the Commissioners, Qajaq Robinson, spoke to me about the call for a basic income for all Canadians (Forget & Owczar, 2021, pp. 109ff; 150ff). The call was not limited to Indigenous people because the poverty and deprivation that restrict opportunities and force people into dangerous work and violent living arrangements are not limited to Indigenous people. Deprived communities, where violence is prevalent, house Indigenous and non-Indigenous people. Industries that exploit marginalized people do not check for Indigenous status. All people without the resources they need to survive are vulnerable. Everyone should, she claimed, have access to what is needed to live an adequate life.

When I asked her why she called for a basic income rather than just greater support through existing income supports or expanded services, she told me that many of the services all Canadians rely upon are created, delivered and evaluated by members of the dominant (white) community. As such, the norms of that community imbue all aspects of service delivery and, as a consequence, many Indigenous people who may live in different kinds of family arrangements, have different educational and social backgrounds, or live in different parts of the country find these services less than welcoming. Many people have been mistreated and, as a consequence, refuse further contact with mainstream health, educational and other services. When forced into the justice system, they see themselves mistreated and believe their initial misapprehensions were accurate. As for existing income support programmes, Robinson noted that they had allowed disproportionate poverty to grow among Indigenous people, and that the conditions imposed on receiving support from such programmes were particularly difficult and demeaning for Indigenous people to meet. Moreover, the staff were most often members of the dominant community and either explicitly or implicitly biased. At best, they were ignorant of Indigenous ways.

Money, on the other hand, is fungible. It can be used however an individual wants to use it. If a mother wants to give her sister a few dollars to take care of a child while she is forced to fly south to access medical care, she can do so. If she lives in a community with no public transport, a few dollars to a neighbour for gasoline can allow her to leave a dangerous situation at home. She can pay for a place to sleep in a community without a shelter. A little bit of money can give her an alternative to hitch-hiking on isolated highways where many murders have taken place.

Another story comes from a somewhat different demographic. I have been told versions of this story by many Indigenous men, but I am going to attach it to one individual because there is some written evidence to support the report. Wab Kinew is an Indigenous man who became premier of the Canadian province of Manitoba in 2023. He is the son of an Anishinaabe father and white mother. His memoir (Kinew, 2017) covers the year 2012 that he spent reconnecting with his father, who had just received a terminal cancer diagnosis. His father was a traditional chief and an elected official who had engaged with the federal government. His traumatic childhood at residential school, where he was physically and sexually abused, left him a loving but distant father. Kinew, a Sun Dancer, former rapper, academic administrator and urban activist, spent his childhood in Winnipeg and on a reserve in northern Ontario. The Sun Dance is an Indigenous ritual that takes place over four days in the summer. The Sun Dance is about prayer and endurance. Sun Dancers fast and seek support from spiritual forces.

Kinew attended a private high school in Winnipeg and graduated from the University of Manitoba. In his twenties, he struggled with the law and drugs, eventually coming before a judge on an assault charge who gave him an opportunity to turn his life around. He used the second chance to devote himself to music and martial arts. The 2023 election campaign was one in which his prior legal issues figured heavily.[6] This story of personal redemption is one Kinew likes to tell, especially to Indigenous boys. On the evening of his inauguration as premier, he reflected on his pride at being in a position of leadership, recounted his story of drugs and arrests and the power of a second chance, and emphasized the need for young Indigenous men to take control of their own lives, to live ethically and never to depend on others to create opportunities for them to succeed.[7]

This narrative is only indirectly related to basic income. In 2019, an election his party lost, Wab Kinew promised to transition the existing system towards a basic income.[8] He has made no similar promise in the

[6] https://www.winnipegfreepress.com/opinion/analysis/2023/02/07/voters-deserve-answers-on-ndp-drug-stance

[7] https://www.cbc.ca/news/canada/manitoba/wab-kinew-profile-premier-election-1.6988740

[8] https://www.cbc.ca/news/canada/manitoba/manitoba-disability-matters-debate-employment-income-assistance-1.5261751

current government. Yet, the story is relevant to basic income primarily because of the repetition of the "independence" trope. Basic income has always appealed to those emphasizing freedom and independence, but it is clear that these words might mean something more profound to people who come from a background of paternalism, generational abuse and oppression than they do to middle-class people who would like to spend more time on hobbies and less in an office. Understanding the depth and implications of independence to this cohort of Indigenous men is profoundly important to policy analysts and to basic income researchers.

A third narrative relevant to the acceptability of basic income among Indigenous people relates to the pandemic income supports created by the Canadian federal government during Covid-19 (Forget, 2020). The key feature was the Canadian Emergency Response Benefit (CERB) that offered workers who had lost their jobs due to closures $2000 a month to meet their basic needs. Unlike pre-existing income supports, there was little bureaucratic oversight. The money was offered on a "trust-but-verify" basis; that is, recipients were granted the cash on application with the understanding that they might be called upon to demonstrate that they were not working during the period in question. The CERB was very effective; the poverty rate fell to 6.4% in 2020 compared with 14.5% in 2015.[9] The poverty rate began to climb once again as pandemic supports were scaled back.

The CERB was not a basic income. It was only available to those who claimed to have been in the workforce before the pandemic and who lost their jobs. Those on income assistance were not eligible, nor were the retired. It did, however, have some features of a basic income, such as a uniform pay-out independent of prior earnings and, especially, the relative lack of conditionality. In the popular mind, the CERB was perceived as a basic income.

One story that began to emerge very quickly was that the CERB was responsible for widespread substance use, especially in Indigenous communities, which caused chaos.[10] There was an increase in drug use and associated deaths during this period, but whether the CERB was responsible is questionable.[11] Many people with serious addictions, particularly

[9] https://www150.statcan.gc.ca/n1/pub/11-627-m/11-627-m2022011-eng.htm

[10] https://newsinteractives.cbc.ca/longform/fort-resolution-cerb/

[11] https://www.readthemaple.com/the-media-keeps-blaming-overdoses-on-the-cerb-theyre-wrong/

the unhoused, would not have qualified for CERB and were unlikely to have had the paperwork to apply in any case; somehow, they managed to fund their substance use before CERB and they continued to use substances during the pandemic. Other people at many different income levels used substances both before and during the pandemic. The cost of drugs to cause serious harm or death is quite low. However, substance use did unquestionably increase during the pandemic, no doubt fuelled by the isolation, the shutdown of regular meeting places and events and other challenges.

This story led many to conclude that basic income is dangerous because it will further marginalize the most vulnerable by providing cash that will be misused. Indigenous communities were particularly, but not exclusively, hard hit by the surge in substance use, largely because of pre-existing poverty and widespread generational trauma. The effect on Indigenous communities reinforced stereotypes long held by some members of the dominant community, but it also worried Indigenous leaders. Would a basic income cause even greater hardship for Indigenous communities?

These three stories regarding the acceptability of basic income among Indigenous people illustrate the various functions of stories outlined by Dillon and Craig. In each case, a unique collective identity emerges. The identification and understanding of these identities are important to public reasoning. Narrative evidence assembled by diverse, multidisciplinary teams could be a valuable addition to syntheses of evidence about behavioural responses to basic income and about the acceptability of basic income as a policy. Moreover, these stories identify new points of view and new research questions for basic income analysts. There is some existing evidence about basic income and substance use (Dwyer et al., 2023; Silver & Zhang, 2022) but little narrative research about the response of the dominant culture on social media, or about the real worry of Indigenous leaders dealing with multiple challenges within their communities. There is quite a lot of research dealing with feminist responses to basic income, but little of it focuses on the needs and responses of Indigenous women. The "independence" trope is well articulated in basic income literature, but how well do we understand the similarities and differences between independence as understood by different groups of Indigenous people in Canada, and those using the same words whose lived experience reflects that of the dominant culture?

A fourth story reflecting the ways in which a different group of Indigenous people in Canada engage with basic income illustrates how a story, even when imperfectly understood by a storylistener, can expand the range of plausible models and offer new opportunities to imagine how the future might evolve with and without the implementation of different basic income formulations.

Most Indigenous people in Canada do not live on reserve, but make their homes in towns and cities. Others live on reserves that are geographically close to larger urban centres. However, there are some groups of Indigenous people in Canada who live in rural and remote areas of the country. One such group includes people living in the Northwest Territories. In 2023, an estimated 44,760 people lived in a region of approximately 144,000 km^2 (442,000 square miles). Its only city is Yellowknife, the capital, with a population of less than 20,000. This is a culturally diverse region in which more than half the population is Indigenous (First Nations, Métis and Inuit), but Tagalog is the sixth most commonly spoken language, and the Official Languages Act recognizes nine Indigenous languages, as well as English and French.

While per capita GDP in the Northwest Territories is quite high relative to other provinces and territories, that is largely the result of mining, which does not result in high incomes for everyone. Outside the city and, especially in more remote regions, some people engage in traditional economic activities such as fishing and hunting. Costs of living, especially food and rent, are very high because most commodities are flown in from the south and there is a perennial and persistent housing shortage.

Alternatives North is a coalition of antipoverty groups, women's organizations, faith groups, family groups, labour unions and environmental groups that supports the creation of a basic income accompanied by other economic policies such as a living wage in order to address widespread poverty. In a recent conversation with southern researchers, they raised two questions: how can a basic income accommodate the widely differing costs of living experienced by those who live in the urban centre and those in the smallest communities; and how might a basic income accommodate the traditional subsistence lifestyle still practiced by Indigenous northerners?

Basic Income modelling has never attempted to accommodate these complexities. Is there any role at all for basic income in such a demographically diverse, geographically challenged community with limited markets? If so, what should it look like? What is cash used for? If a basic income is not appropriate, what is the alternative? Public services are severely constrained outside Yellowknife, with no transportation except air and few roads at all. Health care is accessed either in Yellowknife or in southern communities. High school students typically board away from their families. Agriculture really does not exist. Existing income support programmes have left many with inadequate housing and food insecurity.

It is not at all clear what a basic income would, or should, look like in such a region, but it is very clear that importing models from the south is not adequate. Addressing these challenges requires significant storytelling and critical storylistening in order to determine how people live in such a region and how they would like to live. What would a future without poverty look like?

Towards a Methodology of Storylistening in Basic Income Research

This analysis began with two, relatively controversial, claims: stories are not simple; and, storylisteners are as involved in the creation of meaning as storytellers. As soon as a story is read or heard, there are at least two people involved in sense-making, and there is no reason to assume they will agree about the meaning or implications of a story. The storylistener brings their own background, their own preoccupations and their own presuppositions to the task of listening to a story. Sometimes they mishear and sometimes they make mistakes. Other times they hear the words just fine, but the words mean something very different to them than whatever the speaker intended. With written material, we see this all the time. Sometimes a commentator is simply wrong about what they thought they read in another's work; sometimes they know what they read, but their background is so different from the original author's background that the meaning they attribute to the words is at odds with that of the storyteller.

Qualitative researchers attempt to deal with these issues by bringing narratives back to the originator for "verification". Sometimes that is not possible because the original storyteller is no longer alive or available, so other methods of verification might be sought. This, however, presupposes that the meaning intended by the storyteller should be privileged.

However, narrative methodology can be advanced by recognizing that meaning does not dwell in a story, but rather emerges through the iterative activity of a conversation between the storyteller and the storylistener. Validating outcomes with the storyteller is static because it assumes that the meaning of a story is codified and the role of the researcher is to reveal that meaning. By contrast, focusing on storylistening recognizes that the meaning of a story will change as it is shared and that the changes themselves lead to innovative modelling and scientific outcomes. The story is no longer just seen as "data", but storytelling becomes a tool of scientific investigation. As a consequence, narrative methodology should be at least as rigorous as other forms of scientific investigation. As challenging as that might seem to a quantitative researcher, examinations of literature representing the 2008 financial crisis have shown that fictional work sometimes reveals truths about a situation, while more apparently factual economic writing contains significant elements of fiction (Shaw, 2015). All scientific investigation uses instruments that include elements of narrative.

Dillon and Craig outline a number of components of a methodology of storylistening:

1. A research team must be multidisciplinary and might include scholars of literature, film and cultural studies, as well as social scientists and anthropologists.
2. Experts should consider a broad range of narrative types in order to discover points of agreement, disagreement and gaps in the literature. These would include reports, interviews, polls and focus group reports, but also poetry, fiction and memoir.
3. Judgements about which stories to include and how to include them in research syntheses should be as evidence-based as quantitative research, including:
    (a) Systematic literature reviews, in which the methodology of story selection is explicitly reported
    (b) Close attention to the narrative using tools and techniques appropriate to that narrative
    (c) A systematic search for new, relevant stories
    (d) Evidence-based conclusions, peer review and disciplinary interrogation
4. A narrative synthesis should be both comprehensive and structured.

A synthesis based on such methods could contribute to public reasoning by posing new questions and opening new areas of investigation, shifting the way in which a debate has been framed, reformulating policy questions in ways that are more accessible to traditional research methods, identifying new collective identities which can both raise new research questions and suggest different forms of engagement, and inviting public deliberation on potential new economic or social arrangements. Inviting humanities scholars into the policymaking framework would allow them to contribute more fully to innovative forms of public engagement that are already common, such as citizens' juries (OECD, 2020).

All this requires a new level of narrative literacy among policymakers and the public. Basic income researchers already make routine use of narratives to explain concepts, demonstrate the impact of experimental or model evidence and address persistent myths. Narratives are collected by survey, interview and focus group. However, by critically examining a broader range of potentially relevant narratives, a nuanced understanding of collective identities could be generated, and new areas of investigation and research problems uncovered. Understanding the ways in which stories are heard as well as the way they are told, enhances the richness of the policy conversation. Engaging a broader range of qualitative expertise to identify relevant narratives reveals the myriad ways that identities, opinions, positions and attitudes are consolidated and shared throughout society.

References

Bidadanure, J., Kline, S., Moore, C., Rainwater, B., & Thomas, C. (2018). *Basic income in cities: A guide to city experiments and pilot projects.* National League of Cities. Accessed 1/22/2024, from https://basicincome.stanford.edu/research/papers/basic-income-cities-toolkit/

Craig, C., & Dillon, S. (2023). "Storylistening" in the science policy ecosystem. Expert analysis of narrative can complement and strengthen scientific evidence. *Science, 379*(6628).

Craig, C., & Dillon, S. (2021). Storylistening: Why narrative evidence matters for public reasoning and how to use it. Date originally posted: 2021-10-13. *Permalink.* https://blogs.lse.ac.uk/impactofsocialsciences/2021/10/13/storylistening-why-narrative-evidence-matters-for-public-reasoning-and-how-to-use-it/

Dillon, S., & Craig, C. (2021). *Storylistening: Narrative evidence and public reasoning.* Routledge.

Dwyer, R., Palepu, A., Williams, C., Daly-Grafstein, D., & Zhao, J. (2023). Unconditional cash transfers reduce homelessness. *Proceedings of the National Academy of Sciences of the United States of America, 120*(36), e2222103120.

Forget, E. L. (2020). *Basic income for Canadians. From the Covid-19 emergency to financial security for all.* Lormer.

Forget, E. L., & Owczar, H. (2021). *Radical trust. Basic income for complicated lives*. ARP.

Kinew, W. (2017). *The reason you walk*. Penguin Canada.

Mair, D., Smillie, L., La Placa, G., Schwendinger, F., Raykovska, M., Pasztor, Z., & Van Bavel, R. (2019). *Understanding our political nature: How to put knowledge and reason at the heart of political decision-making*. EUR 29783 EN, Publications Office of the European Union, Luxembourg, 2019, ISBN 978-92-76-08620-8. https://doi.org/10.2760/910822, JRC117161. Accessed January 22, 2024, from https://publications.jrc.ec.europa.eu/repository/handle/JRC117161

National Inquiry into Missing and Murdered Indigenous Women and Girls. (2019). Reclaiming power and place. The final report of the national inquiry into missing and murdered indigenous women and girls. *The National Inquiry*. Accessed January 22, 2024, from https://www.mmiwg-ffada.ca/final-report/

OECD. (2020). *Innovative citizen participation and new democratic institutions: Catching the deliberative wave*. OECD Publishing.

Shaw, K. (2015). *Crunch lit*. Bloomsbury.

Silver, D., & Zhang, J. (2022). *Impacts of basic income on health and economic well-being: Evidence from the VA'S disability compensation program* (No. w29877). National Bureau of Economic Research.

CHAPTER 7

One Size Does Not Fit All: Universal Basic Income and Country Context

Pedro Vaz Goulart and Carla Guapo Costa

Introduction

Distributional issues have marked the start of the twenty-first century, particularly after the Great Recession (Claveria & Sorić, 2024; Goulart et al., 2023). Unconditional basic income (UBI), a "hotly debated idea" (Gentilini et al., 2020, p. 1), has been put forward as a panacea for issues ranging from redistribution, ending poverty, economic security and labour market flexibility to social justice and individual freedom and autonomy (Van Parijs & Vanderborght, 2017; Standing, 2017; Wright, 2010).[1]

[1] The literature has used both "universal basic income" and "unconditional basic income" terms. In this chapter, we follow the term used by the other contributors in this book: unconditional basic income.

We both thank the financial support of the Portuguese Foundation for Science and Technology under the project [2022.02143.PTDC].

P. Vaz Goulart (✉) • C. Guapo Costa
Universidade de Lisboa, Institute of Social and Political Sciences, Centre for Public Administration and Public Policies, Lisbon, Portugal
e-mail: pgoulart@edu.ulisboa.pt

R. Merrill, C. Neves (eds.), *Determining the Value of Universal Basic Income*, Exploring the Basic Income Guarantee,
https://doi.org/10.1007/978-3-032-04004-6_7

While some authors have supported UBI schemes, others have firmly opposed this policy (Greenstein, 2019; Tanner, 2015; Alston, 2017). The main arguments against it are that people will work less, ranging from a neutral tone to that it is a subsidy to laziness, the sheer financial cost of the initiative, and the political economy argument that some people will lose after the change. Therefore, the most compelling arguments regard labour market, funding and political economy issues and are particularly prone to being tested according to their likely political feasibility.

In the past, authors applied a typology to classify countries, such as the famous typology of Esping-Andersen (1990), which could help identify the challenges and opportunities that UBI presents in different settings and provide a relevant framework for understanding contexts more likely to implement UBI schemes.[2] Extending Esping-Andersen's typology, Ferrera (1996) also discusses the challenges facing these welfare states, such as ageing populations and high unemployment rates, in the context of globalisation and European integration, and concludes that adapting to these challenges will be difficult both socially and politically for the Southern European welfare states, namely due to features such as corporatist income maintenance systems, universal health care systems or clientelism and patronising in the provision of public goods. Although insightful to our research, these analyses and their applications are made for fixed groups of countries, often not considering country idiosyncrasies and changes over time.

Individual empirical approaches specific to UBI have looked into implementing these schemes or similar in countries or regions but are often dispersed and not meant for generalisation. In contrast, we follow Aerts et al. (2023), who stress that outcomes will depend on the "level, design and context". Our approach is empirical, and we focus on addressing the issue of context for individual countries and across time. We aim to identify which countries present more adequate characteristics to politically implement an unconditional basic income programme according to these identified arguments. We will give particular emphasis to the issue of labour supply.

[2] Esping-Andersen (1990) categorises welfare states into liberal, conservative-corporatist, and social democratic regimes. Complementarily, Ferrera (1996) identifies and analyses the distinctive features of welfare states in Southern European countries (Italy, Spain, Portugal, and Greece) and outlines several characteristics that set these welfare states apart from their Northern and Western European counterparts.

In the chapter, we start by discussing the history of the UBI and then move to the arguments in favour and against UBI. We then review evidence from previous UBIs or similar experiences in developed and developing countries. The following section bridges the data approach and description. Next, each argument is then empirically compared across countries through selected indicators. Finally, we present some exploratory conclusions.

The History of an Eclectic UBI

From the Past

As Camporesi states (2023, p. 77), "*Ideas cannot be considered as artifacts that travel persistently throughout history with a static meaning, independent of their historical context.*" The concept of UBI has a rich and varied history, which spreads unevenly across philosophy, economics, politics, sociology, and history. UBI is not new. Early proposals of a basic income guarantee were first presented over two centuries ago.

In its most ancient philosophical and economic roots, we could consider the works of Thomas Moore (1516) or Johannes Vives (1526) in the sixteenth century, appealing to some state insurance of minimum income for all citizens (Camporesi, 2023; Widerquist et al., 2013). However, the eighteenth and nineteenth centuries saw the determinant impetus, with the contributions of Thomas Paine in his famous pamphlet *Agrarian Justice*. There, he proposed a system of social welfare funded by tax landowners to provide a basic income to all citizens as compensation for the loss of natural inheritance. In the nineteenth century, John Stuart Mill discussed the distribution of wealth and pledged that the state should provide every citizen with a basic level of subsistence.

In the twentieth century, the range of contributions widened and context issues became more significant. At the beginning of the century, Bertrand Russell equated basic income with freedom since it allowed people to free themselves from the claws of subsistence and economic necessity. Instead, they could pursue more creative goals, including intellectual and personal development. However, the idea of a basic income only started gaining greater attention in the political debate during the 1960s. Many different proposals were produced over the years, backed by advocates of the welfare state, such as John Kenneth Galbraith and Anthony

Atkinson, as well as numerous free-market and libertarian economists, including Friedrich Hayek and Milton Friedman (Tanner, 2015).

Some of these proposals are not pure UBI. Authors such as Atkinson (1996) propose a different instrument, the Participatory Income (PI), arguing that, instead of granting unconditional and universal grants, individuals should receive income only if they contribute to socially beneficial activities. In this way, it would be possible to articulate the financial security offered by a basic income with a commitment to reciprocal engagement in society and, thus, contribute to addressing both economic insecurity and social cohesion. In short, there is controversy about the proposed solutions, and details are important.

From Liberal to Socialist Influences

Therefore, the issue of UBI is, foremost, an eclectic one from a theoretical perspective. Although it has received support from several theoretical perspectives, ranging from a more liberal perspective to a socialist one, not forsaking others, such as technocratic, feminist, or ecological ones, it has also been severely argued against by objectors from these same theoretical and ideological spaces. The complexity of the arguments suggests that implementing UBI would need careful consideration of economic, social, and cultural factors.

Neo-liberal economists such as Milton Friedman or Charles Murray argue that a UBI enhances individual freedom without increasing state control or economic intervention, improving economic efficiency and reducing poverty. Friedman (1962) advocated for a negative income tax, simplifying welfare systems, reducing bureaucratic procedures and enabling people to make their own choices with direct cash transfers. Murray (2016) proposed that UBI replace the existing welfare state to reduce the state's role in the economy and society.

The social-democratic stance of Wright, Van Parijs, or Atkinson views UBI as a tool for achieving economic equality and social justice. Wright (2010) discussed UBI as a mechanism to redistribute wealth more equitably, reduce poverty, and provide everyone with a safety net, promoting social justice and reducing class disparities. Van Parijs (1995) argues that UBI ensures effective freedom by providing individuals with the economic means to pursue their own goals, free from the constraints of poverty and economic insecurity.

The critical perspective, led by Standing (2011), considers UBI a way of transforming capitalist structures and a tool to empower a growing class of insecure and underemployed individuals who face precarity in their professional careers. Standing (2017) and Widerquist et al. (2013) consider that UBI schemes could grant individuals the economic security to refuse exploitative labour conditions.

Worldviews for the Future

Proponents argue that UBI can provide a fairer and more stable solution. Given the debate's vivid and multifaceted nature, its cross-cutting support from different worldviews sometimes leads to contradictory arguments.

Some authors stress that UBI can improve material well-being. UBI is seen as a means for alleviating poverty, reducing income inequality and promoting economic growth. UBI ensures a minimum income level for all, directly addressing poverty (Widerquist, 2013). By providing a basic income to everyone, UBI can reduce income inequality and support those at the lower end of the income spectrum (Van Parijs & Vanderborght, 2017). By increasing disposable income, UBI can boost consumer spending, stimulating economic growth and the system's funding (Banerjee & Duflo, 2019). UBI can stabilise demand and mitigate recession impacts during economic downturns by providing a steady income flow (Standing, 2017).

In contrast, a more ecological strand sees UBI as promoting environmental sustainability and reducing ecological footprints (Battistoni, 2021). Mulvale (2019) and Lawhon and McCreay (2020) suggested that UBI could support a shift towards a more sustainable economy by decoupling income from employment, thus allowing people to engage in environmentally beneficial activities and reduce consumerism. Jackson (2009) advocates for UBI as part of a broader strategy to create a sustainable economy by ensuring basic economic security; people could be encouraged to pursue lifestyles and occupations that are less resource-intensive and more environmentally friendly.

The Arguments About UBI

The debate over UBI chiefly concerns issues such as work incentives, sheer cost, and political feasibility while comparing UBI to traditional social policy alternatives,[3] which we examine in more detail.

Work Incentive Arguments

Does UBI reduce the incentive to work? Some academics have turned to prior studies on the effects of universal cash transfers or lottery winners. Earlier experiments with negative income tax find a reduction in the labour supply of the targeted households (Burtless & Greenberg, 1983). Marinescu (2018), however, suggests that most studies do not find an effect of unconditional cash transfers on labour supply, and when they do, this effect is negligible. Paz-Báñez et al. (2020) provide a nuanced view of the relationship between UBI and labour supply, stating that while there is evidence of some reduction in labour participation, the magnitude and significance of this effect vary widely depending on contextual factors and demographic characteristics. The effect of UBI on labour supply is quite ambiguous (Almeida, 2023). From existing studies, we conclude that there might be a reduction in labour supply in the short term (Bibler et al., 2019; Hoynes & Rothstein, 2019), but there is no empirical evidence for this to happen in the long term (Paz-Banez et al., 2020).

UBI can provide an incentive to work, including private and social entrepreneurship. UBI can eliminate welfare traps that disincentivise work, encouraging labour market participation (Banerjee & Duflo, 2019). Regarding labour flexibility and entrepreneurship, UBI can lower the barriers to starting new businesses by providing a financial safety net and encouraging innovation and risk-taking (Banerjee & Duflo, 2019). UBI recognises and values engagement in unpaid activities like caregiving and volunteering by providing financial support (Standing, 2017). Because most of these are women, UBI is also considered a means to achieve gender equality, reduce gender disparities in income, and improve economic security (Pateman, 2004).

In contrast, UBI could become a disincentive to workers. A guaranteed income could reduce the incentive to work, potentially decreasing overall

[3] These may include targeted programmes, such as conditional cash transfers, in-kind programmes, or public services.

labour market participation (Moffit, 2003). Personnel and labour economics textbooks suggest that individuals tend to work less with a rise in non-labour income (Borjas, 2020). Economists do not attach a positive or negative value to this effect, as leisure is as legitimate as work, providing utility to agents. Economists remind us of the outcome of working less and reaching higher utility levels. UBI providing a disincentive to work can be a strong argument against it when many developed countries and organisations are facing difficulties in recruiting (The Economist, 2024).

Going further, UBI could foster a dependency culture where individuals rely on basic income rather than seeking employment (Murray, 2016). In a more rational choice approach, there is a concern that UBI might create a moral hazard, where individuals do not take responsibility for their economic well-being and rely on this given income (Torry, 2022). Some critics even further argue that UBI could undermine the social contract and the value of work, leading to less social cohesion and community engagement (Murray, 2016). Previous similar programmes suggest UBI could actually entrench women in low-income jobs and reinforce traditional gender norms if not tied to an agenda for societal transformation (Iturriza et al., 2011).

In practice, some extreme views declare that not all persons (if any) deserve a non-labour income, as it is a subsidy to laziness. While for most of these leaders, it is not obvious what they would do if they were effectively in government, Meloni's government in Italy provides anecdotal evidence. With the motto of supporting "who wants to work", the Italian government has just terminated state subsidies to persons in need (Birchard, 2023). For example, extreme right-led governments can impede or revert the adoption of UBI schemes.

Funding Arguments

Funding has been a significant obstacle to the implementation of UBI. The funding argument raises the idea that the programmes may be too costly. In Southern Europe, the setting up a minimum income targeting the poorest in Portugal in the 1990s raised a significant debate about relatively low funding (Pereira, 2023; Castro, 2018). Austerity policies reduced social stipends during the Great Recession. Implementing an unconditional stipend much higher than the current one for the poorest will certainly present additional challenges. Notably, it would compete for funding with the traditional public sector, which some argue is already underfunded. Allocating resources to UBI might mean less funding for other essential services that effectively address poverty and inequality (Torry, 2023). Other authors argue that targeted social welfare programmes address specific needs, such as housing, healthcare, and food security, more efficiently than an unconditional basic income (Hoynes & Rothstein, 2019). Thus, there might even be a rise in inefficiency due to the focus on distributing resources universally rather than targeting those in need (Feldstein, 2005; Bidadanure, 2019).

Critics further argue that funding UBI would require substantial increases in taxes or reallocation of funds from other social programmes, which might not be economically feasible or even originate welfare losses (Conesa et al., 2023; Hoynes & Rothstein, 2019). UBI could also have an impact on wages and prices. UBI could lead to upward pressure on wages, which could increase production costs and reduce the competitiveness of businesses (Ghatak & Maniquet, 2019). Wage increases could lead to inflation if the increase in consumer demand is not matched by a corresponding increase in the supply of goods and services (Torry, 2022). There is a risk that higher prices for goods and services, particularly in housing and other essential markets, could offset the benefits of the additional income (Hoynes & Rothstein, 2019).

Political Economy Arguments

Political economy tells us that when introducing a UBI, change will lead to winners and losers.

UBI can have a key role in the sustainability of work by shifting the balance of the labour agenda towards workers. UBI can increase workers' bargaining power and labour rights. Workers have more negotiating power with a basic income, leading to better wages and working conditions (Wright, 2010). UBI also provides income stability for gig workers, who often face irregular earnings, allowing them to pursue flexible work arrangements without financial insecurity (Standing, 2017). Financial security could promote health and well-being by reducing stress and anxiety (Widerquist, 2013). UBI allows individuals to achieve a better work-life balance, potentially reducing burnout and increasing long-term productivity (Van Parijs & Vanderborght, 2017).

But is UBI a necessary and sufficient instrument for workers to have the real freedom to "say no"? Widerquist et al. (2013) see UBI as a transformative tool that grants individuals real freedom to refuse degrading work, strengthening their bargaining power. By decoupling income security from employment, workers would be less dependent on any single employer and better positioned to negotiate improved wages or conditions, and enhancing the worker's overall freedom and dignity. However, Birnbaum and De Wispelaere (2016) argue that the effectiveness of the worker's bargaining power could actually be contingent on the presence of complementary background institutions. For workers—especially those in precarious positions—the basic income alone may be insufficient to alter the power dynamics if alternative employment opportunities or strong labour market protections are lacking. Thus, according to Birnbaum and De Wispelaere (2016), the promise of enhanced bargaining power through a basic income can only be realised when it is embedded within a broader framework of supportive policies and institutions.

UBI also secures a stable income for vulnerable workers. Trends in automation and technological development may lead to significant job displacement. While recent estimates suggest these concerns may be overrated (Ramos et al., 2023), the transition to more automation should be regulated with care (Acemoglu & Lensman, 2023). The technocratic perspective sees UBI as a way to provide financial security during these transitions (Ford, 2015; Yang, 2018). A basic income could also support displaced workers as they retrain for new jobs, reducing the economic friction caused by technological changes (Brynjolfsson et al., 2014).

In contrast, losers may try to block the change (Alston, 2017; Standing, 2017; Van Parijs & Vanderborght, 2017; Widerquist, 2013; Widerquist et al., 2013). In particular, will there still be a need for public services with UBI? Will there still be a need for public sector workers? The answer to these questions concerns the low likelihood that UBI will find support among public sector workers and their representative trade unions. The competition for public funding could risk large sectors of the public sector, and, naturally, this would mean fewer job posts and services. Public sector workers or even public service users could be at a loss.

The current state of the art of UBI literature is still tentative. Given the recent surge in studies on UBI schemes, many of these studies have not yet undergone serious peer review processes. The adaptation of the findings from other programmes, such as other unconditional cash transfers or lottery schemes, should be seen cautiously. In addition, the recent surge also suggests a hype, with a profusion of academics writing on the matter, which is always dangerous for scientific scrutiny and academic significance (McKloskey, 2000).

Experiences on UBI

While the above studies focus on individual country studies and causation or correlational relationships between UBI schemes, particularly labour supply, our approach differs. We prefer to compare countries and identify country cases where it is less likely that eventual labour supply effects will be detrimental. These countries will be ideal for an initial introduction of UBI schemes and experimentation for the eventual scaling up of this policy instrument. Before that, learning more about the consequences of introducing UBI in specific countries is instrumental.

UBI in Developed Countries

The 1960s witnessed the upsurge of the first documented experiences of a UBI in places such as the *Mincome* project in Canada, in the rural province of Manitoba, in the second half of the 1970s. It guaranteed the average family an annual income of circa 16,000 Canadian dollars, which positively affected health and educational outcomes and was a way to address rural poverty. At the time, it was considered the most ambitious social experiment ever to take place in Canada, as rates of hospitalisation fell, with improvements in mental health and a rise in the number of children completing high school, besides an increase in investment in human capital from families (Forget, 2011). Results also show a modest reduction in labour supply in the groups of new mothers and teenagers who would remain in school instead of joining the labour force earlier. With the abandonment of the programme at the end of the decade due to stringent inflation shocks, unemployment rose, and people's quality of living returned to the early 1970s (Calinitsky, 2016; Forget, 2011).

At the beginning of the twenty-first century, there was a resurgent interest in UBI experiments. Again, contextual issues played a determining role, as technological development, artificial intelligence, and globalisation's collateral effects brought to light the asymmetrical consequences of automation, job displacement, and economic inequality. The trend is that it becomes ever more critical to ensure a basic standard of living in increasingly automated economies (Ford, 2015; Standing, 2017; Srnicek & Williams, 2015).

The most famous experience occurred in Finland between 2017 and 2018, when a nationwide experiment was conducted. Circa 2000 unemployed citizens, aged 25 to 58, were provided with a monthly stipend of

560 €. Results were mixed, although insightful. The payments were unconditional, and recipients continued to receive the money even if they started working. The primary goals were to investigate the impact on employment, economic well-being, and overall life satisfaction (Kangas et al., 2019). There was no significant impact on employment levels. Some participants reported increased motivation to work, but this did not translate into statistically significant changes in employment rates. Recipients reported higher levels of well-being and reduced stress compared to the control group. They also felt more secure about their financial situation.

However, it is worth noting that the Finnish experiment was not a UBI experiment since it was not "universal" and was not available to all residents regardless of their employment status. It did provide unconditional cash payments and offered valuable insights into the potential benefits of income support for the unemployed, but it did not target the entire Finnish population.

In a different longitude, **Alaska**'s **Permanent Fund Dividend (PFD)** programme provides a UBI example in the United States. The Alaska Permanent Fund was established in 1976 and funded by oil revenues. The PFD, introduced in 1982, provides annual dividends to all Alaska residents. The dividend amount varies yearly based on the fund's performance: in 2021, the PFD was approximately $1,114 per person. The dividend has positively impacted reducing income inequality and poverty levels (Goldsmith, 2010). According to Guettabi, the PFD provides a stable source of income for Alaskans, contributing to economic stability, especially in rural areas where job opportunities are limited (Guettabi, 2019). Other studies show that the PFD has not significantly reduced work incentives, supporting local economies by increasing consumer spending (Jones & Marinescu, 2022). Overall, the PFD has been a successful wealth redistribution model from natural resources to the public, ensuring that oil revenues benefit all residents (Goldsmith, 2010) and contributing to improved health outcomes and reduced inequality.

Also, in the United States, the *Stockton Economic Empowerment Experience* (SEED) provided 125 randomly selected residents in California between 2019 and 2021 with a monthly stipend of 500 US dollars. The income was unconditional and could be spent freely. The objective was to assess the impact on financial security, mental health, and employment. In terms of outcomes, participants showed increased employment stability and full-time employment rates. The income allowed recipients to pursue better job opportunities and invest in personal development. There were also significant improvements in mental health, with reductions in anxiety and depression. Participants reported greater economic security and the ability to meet basic needs (West et al., 2021).

UBI in Developing Countries

UBI experiments were also conducted in Africa, Asia, and South America. Between 2008 and 2009, Namibia's *Otjivero-Omitara* Pilot experience provided N$100 monthly to every resident below 60. The objectives were to alleviate poverty and improve health, education, and economic activity in the region (Haarmann & Haarmann, 2012). There was a significant reduction in poverty levels and malnutrition. Health outcomes improved, with fewer people needing medical treatment for malnutrition-related issues. Increased economic activity was observed as recipients could invest in small businesses and farming. School attendance rates also improved.

In Kenya, the *GiveDirectly* UBI Experiment (ongoing since 2016), the largest and longest-term UBI experiment in Kenya, provides over 20,000 individuals in rural villages with regular cash payments. The experiment includes various treatment groups receiving payments for different durations. The aim was to evaluate the impact on poverty, economic activity, health, and social outcomes over a long period (GiveDirectly, 2020). Early results show improvements in economic stability, increased entrepreneurial activity, better nutrition, and higher school attendance rates. Long-term impacts are still under study.

In India, SEWA Bharat and UNICEF conducted the *Madhya Pradesh Pilot* (2011–2013), which provided a basic income to over 6,000 individuals in eight villages in Madhya Pradesh (Davala et al., 2015). The amount varied, but it was designed to cover basic needs. The objectives were to study the effects on poverty, health, education, and economic activity. There was a significant reduction in poverty and improvements in health indicators. Recipients had better nutrition and healthcare access, increased investment in productive assets, higher school attendance, and improved sanitation. Women showed increased financial independence.

Brazil has been a notable example due to its economic inequality and poverty. The concept of UBI has gained traction through smaller-scale programmes and pilot projects. Some key programmes and pilots were *Bolsa Familia* and *Basic Income Pilots*. While not a UBI, *Bolsa Família* is a conditional cash transfer programme. The programme was implemented on a large scale and has been influential in Brazil's social policy. It provides monthly financial aid to low-income families, contingent on certain conditions such as children's school attendance and vaccinations. *Bolsa Família* has significantly reduced poverty and inequality, improving educational outcomes and reducing child labour (Lindert et al., 2007).

In 2020, in the city of Maricá, Rio de Janeiro, authorities launched a programme that provided basic income to residents, funded by oil royalties. Although it embodied several features of a basic income (regular, unconditional cash transfers that improve well-being), similar to the Finnish case, it cannot be considered truly "universal" in the strict sense because it targets residents who meet specific income and residency criteria, namely poor and deprived people. Although considered a significant experience, it is often described as a large-scale, unconditional cash transfer or guaranteed income programme rather than a fully universal basic income. Preliminary findings suggested improved well-being and economic security among participants (Katz & Ferreira, 2020), and more recent literature has assessed the programme's impact on income, labour supply, and well-being. It is relatively consensual that Maricá's programme delivered several benefits anticipated from a UBI (such as improving household stability and reducing poverty-related stress), although displaying a targeted nature (De Wispelaere et al., 2024; Jain Family Institute, 2022).

Brazil is quite an interesting case since implementing a nationwide UBI in Brazil poses significant challenges due to fiscal constraints and the need for substantial public expenditure (Lavinas, 2018). Advocates argue that a well-designed UBI could simplify and enhance the effectiveness of Brazil's social safety net (Lavinas, 2006). The political will for UBI is mixed, with some support among progressive politicians, but scepticism remains regarding funding and long-term sustainability.

The experiences with UBI across different countries provide valuable insights into its potential benefits and challenges. While results vary based on the design and context of each experiment, common themes include improvements in well-being, reductions in poverty and economic insecurity, and mixed impacts on employment. These experiments highlight the importance of context-specific implementations and the need for further research to understand the long-term effects of UBI. Implementing UBI requires careful consideration of various socio-economic factors, including the features of labour markets, economic stability, administrative capacity, existing social welfare systems, or public support. Countries like Finland or Canada seem better suited to implement UBI due to their economic stability, robust welfare systems, political and public interest, social structures, and efficient administrative capabilities. These factors can significantly enhance the feasibility and effectiveness of UBI implementations in pilot experiences or country-wide.

Data Approach and Description

We have identified three significant arguments with contention on UBI in the literature: reduced labour supply, unsustainability of funding, and political support. Therefore, we will link each argument to indicators to measure the potential for the implementation of UBI, with emphasis on the former. We compare European countries regarding the indicator levels and use several visual techniques to highlight the relationship between the relevant indicators. The respective countries are unlikely candidates if these indicators are already at critical levels.

The broadness of the arguments against UBI schemes makes it challenging to select indicators, given that there are several potential indicators for each argument. Table 7.1 presents the indicators, their identification,

Table 7.1 Indicators and sources

Dimension	*Indicator*	*Description*
Labour supply	Active population rate (%)	Population employed or unemployed but seeking a job
Labour supply	Unemployment rate (%)	Persons aged 15 to 74 years who were not employed, currently available for work, and actively seeking work over active population
Labour supply	Job vacancy rate (%)	Job vacancies (paid posts that is newly created, unoccupied, or about to become vacant) over the sum of occupied posts and of job vacancies
Public funding	Public deficit (% GDP)	Government revenue minus government expenditures (deficit implies expenditures higher than revenues)
Public funding	Public debt (% GDP)	Value of total gross public debt outstanding over the GDP
Political economy	Workers in public sector (% total employment)	Workers in public sector over total employed workers
Political economy	Union density (% of workers)	Wage earners trade union members, over the total number of wage and salary earners

Note: All indicators are from Eurostat with exception from Workers in public sector (OECD) and union density (ICTWSS6.0)

explanation, and unit of measurement. Three indicators were selected to represent labour supply: active population, unemployment, and job vacancy rates. In countries with low activity rates, low unemployment, or high job vacancy rates, it is unlikely that programmes that may diminish the incentive to work are adopted. Regarding funding, the indicators selected were public deficit and public debt as a percentage of GDP. Countries with high public deficits and debt will be unlikely candidates for expensive programmes. The *a priori* interpretation of low likelihood may not apply when radical political changes occur, such as in Argentina. The indicators of the political economy are the percentage of workers in the public sector and union density. Both suggest that changes that harm public employment or traditional public services will be fought harder in countries with high values in these indicators.

Given that we have selected more than one indicator for each argument, this may lead to ambiguous predictions, as we shall see in the empirical part. The interpretation of each indicator can also be challenging, as it can be ambiguous in terms of affecting the likelihood of UBI implementation, given that the economy fluctuates substantially across the economic cycle; when relevant, we provide information for the peak (2019) and trough (2013). We highlight the case of Finland, where UBI was tested, and the case of Portugal, the country that funds our research, and where no UBI was tested yet.

A cross-tabulation of these indicators tells us which countries would be more politically feasible for implementing UBI programmes.

The Empirics of the Labour Supply Argument

Single Indicator Results

Considering the indicators individually, we find which countries are less or more likely to succeed regarding this criterion in implementing an unconditional basic income. We present information for 2013 and 2019, a minimum point of the recession and a maximum point of the expansion, as these indicators may change throughout the business cycle. See Tables 7.2a and 7.2b.

In 2013, Romania, Italy, Croatia, Poland, and Hungary had the lowest levels of active population, while Greece, Spain, Croatia, Portugal, and Cyprus had high unemployment levels. Norway, Germany, Latvia, Estonia, and Sweden exhibited high job vacancy levels. In 2019, Romania, Italy,

Table 7.2a Indicators of labour supply, 2013

Less likely	*Active population (%)*	*Unemployment (%)*	*Job vacancy (%)*
1	Romania	Greece	Norway
2	Italy	Spain	Germany
3	Croatia	Croatia	Latvia
4	Poland	Portugal	Estonia
5	Hungary	Cyprus	Sweden
More likely			
1	Iceland	Norway	Poland
2	Switzerland	Switzerland	Portugal
3	Netherlands	Germany	Bulgaria
4	Sweden	Iceland	Luxembourg
5	Norway	Austria	Romania

Note: Job vacancy has several missing observations reducing the sample of countries

Table 7.2b Indicators of labour supply, 2019

Less likely	*Active population (%)*	*Unemployment (%)*	*Job vacancy (%)*
1	Romania	Greece	Czechia
2	Italy	Spain	Germany
3	Croatia	Italy	Netherlands
4	Greece	France	Latvia
5	Belgium	Cyprus	Hungary
More likely			
1	Iceland	Czechia	Bulgaria
2	Switzerland	Germany	Portugal
3	Netherlands	Hungary	Poland
4	Sweden	Poland	Romania
5	Norway	Iceland	Slovakia

Note: Job vacancy has several missing observations reducing the sample of countries

and Croatia again had the lowest levels of active population, followed by Greece and Belgium. Regarding high unemployment levels, Greece, Spain, and Cyprus were joined by Italy and France. As for high job vacancies, the situation in Germany and Latvia was similar to that in Czechia, the Netherlands, and Hungary. These indicators discourage the implementation of unconditional basic income in these countries, as it may exacerbate its disadvantages.

In contrast, Iceland, Switzerland, the Netherlands, Sweden, and Norway presented high levels of active population in 2013 and 2019.

Norway, Switzerland, Germany, Iceland, and Austria exhibited low levels of unemployment in 2013, while in 2019, Germany and Iceland were joined by the Czech Republic, Hungary, and Poland. Poland, Portugal, Bulgaria, Luxembourg, and Romania held low job vacancy levels in 2013, with Slovakia replacing Luxembourg in 2019. Implementing an unconditional basic income would be more likely successful in these countries, as they are performing well in these indicators of labour supply.

Because some countries are mentioned more than once in different situations, this leads to individual highlights. Iceland (2013 and 2019), Switzerland (2013), and Poland (2019), followed by Norway (2013), are the best candidates in terms of the labour supply argument. Therefore, performing well in two indicators presents a lower probability of downsides to implementing an unconditional basic income. Romania and Germany (2013 and 2019), Sweden, Poland, Portugal, Norway (2013), and Czechia, Hungary, and The Netherlands (2019) present an undetermined situation, performing relatively well and poorly at different indicators. The indicators suggest Italy and Greece are unlikely candidates for unconditional basic income, as they performed poorly in two indicators in 2019.

Cross-Tabulation of Single Indicators

In the previous sections, we identified consensual and ambiguous situations in different countries. It is interesting to cross-tabulate the selected indicators to better understand the correlations between single indicators (within the same argument).

Figures 7.1a, b compare information for the activity and unemployment rates for 2013 and 2019, respectively. Three groups stand out from the majority of countries gathered in the middle. Greece and Spain present a middle-level activity rate and a very high unemployment rate. Croatia, Italy, and particularly Romania show low activity and middle-level unemployment rates. Iceland, The Netherlands, Sweden, and Switzerland present very high activity and low unemployment rates.

The position of these countries does not vary much from the trough (2013) to the peak (2019), although it is possible to identify a compression of the interval of outcomes. Notably, the upper limit of the unemployment rate declines from 28% to 18%, and the lower limit of the activity rate increases from 58% to 63%. The stability of the relative results of

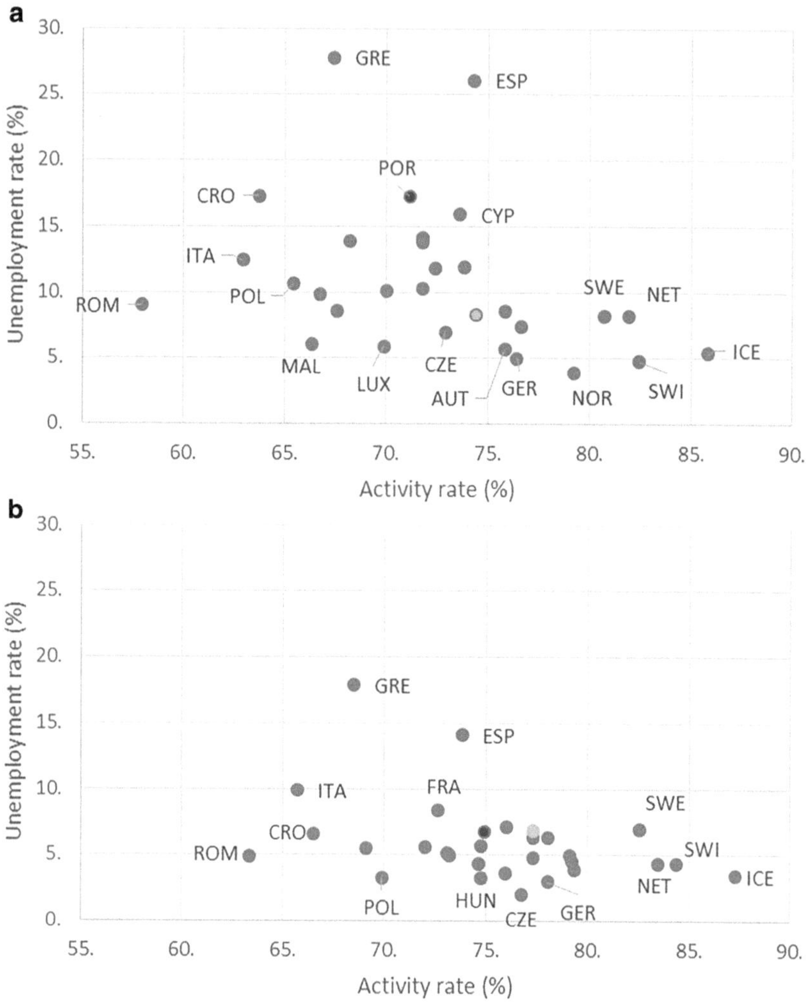

Fig. 7.1 (**a**) Activity vs. Unemployment rate, 2013. (**b**) Activity vs. Unemployment rate, 2019

countries points to structural features of each country's economy, such as the women's activity rate.

The Beveridge curve is a more traditional graphical relationship that contrasts unemployment with the job vacancy rate (see Fig. 7.2a, b).

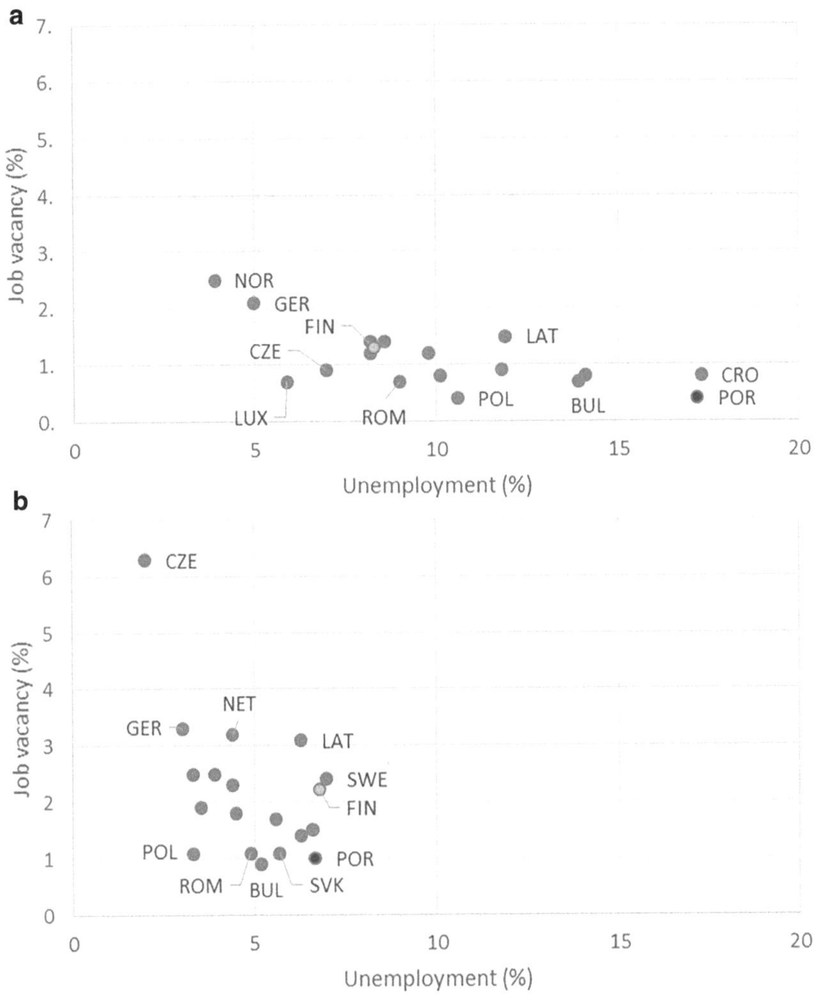

Fig. 7.2 (**a**) Beveridge curve (Job vacancy vs. unemployment rate), 2013. (**b**) Beveridge curve (Job vacancy vs. unemployment rate), 2019

Nevertheless, fewer countries are shown, given that job vacancies are available in fewer countries. In contrast to the activity and unemployment rate results in Fig. 7.1a, b, the very different shape of the relationship between unemployment and job vacancy rates in times of crisis or boom stands out.

Because of the trough of the recession (Fig. 7.2a), most countries did not show evidence of job vacancies, with two exceptions. Norway and Germany presented both low unemployment rates and some level of job vacancy. Despite the crisis, the unemployment rate varied much.

Croatia and Portugal had very high unemployment, while Luxembourg and Czechia had low unemployment rates. At the peak in 2019, the countries were positioned differently—Fig. 7.2b. The lower and upper limits of the unemployment rate halved, and job vacancies increased. Czechia stands out, with almost double that of the second-ranked country. Juxtaposing Fig. 7.2a, b, most observations fit well with the traditional Beveridge curve shape. The exceptions are Finland, Latvia, and Sweden, which present relatively high unemployment and high vacancy rates, an unusual coexistence.

The Empirics of the Public Funding and the Political Economy Arguments

Regarding the funding sustainability of a UBI scheme, Figs. 7.3 and 7.4 cross-tab budget deficit/surplus against government debt across European countries. The difference between both is that the former uses the information for 2019, the peak year, which is more sensitive to cyclical and idiosyncratic reasons, while the latter uses a 5-year average. Both indicate a negative association between budget surplus and government debt. Figure 7.4 identifies three countries with high budget deficits and government debt: Italy, Spain, and France. In contrast, Denmark, Luxembourg, and Sweden present a budget surplus and low government debt.

The political economy of implementing UBI is also relevant. Workers in the public sector and union density (%) are indicators that vary considerably according to the economic model proposed. The interpretation of their meaning also varies sharply depending on world views and the purpose for which we use them. For example, union density has been used to measure labour bargaining power (Freeman & Medoff, 1984). For this paper, we use union density and the level of public employment as a sign of protection for the status quo. UBI schemes may lead to changes in the

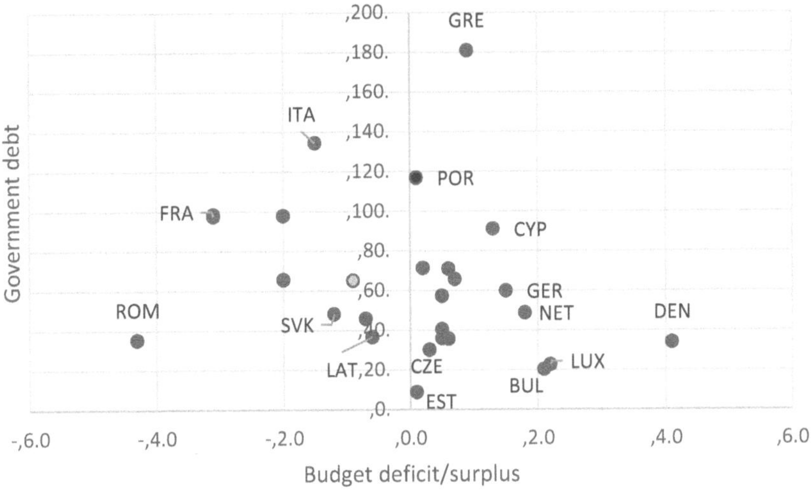

Fig. 7.3 Budget deficit/surplus and Government debt, 2019

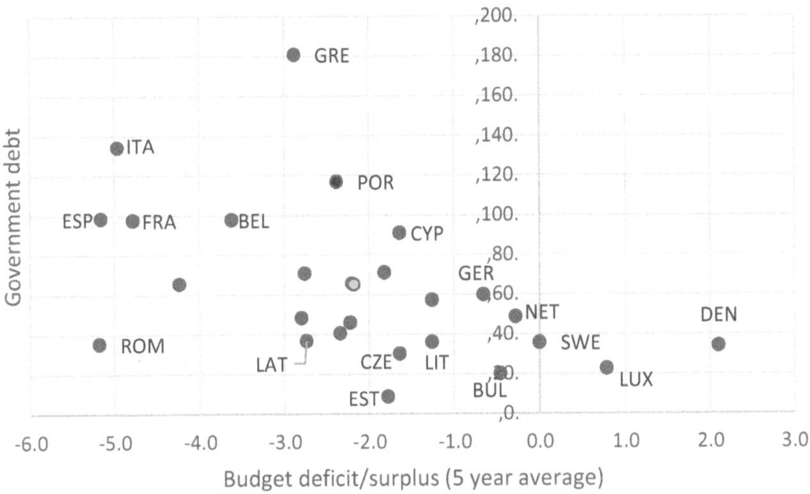

Fig. 7.4 Budget deficit/surplus (5 year average) and Government debt, 2019

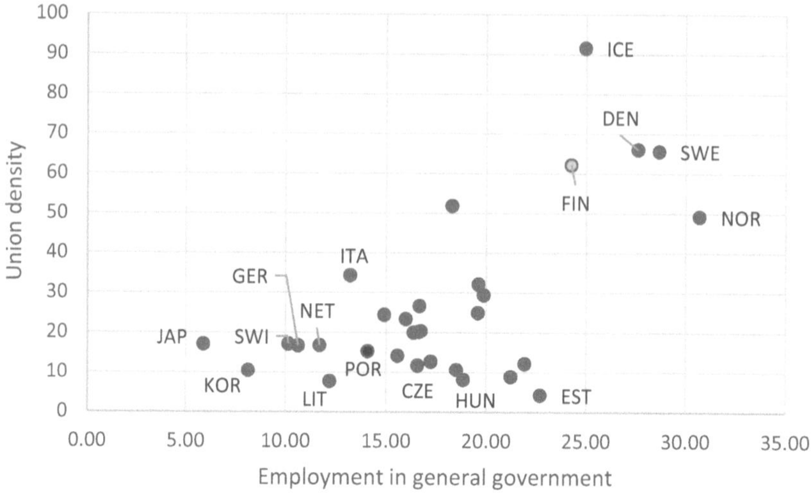

Fig. 7.5 Employment in general government and union density, 2019

need for public sector services or their type, which may not be seen lightly by current public sector workers, and unions may resist these changes. This argument against UBI in this literature suggests that the higher the public sector employment and/or the higher the union density, the higher the resistance to change for a UBI-based scheme.

Figure 7.5 presents employment in general government and union density, and the results are in sharp contrast with the previous analysis. Employment in the general government does not vary much across time.[4] Union density declines, particularly in former socialist countries. Countries with high public sector employment and union density include Iceland, Denmark, Sweden, and Norway, which have been identified as good candidates to test UBI regarding the labour supply argument. In contrast, the Netherlands and Switzerland are good candidates for both arguments. Portugal presents a low-middle level of general government employment and a low union density. However, it is important to note that unions are the strongest in the public sector.

[4] Exceptions include Israel and Great Britain, which saw reductions of 3 percentage points, and Estonia and Spain, which saw increases of around 2 percentage points.

Concluding Remarks

Discussion of Results

In which countries is UBI most likely to succeed? Which countries are less likely to implement UBI? Which is the ideal candidate country to test UBI? These are difficult questions that we will tentatively explore in this section. Our analysis often finds the usual suspects as the best performers for most indicators. Nevertheless, the country blocks following Esping-Andersen (1990) or Ferrera (1996) typologies do not hold to a multi-indicator analysis.

The empirics of the different criticisms led to different country alignments in what one can call criticism differences. The first results regarding the labour supply and the funding arguments suggest that Finland was not the best candidate for experimentation. Finland was an average candidate with a lower probability of succeeding than countries such as Iceland, Switzerland, the Netherlands, and Czechia (labour supply); Denmark, Luxembourg, Bulgaria, and Estonia (funding); or Switzerland, Lithuania, Germany, and the Netherlands (political economy).

This exploratory analysis varies across indicators, which we can call within-criticism differences. This divergence stresses the relevance of the choice of indicators and the time of measurement. Regarding the choice, different indicators provide different rankings, particularly evident in the labour supply indicators in Tables 7.2a and 7.2b. In terms of the timing, being in times of crisis or boom makes a difference and alters the rankings between countries.

Being an average candidate is not necessarily bad for experimentation, as it faces more real problems and, therefore, increases the chances of replication than the ideal candidate but reduces the likelihood of success of the experiment. In this sense, regarding these two arguments, Portugal is a worse candidate than Finland, as it presents a lower activity rate and higher government debt. Portugal is a better candidate than Finland in terms of the political economy, with lower union density and public sector employees. None has an exogenous source of income that helps a country succeed in implementing a UBI scheme. Of the other countries, Switzerland is a likely good candidate to excel in its implementation, given a combination of the selected indicators and abundant capital inflows.

Future Steps

Relevant research avenues need to be pursued. Following our methodology, we need to fine-tune and consolidate the choice of indicators and the robustness of its results. For example, current indicators can be complemented with additional ones regarding working hours (labour supply) or taxation levels (funding).

Arguments for pro-UBI schemes, such as it will reduce inequality, suggest that countries with higher inequality may gain from this and that an additional indicator should include this dimension. Regarding the ideal country profile for UBI experimentation, one needs to identify the objective: Is it to maximise the success of the experience or the success of replication? de Paz-Báñez et al. (2020) highlight the importance of rigorous experimental designs in assessing the impacts of UBI and call for more randomised controlled trials (RCTs) and longitudinal studies to better understand the long-term effects of UBI on labour supply. The authors call for more comprehensive and methodologically robust studies to fully understand the implications of UBI on labour markets.

Acknowledgements We thank the participants of the 22nd BIEN Congress in Seoul.

References

Acemoglu, D., & Lensman, T. (2023). Regulating transformative technologies. *American Economic Review: Insights*. https://www.nber.org/system/files/working_papers/w31461/w31461.pdf

Aerts, E., Marx, I., & Verbist, G. (2023). Not that basic: How level, design, and context matter for the redistributive outcomes of universal basic income. *Journal of Social Policy, 1–23*. https://doi.org/10.1017/S0047279423000582

Almeida, M. A. (2023). *Rendimento Básico Incondicional: Uma Medida Eficaz e Sustentável? Tese de Mestrado em Economia*. Universidade do Porto.

Alston, P. (2017). Universal basic income as a social rights-based antidote to growing economic insecurity. In K. G. Young (Ed.), *The future of social rights* (pp. 377–404). Cambridge University Press. https://doi.org/10.1017/9781108284653.015

Atkinson, A. B. (1996). The case for a participation income. *The Political Quarterly, 67*(1), 67–70. https://doi.org/10.1111/j.1467-923X.1996.tb01568.x

Banerjee, A., & Duflo, E. (2019). *Good economics for hard times: Better answers to our biggest problems*. Penguin UK.

Battistoni, A. (2021). The other side of abundance: Feminist and ecological arguments for guaranteed income in the United States, c. 1960–1980. In P. Sloman, D. Zamora Vargas, & P. Ramos Pinto (Eds.), *Universal basic income in historical perspective*. Palgrave Macmillan. https://doi.org/10.1007/978-3-030-75706-9_5

Bibler, A., Guettabi, M., & Reimer, M. (2019). *Short-term labour responses to unconditional cash transfers*. Institute of Social and Economic Research Working Paper: Anchorage, AK, USA.

Bidadanure, J. (2019). The political theory of universal basic income. *Annual Review of Political Science, 22*, 481–501. https://doi.org/10.1146/annurev-polisci-050317-070954

Birchard, R. (2023). *Italy: Meloni pressured by welfare cuts and slowing economy* – DW – 08/04/2023

Birnbaum, S., & De Wispelaere, J. (2016). Basic income in the capitalist economy: The mirage of "exit" from employment. *Basic Income Studies, 11*(1), 61–74.

Borjas, G. (2020). *Labour economics* (8th ed.). McGraw-Hill Education.

Brynjolfsson, E., McAfee, A., & Spence, M. (2014). New World order: Labour, capital, and ideas in the power law economy. *Foreign Affairs, 93*(4), 44–53.

Burtless, G., & Greenberg, D. (1983). Measuring the impact of NIT experiments on work effort. *Industrial and Labour Relations Review, 36*(4), 592–605. https://doi.org/10.2307/2522932

Calinitsky, D. (2016). 'More normal than welfare': The Mincome experiment, stigma, and community experience. *Canadian Journal of Sociology, 53*(1), 26–71. https://doi.org/10.1111/cars.12091

Camporesi, A. T. (2023). Rethinking Thomas Paine and the origins of the basic income proposal. *History of Political Economy, 55*(1), 77–102. https://doi.org/10.1215/00182702-10213639

Castro, M. (2018). Será possível financiar um Rendimento Básico Incondicional em Portugal? Análise de três cenários. *Revista Portuguesa de Filosofia, 74*(2–3), 627–660. https://doi.org/10.17990/RPF/2018_74_2_0627

Claveria, O., & Sorić, P. (2024). Inequality and redistribution: Evidence from Scandinavian and Mediterranean countries. *Applied economic analysis, 32*(94), 1–22.

Conesa, J. C., Li, B., & Li, Q. (2023). A quantitative evaluation of universal basic income. *Journal of Public Economics*. https://doi.org/10.1016/j.jpubeco.2023.104881

Davala, S., Jhabvala, R., Mehta, S. K., & Standing, G. (2015). *Basic income: A transformative policy for India*. Bloomsbury.

de Paz-Báñez, M. A., Asensio-Coto, M. J., Sánchez-López, C., et al. (2020). Is there empirical evidence on how the implementation of a universal basic income (UBI) affects labour supply? A systematic review. *Sustainability, 12*(22), 9459. https://doi.org/10.3390/su12229459

De Wispelaere, J., Morales, L., & Waltenberg, F. (2024). Basic income as a pandemic social protection instrument: Lessons from Maricá, Brazil. *International Social Security Review, 77*, 121–136. https://doi.org/10.1111/issr.12352
Esping-Andersen, G. (1990). *The three worlds of welfare capitalism*. Princeton University Press.
Feldstein, M. (2005). Rethinking social insurance. *American Economic Review, 95*(1), 1–24. https://doi.org/10.1257/0002828053828545
Ferrera, M. (1996). The "southern model" of welfare in social Europe. *Journal of European Social Policy, 6*(1), 17–37. https://doi.org/10.1177/095892879600600102
Ford, M. (2015). *The rise of the robots: Technology and the threat of a jobless future*. Basic Books.
Forget, E. L. (2011). The town with no poverty: The health effects of a Canadian guaranteed annual income field experiment. *Canadian Public Policy, 37*(3), 283–305. https://doi.org/10.3138/cpp.37.3.283
Freeman, R. B., & Medoff, J. L. (1984). *What do unions do?* Basic Books.
Frieman, M. (1962). *Capitalism and freedom*. University of Chicago Press.
Gentilini, U., Grosh, M., Rigolini, J. et al. (2020). *Exploring universal basic income: A guide to navigating concepts, evidence, and practices*. World Bank. https://openknowledge.worldbank.org/handle/10986/32677
Ghatak, M., & Maniquet, F. (2019). Universal basic income – Some theoretical aspects. *Annual Review of Economics, 11*(1), 895–928. https://doi.org/10.1146/annurev-economics-080218-030220
GiveDirectly. (2020). *Universal basic income: Early lessons from Kenya*. Universal Basic Income Programs (UBI) | GiveDirectly
Goldsmith, S. (2010). *The Alaska permanent fund dividend: A case study in implementation of a basic income guarantee*. Paper presented at the 13th BIEN Congress, Sao Paulo, Brazil.
Goulart, P., Ferrittu, G., & Ramos, R. (2023). Income inequality and effectiveness in redistribution. In P. Goulart, R. Ramos, & G. Ferrittu (Eds.), *Global labour in distress. Volume II: Earnings, (in)decent work and institutions* (pp 13–25). Palgrave.
Greenstein, R. (2019). *Commentary: Universal basic income may sound attractive but, if it occurred, would likelier increase poverty than reduce it*. Center on Budget and Policy Priorities.
Guettabi, M. (2019). *What do we know about the effects of the Alaska permanent fund dividend?* Institute of Social and Economic Research, University of Alaska Anchorage.
Haarmann, C., & Haarmann, D. (2012). Namibia: Seeing the sun rise – The realities and hopes of the basic income grant pilot project. In M. C. Murray & C. Pateman (Eds.), *Basic income worldwide. International political economy series*. Palgrave Macmillan. https://doi.org/10.1057/9781137265227_3

Hoynes, H., & Rothstein, J. (2019). Universal basic income in the United States and advanced countries. *Annual Review of Economics, 11*, 929–958. https://doi.org/10.1146/annurev-economics-080218-030237

Iturriza, A., Bedi, A. S., & Sparrow, R. (2011). Unemployment assistance and transition to employment in Argentina. *Economic Development and Cultural Change, 59*(4), 811–837. https://doi.org/10.1086/660004

Jackson, T. (2009). *Prosperity without growth – Economics for a finite planet.* Routledge.

Jain Family. (2022). Fact sheet Marica basic income, August. https://jainfamily-institute.org/wp-content/uploads/pdf/fact-sheet-august-2022.pdf

Jones, D., & Marinescu, I. (2022). The labour market impacts of universal and permanent cash transfers: Evidence from the Alaska permanent fund. *American Economic Journal: Economic Policy, 14*(2), 315–340. https://doi.org/10.1257/pol.20190299

Kangas, O., Jauhiainen, S., Simanainen, M. et al. (2019). The basic income experiment 2017–2018 in Finland: Preliminary results report. *Reports and Memorandums of the Ministry of Social Affairs and Health 2019:9*.

Katz, P., & Ferreira, L. (2020). The history of basic income in Brazil and how the City of Marica points the way forward. *The Boston Review, The Universal Basic Income Hub.* April 14. Retrieved from https://basicincometoday.com/

Lavinas, L. (2006). From means-test schemes to basic income in Brazil: Exceptionality and paradox. *International Social Security Review, 59*, 103–125. https://doi.org/10.1111/j.1468-246X.2006.00249.x

Lavinas, L. (2018). The collateralization of fiscal policy under financialized capitalism. *Development and Change, 49*(2), 502–517. https://doi.org/10.1111/dech.12370

Lawhon, M., & McCreay, T. (2020). Beyond jobs vs environment: On the potential of universal basic income to reconfigure environmental politics. *Antipode, 52*(2), 452–474. https://doi.org/10.1111/anti.12604

Lindert, K., Linder, A., Hobbs, J., & la Brière, B. (2007). *The nuts and bolts of Brazil's Bolsa Família program: Implementing conditional cash transfers in a decentralised context.* Social Protection Discussion Paper 39853. World Bank.

Marinescu, I. (2018). *No strings attached: The behavioral effects of U.S. unconditional cash transfer programs.* NBER working paper 24337. https://www.nber.org/papers/w24337

McKloskey, D. (2000). *How to be human. Though an economist.* University of Michigan Press.

Moffit, R. A. (2003). The negative income tax and the evolution of US welfare policy. *Journal of Economic Perspectives, 17*(3), 119–140.

Mulvale, P. (2019). Social-ecological transformation and the necessity of universal basic income. *Social Alternatives, 38*(2), 39–46. https://doi.org/10.3316/informit.597471928210769

Murray, C. (2016). *In our hands - a plan to replace the welfare state.* Revised and Updated. The American Enterprise Institute.
Pateman, C. (2004). Democratising citizenship: Some advantages of a basic income. *Politics and Society, 32*(1), 89–105. https://doi.org/10.1177/0032329203261100
Pereira, R. (2023). *Financing basic income – A dual income proposal.* Palgrave Macmillan. https://doi.org/10.1007/978-3-031-29012-1
Ramos, R., Ferrittu, G., & Goulart, P. (2023). Technological change and the future of work. In P. Goulart, R. Ramos, & G. Ferrittu (Eds.), *Global labour in distress. Volume I: Globalization, technology and labour resilience* (pp. 203–212). Palgrave.
Srnicek, N., & Williams, A. (2015). Inventing the future: Postcapitalism and a world without work. Verso Books.
Standing, G. (2011). Workfare and the precariat. *Soundings, 47*(47), 35–43.
Standing, G. (2011). The Precariat: The New Dangerous Class. Bloomsbury Academic, London.
Standing, G. (2017). *Basic income: And how we can make it happen.* Penguin.
Tanner, M. (2015). The pros and cons of a guaranteed national income. *Cato Institute Policy Analysis, 773*, 1–24.
The Economist. (2024). *Talent is scarce. Yet many countries spurn it.* Aug 15th 2024.
Torry, M. (2022). *Basic income—What, why, and how? Aspects of the global basic income debate. Exploring the basic income guarantee.* Palgrave Macmillan. https://doi.org/10.1007/978-3-031-14248-2
Torry, M. (2023). Feasibility and implementation. In M. Torry (Ed.), *The Palgrave international handbook of basic income. Exploring the basic income guarantee.* Palgrave Macmillan. https://doi.org/10.1007/978-3-031-41001-7_11
Van Parijs, P. (1995). Real freedom for all: What (if anything) can justify capitalism?. Clarendon Press.
Van Parijs, P., & Vanderborght, Y. (2017). *Basic income: A radical proposal for a free society and a sane economy.* Harvard University Press.
West, S., Baker, A. C., Samra, S., & Coltrera, E. (2021). *Stockton economic empowerment demonstration (SEED) – Preliminary Analysis – SEED's First Year.* SEED_Preliminary+Analysis-SEEDs+First+Year_Final+Report_Individual+Pages+.pdf (squarespace.com)
Widerquist, K. (2013). *Independence, Propertylessness, and basic income: A theory of freedom as the power to say no (exploring the basic income guarantee).* Palgrave McMillan.
Widerquist, K., Noguera, J. A., Vanderborght, Y., et al. (2013). The idea of unconditional income for everyone. In K. Widerquist, J. A. Noguera, Y. Vanderborght, et al. (Eds.), *Basic income: An anthology of contemporary research* (pp. 6–21). Blackwell.

Wright, E. O. (2010). *Envisioning real utopias*. Verso.
Yang, A. (2018). *The war on Normal people: The truth about America's disappearing jobs and why universal basic income is our future*. Hachette Books.

CHAPTER 8

Beyond the Prototype, Towards the Varieties of Basic Income Experiences

Soomi Lee

Introduction

The financial feasibility of implementing a Universal Basic Income (UBI) program determines its political viability. While local UBI pilots have shown promise in enhancing well-being by providing unconditional cash transfers to low-income households, there are limitations to scaling these efforts to a national level. Successfully implementing a large-scale UBI requires more than the financial feasibility of a *program cost*; it demands an integration of UBI principles with existing tax and transfer programs in its design and the development of administrative capacity in its implementation. The challenge of UBI cost estimation is in designing a national UBI *program* guided by the principles of basic income and the assessment of the existing welfare system.

The distinction between public policy and public programs is crucial. *Public policy* establishes the general frameworks that set the goals and direction of government actions, while *public programs* represent specific activities designed to achieve those policy objectives. Therefore, it is

S. Lee (✉)
University of La Verne, La Verne, CA, USA
e-mail: slee4@laverne.edu

R. Merrill, C. Neves (eds.), *Determining the Value of Universal Basic Income*, Exploring the Basic Income Guarantee,
https://doi.org/10.1007/978-3-032-04004-6_8

essential to address the specific problems that a UBI is intended to solve and how it relates to existing programs (Hoynes & Rothstein, 2019). I argue that the design of a UBI program should consider the current social safety net and tax system, explore how the program interacts with other programs, and ensure that how basic income principles can be integrated into these frameworks. This suggests that the welfare system, including basic income programs, can vary significantly between countries. However, any system that adheres to the fundamental principle of basic income should ensure everyone experiences financial security with dignity and freedom.

What We See from the UBI Cost Discussions

Estimates of the cost of a basic income program vary widely. They stem from different assumptions in program designs. One of the critical factors influencing these estimates is the gross versus net cost debate—whether to use the prototype UBI program ("prototype UBI" hereafter) or a design based on the Negative Income Tax (NIT) program.

The cost of a prototype UBI program is typically calculated using a straightforward method, though the exact figures can vary based on specific assumptions. For instance, the proposed Prototype UBI program, which would distribute $1,000 per month to every adult and $500 per month to every child in the United States, carries a substantial gross cost. Based on the 2024 population projection from the U.S. Census Bureau, this program would require an annual budget of $3.57 trillion. It equates to 14% of the projected GDP and 53% of the federal budget in 2024. For those who are fiscally conservative, the sheer magnitude of the cost would appear reckless. For the progressives, it may appear unwise to allocate scarce resources to those not in need, which leaves those in need worse off with fewer resources (Greenstein, 2019; Hoynes & Rothstein, 2019).

Researchers argue that through an appropriate income tax structure, NIT programs can produce similar distributional outcomes as the prototype UBI with a much smaller budget (Mankiw, 2021; Zwolinski & Fleischer, 2023; Widerquist, 2017; Chang et al., 2024). The contrast between gross versus net cost is often illustrated to show the fiscal feasibility of a UBI program. In a stylized demonstration, for instance, Widerquist (2017) shows that when considering taxes, the net cost of a UBI in the United States can be much lower than the gross cost. He demonstrates that a UBI program with a total cost of more than $3 trillion results in a net cost of $500 billion, based on his assumptions regarding benefit levels and a flat income tax rate of 50%. Chang et al. (2024) show the feasibility of NIT designed to imitate the effects of the prototype UBI. In their quantitative general equilibrium model that simulates the U.S. income and wealth distributions, NIT can replicate the prototype UBI program. However, despite their similar distributional outcomes, the NIT program always operates with a smaller budget than the prototype UBI program. Nonetheless, the authors caution against the practicality of NIT in their model, as it assumes an unrealistic linear income tax structure and no administrative cost.

The equivalency of UBI and NIT faces criticism. First, some argue that the two are not truly equivalent if administrative costs are considered. Because of the high cost involved in means testing, NIT is more expensive than UBI (Santens, 2022). Second, since the equivalency is presented in a highly stylized manner, NIT is inapplicable to practical policymaking. In fact, real-world tax codes are significantly more complex than a flat income tax used in many models.

Note that the equivalency analysis assumes that there are no interactions between the proposed UBI or NIT programs and the existing welfare and tax systems. This means that the UBI/NIT costs are evaluated as if they operate independently, without considering how they might fit into the current welfare structures. Additionally, the analysis disregards how implementing a UBI-like program could embody the fundamental principles of UBI. While UBI and NIT might lead to similar distributional effects, they would not change the stigmatizing nature or the onerous administration burden of current welfare programs.

What to Consider

1. Targeting Within Universalism

As suggested by Skocpol (1991), the "targeting within universalism" approach in social policy combines the strengths of both universal and targeted programs. Her idea starts with a universal service framework that benefits a large population. Within this framework, extra or more intensive services target disadvantaged groups. By doing this, programs can maintain broad political support through their universality while directing more resources to those with greater needs. Furthermore, this approach reduces the stigma and political vulnerability of purely targeted programs.

A notable example is the U.S. Child Tax Credit (CTC) program, expanded during the COVID-19 pandemic. The expansion made the credit fully refundable, increased the maximum amount per child, and allowed for monthly cash payments instead of waiting for refunds during tax filing season. By making it fully refundable, low-income families receive refunds, which ensures that the benefits are directed towards them. As a result, it benefited 61 million children across 36 million families, reaching 84% of children in the country. The expansion reduced child poverty by more than 40% while it was in effect. Its nearly universal coverage helped to build a broad political coalition in support of the program. If the expansion is made permanent, it is estimated that child poverty could fall by 28% and extreme child poverty by 49% (Bastian, 2024).

One way to incorporate the "targeting within universalism" approach in designing a guaranteed income program is by establishing a baseline level of financial security for all citizens. To effectively target resources, complementary programs can provide additional benefits for specific disadvantaged groups. Careful data collection and analysis can guide the targeting aspect, ensuring that the program effectively identifies and supports those who need it most while maintaining the broader universal framework.

2. Simultaneous Examination of Tax and Spending Programs

In his 2021 work, Mankiw (2021) argues that it is misleading to consider taxes and transfers separately when evaluating their impact on different income groups. The complexity of the tax code and the fragmented nature of government transfer programs often obscure their overall impact. He points out that many public benefits are delivered through the tax system, making it essential to examine them together for a clearer understanding of their distributional effects.

The Organization for Economic Co-operation and Development (OECD) has recently started reporting gross and net social spending. Figure 8.1 highlights the importance of considering the effects of taxes (both direct and indirect) and "tax breaks with a social purpose (TBSPs)" on social expenditure. The bars represent gross public social expenditure, while the circles indicate net social spending as a percentage of GDP after accounting for TBSPs. The country rankings for gross and net spending are shown in parentheses.

The OECD average for gross and net social spending is 20% of GDP. France ranks first in both categories. Germany and Portugal show

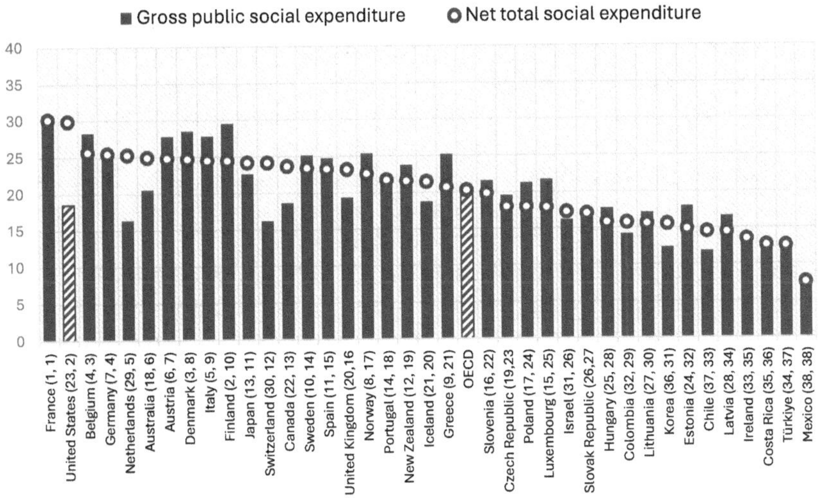

Fig. 8.1 Gross and net social spending, as % of GDP in 2019. Source: OECD (2023), Social Expenditure (SOCX) Update 2023: Private social expenditure and the influence of tax systems, OECD, Paris, http://www.oecd.org/social/expenditure.htm

identical levels of gross and net social spending. Interestingly, when factoring in the impact of TBSPs, the United States becomes the second-largest social spender, while Finland ranks second in gross spending. Similarly, in the Netherlands, Switzerland, Canada, and the United Kingdom, net expenditures exceed gross expenditures. In contrast, in countries such as Finland, Denmark, and Greece, net social spending is lower than gross spending, possibly due to cash benefits being taxed away.

3. Existing Social Safety Net and a Basic Income Program

Assessing a country's current social safety net is essential for understanding the politics of basic income. Lee (2018) analyses the 2016 European Social Survey, which was the first cross-country survey to ask respondents about the introduction of a UBI program in 21 European countries. She finds that countries with weak social safety nets show stronger support for UBI, as they may see it as enhancing their social safety nets. In contrast, UBI receives less support in universalistic welfare states like Norway and

Sweden. This is likely because the survey explicitly describes UBI as replacing "many other social benefits", which many people in more robust social safety systems prefer to keep.

Political support for UBI partly depends on how it is integrated with the current welfare system. Using the same survey data, I created Fig. 8.2 to illustrate the relationship between the effectiveness of social transfer programs in reducing poverty (on the X axis) and support for UBI (on the Y axis). It demonstrates that a more effective social safety net in alleviating poverty is correlated with lower support for UBI, as respondents believe it might replace many existing social services. This relationship suggests that gaining political support for UBI requires the strategic integration of a UBI program into the nation's welfare system.

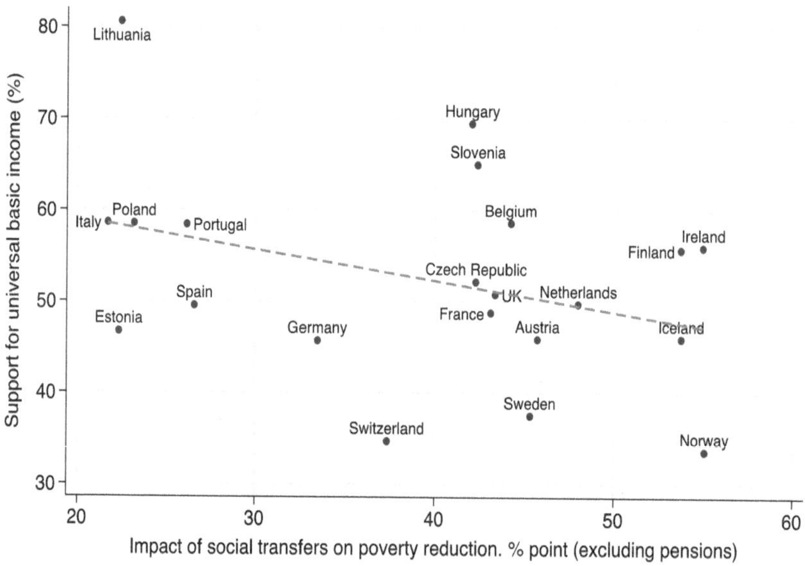

Fig. 8.2 Effect of social safety net and support for UBI in 21 European Countries. Data sources: European Social Survey Round 8 (2016) and Eurostat

U.S. Example

This section explores how the United States could implement a basic income program rooted in UBI principles and the framework of "targeting within universalism". This approach mainly utilizes tax credit programs within the U.S. federal income tax system. The idea is to transform the current standard deduction into a fully refundable standard tax credit for all adults, offer a fully refundable Child Tax Credit (CTC) for every child, expand the work-incentivizing Earned Income Tax Credit (EITC) program, enhance countercyclical in-kind transfer programs, and abolish ineffective, stigmatizing welfare programs.

The proposal aims to ensure financial stability for individuals by introducing a universal basic income program while concurrently enhancing the programs that effectively respond to economic fluctuations and incentivize employment. It is designed to introduce a basic income program by making incremental changes to the current system, which makes the proposal politically palatable to American voters.

1. Plan and the Cost

Many researchers find that the cost of a basic income program can vary significantly depending on its design. I estimate that implementing a guaranteed annual income of $13,000 per adult and $2,000 per child would total approximately $525.4 billion each year.

This cost estimate considers multiple factors. The benefit level aligns with the U.S. federal tax policy. The $13,000 for an adult (monthly payments of about $1,083 in 2023 USD) closely matches the standard deduction in the U.S. federal income tax code. The child tax credit of $2,000 per child is derived from the child tax credit amount during the COVID-19 pandemic. The population estimate relies on the 2023 American Community Survey. Of the 327 million total population, approximately 71.6 million are children under 18. Since the refundable Child Tax Credit (CTC) is not income-based, every child receives $2,000 annually, totalling $143.2 billion.

For adults, I assume that about 11.5% of all adults will receive the net cash transfer based on the pre-tax poverty measure known as the Official Poverty Measure (OPM). This means that 29.3 million individuals are counted as living in poverty when their annual pre-tax income falls below $14,580 in 2023. Thus, 11.5% of 255.5 million adults, or 29.4 million adults in poverty, will receive the net cash benefit as a tax refund. While some of these individuals may have earned income, I assume they will receive the full benefit of $13,000 for simplicity, which may inflate the overall cost. However, this represents an upper bound that is preferable to underestimating the amount.

Adults: 31.5 million × $13,000 = $382.2 billion
Children: 71.6 million × $2,000 = $143.2 billion
Total: $382.2 billion + $143.2 billion = $525.4 billion

The total expenditure of $525.4 billion will result from reduced income tax revenue or be distributed as tax credit refunds, especially for the CTC segment. For example, in 2023, the federal government invested $122 billion in the CTC, which included $74 billion from decreased tax revenue and $48 billion in tax credit refunds (Joint Committee on Taxation, 2023). The total spending on the CTC was probably less than expected, as some individuals either did not file taxes or did not utilize the credit, which I will elaborate on further below.

2. Refundable Tax Credit Programs for Adults and Children

I propose that the U.S. federal government establish a guaranteed income program by converting the standard deduction into a refundable standard tax credit within the existing federal income tax system. Currently, U.S. taxpayers can reduce their taxable income by using either the standard deduction or itemized deductions.[1] To explain this idea, it is essential to first understand how the standard deduction operates.

The standard deduction is a specific amount that reduces an individual's taxable income. It is available to all taxpayers who choose to take it. The primary goal is to simplify the tax filing process and ensure that a portion of income is not taxed at the federal level. The amount of the standard deduction varies according to one's filing status, and additional deductions may apply based on age or disability status, as detailed in Table 8.1.

[1] Itemized deductions allow taxpayers to list specific expenses such as mortgage interest, state and local tax payments, charitable contributions, and certain medical or educational expenses. It requires record-keeping with receipts. It can be more beneficial for some taxpayers if their itemized deductions exceed the standard deduction amount.

Table 8.1 2023 Filing requirements and standard deduction

Filing status	*Age*	*Gross income required to file*	*Standard deduction*
Single	Under 65	$13,850	$13,850
	65 or older	$15,700	$15,700
Head of household	Under 65	$20,800	$20,800
	65 or older	$22,650	$22,650–24,500
Married filing jointly	Under 65 (both spouses)	$27,700	$27,700
	65 or older (one spouse)	$29,200	$29,200–32,200
	65 or older (both spouses)	$30,700	$30,700–33,700
Married filing separately	Any age	$5	$15,350–19,850
Qualifying surviving spouse	Under 65	$27,700	$27,700
	65 or older	$29,200	$29,200–30,700

Source: Internal Revenue Service (2023). Publication 554, Tax guide for seniors. U.S. Department of the Treasury

For example, consider a single person under the age of 65 who earns a pre-tax income of $53,850. This individual is required to file federal income tax. With the standard deduction for her age and filing status being $13,850, her taxable income would be calculated as follows: $53,850 minus $13,850 equals $40,000. This means that the standard deduction unconditionally eliminates the tax liability for the first $13,850 of her income, regardless of the income source.

The standard deduction represents the minimum income level exempt from federal income taxation, essentially functioning as an "income floor". This provision ensures that individuals are not taxed on the essential income needed to cover basic living expenses, even though it is not explicitly labelled as such. Moreover, the standard deduction is adaptable; the threshold can be increased for older individuals or those with disabilities. For example, in 2023, the standard deduction for a single adult was $13,850, while older adults and individuals with disabilities could deduct approximately $2,000 more.

It is worth noting that the standard deduction amount is adjusted each year to account for inflation. This stands in contrast to the federal minimum wage and certain cash assistance programs for low-income individuals. Furthermore, the standard deduction is available to nearly all taxpayers who file a tax return, without any conditions. It supports the principle of a fairer tax system.

Although the standard deduction has some appealing features, it does not significantly benefit low-income individuals who do not file federal income tax returns. The primary beneficiaries of the standard deduction are middle-class taxpayers, while high-income individuals often benefit from itemized deductions. Many lower-income households do not (have to) file federal taxes because their income falls below the required filing threshold (see Table 8.1). Note that the standard deduction is non-refundable, which means that it can only lower taxable income and cannot result in a refund for those who do not owe federal taxes. Consequently, the standard deduction does not improve the financial situation of the poorest households.

The idea of converting the standard deduction into a refundable tax credit has been suggested before. Widerquist and Sheahen (2012) proposed to Congress the creation of a "standard tax credit" of $2,000 for each adult and $1,000 for each child. They argue that this proposal is a small step towards establishing a basic income program. I support this incremental approach, as any program resembling a basic income is preferable to develop within the framework of the existing federal system for political and administrative feasibility.

A federal-level program could help address the vast differences in anti-poverty programs across various states. The variations in cash transfer benefit levels, eligibility requirements, and rules lead to considerable spatial disparities. For instance, a family of three could have greatly different earning limits to remain eligible for Temporary Assistance for Needy Families (TANF). In Wisconsin, any earnings over $0 disqualify them from cash assistance, while in Alabama, the limit is $268, and in Minnesota, it is as high as $2,359 (Welfare Rules Database 2022). Moreover, the maximum monthly benefits for a family of three also vary greatly, ranging from $170 in Mississippi and $204 in Arkansas to $1,086 in New Hampshire. In addition, in 30 states, failing to meet work requirements results in the entire family losing their benefits and having their case closed, whereas five states continue to provide some portion of the benefit despite non-compliance.

A major benefit of the proposal is that it operates as a federal program, addressing inconsistencies in state and local income maintenance policies. Currently, the standard deduction is the only universal and unconditional tax benefit available to all citizens and permanent residents. Additionally, the federal government already has the Internal Revenue Service established to manage it. The experience with the Advance Child Tax Credit payments during the COVID-19 pandemic shows that implementing monthly cash payments is administratively feasible.[2] Recipients obtained monthly payments during the year instead of waiting for a tax refund at year-end.

The Child Tax Credit (CTC) could serve as a foundation for providing a basic income to children. Starting with a benefit of $2,000 per child per year could be an effective approach. During the pandemic, many families experienced significant advantages from this benefit, using the funds for essential expenses such as food, utilities, and rent or mortgages. The amount of the benefit can be negotiated politically, but it is crucial to make it fully refundable. In this way, low-income households can receive the same advantages as middle- and upper-income groups, which may address the disparities in participation rates among different income groups (Goldin & Michelmore, 2022).

The proposal's incremental approach may attract more political support from the middle class and low-income individuals. In the United States, social programs are often delivered through the tax system rather than direct spending, as shown in Fig. 8.1. Americans generally appear more supportive of tax credit programs, such as the EITC and CTC, than traditional direct spending programs, as they continue to receive bipartisan support.

One of the main challenges with this proposal is identifying low-income non-filers. Approximately 10% of households do not submit their tax returns. Many of these individuals are not required to file tax returns or might find the filing process too complicated, worry that they owe money, or lack the required documentation. As shown in Fig. 8.3, low-income individuals are less likely to file federal income taxes. Since my proposal aims to provide direct credit refunds to low-income individuals, it is necessary to undertake political and administrative efforts to reach out and encourage them to register in the system.

[2] The Advanced Child Tax Credit was a 2021 pandemic relief program that provided enhanced tax benefits in the form of monthly advance payments to eligible families. This initiative promoted financial stability and predictability, enabling families to better manage their ongoing expenses.

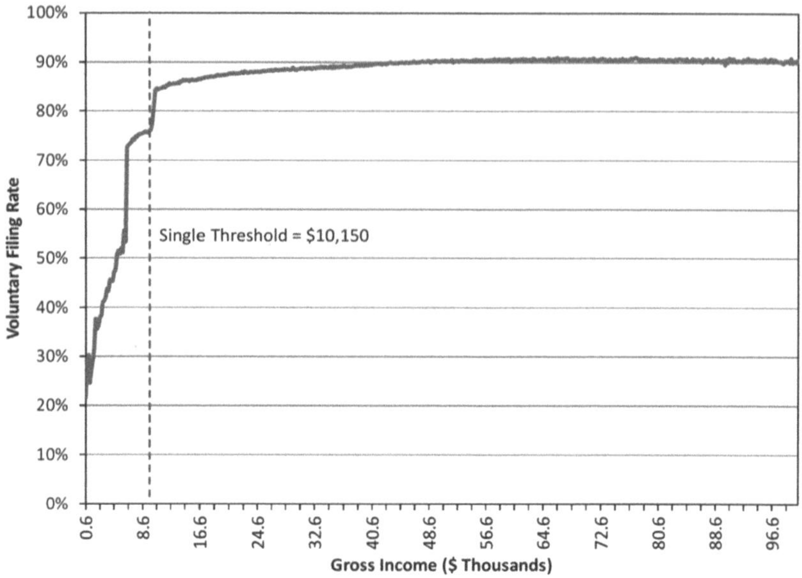

Fig. 8.3 Voluntary filing rate of single taxpayers under 65 Years Old by Gross Income, 2014. Source: Langetieg et al. (2017)

During the COVID-19 pandemic, many people who had not previously filed taxes lacked a bank account or an address to receive the Economic Impact Payments, commonly known as "COVID checks". This was primarily because the IRS did not have their information. To address this issue, the Treasury and IRS introduced an online tool for non-filers to register for these payments. Individuals could use the tool to input their basic personal and financial information to claim their payments. This is a laudable effort, but challenges persist, including access to broadband, computers, and the skills needed to use them effectively. The Center on Budget and Policy Priorities (2020) proposed that the IRS and the federal government collaborate with state agencies operating welfare benefits to reach the 12 million non-filers. Many recipients of food (SNAP) and medical (Medicaid) assistance do file taxes for low gross income. By collaborating with the IRS, these organizations could create a more effective system for delivering tax credit refunds to those hard-to-reach populations. While it would require a significant outreach campaign and coordinated efforts among various agencies, it is a necessary step towards improving benefit delivery through administrative coordination.

3. Transfer Programs

Basic income should not replace all existing social services for two main reasons. First, basic income is not intended to encourage people to work. If this is a concern, additional work incentive programs should be established alongside it. Second, basic income provides a fixed amount that does not adjust for macroeconomic changes, making it inadequate as a safety net during economic downturns. Therefore, introducing a basic income program involves exploring potential consolidations, supplemental programs with clearly distinctive goals, and other strategies to create a cohesive system for providing income support. This section will examine the major social programs offered by the U.S. federal government and their potential interactions with a basic income program.

Poverty rates in the United States based on market income have remained consistent since the 1980s (Furman, 2021). In response, the U.S. government has sought to decrease them by expanding income maintenance programs. Table 8.2 outlines some of the key income support programs included in the 2023 budget. These programs consist of cash transfers and in-kind assistance for essential needs such as food, housing, and utilities.

In 2023, the U.S. federal government had a budget of \$6.3 trillion. About 8.8% of the budget, approximately \$827.3 billion, was allocated for "economic security" expenditures (USAspending.gov., n.d.). However, the budget is significantly smaller if contribution-based programs like

Table 8.2 Major federal programs for economic security for the low-income

Budget function	*2023 Expenditures (billions)*
Food and nutrition assistance (SNAP, WIC, etc.)	\$201.2
Temporary Assistance for Needy Families (TANF)	\$16.8
Supplemental Security Income (SSI)	\$68.5
Payment Where EITC Exceeds Liability for Tax	\$55.5
Housing and utility assistance	\$69.8

Source: U.S. Treasury Fiscal Data website, https://fiscaldata.treasury.gov/

Notes: SNAP (Supplemental Nutrition Assistance Program), WIC (Special Supplemental Nutrition Program for Women, Infants, and Children), EITC (Earned Income Tax Credit)

unemployment insurance are excluded. The guiding principles of U.S. welfare programs involve promoting employment, reducing benefit amounts, strengthening state oversight, and aiding children (Jason Furman, 2021). The programs have varying effects on poverty reduction. Figure 8.4 illustrates their impacts.[3]

- Earned Income Tax Credit (EITC) Program

The EITC is considered one of the most effective anti-poverty programs in U.S. history. Figure 8.4 illustrates that the Earned Income Tax Credit (EITC) has the most significant impact on poverty reduction. In 2021, it decreased poverty by 1.22 percentage points, while in 2022, its effect nearly reached 3 percentage points (Holmes & Berube, 2015). Additionally, in-kind assistance programs have also made a substantial contribution to poverty reduction; however, the impact of Temporary Assistance for Needy Families (TANF) is minimal.

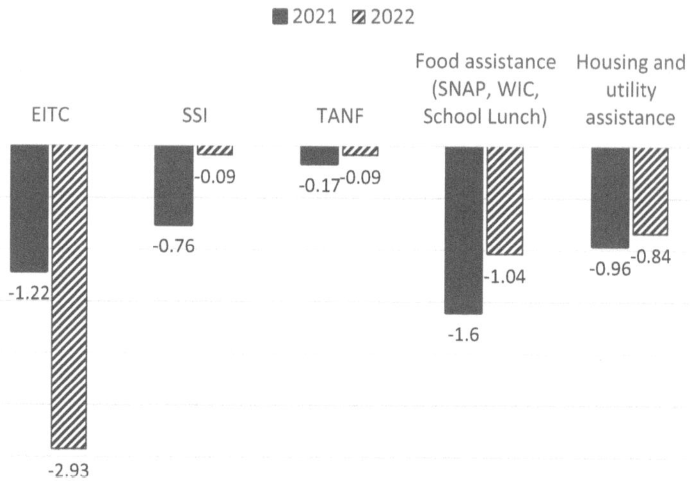

Fig. 8.4 Effects of programs on supplemental poverty measure, 2021–2022. Source: U.S. Census Bureau. (2022). *Poverty in the United States: Table B-7. Effect of individual elements on supplemental poverty measure rates: 2021 and 2022*

[3] It is known as the Supplemental Poverty Measure (SPM), which accounts for benefits and taxes.

There are two key reasons why any basic income program may need to be combined with a separate work incentive program. First, a guaranteed income program, such as a refundable standard tax credit, must adhere to unconditionality, the core principle of basic income policy. The ongoing debates surrounding work participation in basic income pilot programs are beside the point. A primary goal of a basic income program is not to increase labour participation. In fact, it aims to give individuals the freedom to step back from the labour market when their participation is unnecessary or potentially harmful.

Current welfare programs impose work requirements that function more as punitive sanctions than positive work incentives. These mandate employment or job training to receive benefits, often threatening reduced or terminated assistance for non-compliance. While such requirements can increase labour market participation on the surface and may motivate some recipients to seek jobs, the negative consequences can outweigh the benefits for many individuals. Research indicates that these requirements often lead to temporary, low-quality employment, pushing some people deeper into poverty (Robert Wood Johnson Foundation, 2023). They also create administrative burdens, lower participation rates, and present challenges for individuals facing significant barriers to employment, particularly those dealing with childcare or health issues.

In contrast, work incentive programs, such as the Earned Income Tax Credit (EITC), use an incentive-based approach to increase earned income by encouraging labour force participation without penalizing individuals. Their primary beneficiaries are low-income households. About 35% of EITC benefits were allocated to individuals earning less than \$15,000 annually, while 86.5% went to those earning under \$30,000 (Bellafiore, 2019).

A well-designed basic income program can serve as a foundation for financial stability, but to ensure that individuals feel motivated to pursue employment, it should be supplemented by the EITC. In addition to offering immediate financial assistance, research indicates that the EITC promotes long-term advantages such as increased savings, asset building, and improved economic mobility (Duncan et al., 2010). This dual approach—pairing a guaranteed income and the EITC—allows enhanced financial security and a sense of autonomy.

- Food and Housing Assistance

Supplemental Nutrition Assistance Program (SNAP)

The Supplemental Nutrition Assistance Program (SNAP) is designed to provide food assistance to low-income individuals and families. Every month, benefits are distributed via an Electronic Benefits Transfer (EBT) card, which recipients can use at authorized retailers to purchase groceries. In 2023, SNAP ensured food security for 42 million Americans. The program boasts a participation rate of approximately 80%, which spiked to as high as 90% during the 2008 recession among eligible people. Notably, 79% of SNAP households included either a child, an elderly individual, or a nonelderly individual with a disability (USDA FNS, 2023). SNAP reduces food insecurity by up to 30%, with an even greater impact observed among children and those experiencing very low food security (Hernandez & Jacknowitz, 2014).

SNAP functions as an automatic economic stabilizer through its various rules without requiring additional legislative action. When economic conditions deteriorate, for example, SNAP eligibility expands, benefit levels increase, and work requirements can be exempted in areas with high unemployment rates. The counter-cyclical nature of SNAP means it provides economic support without the typical delays associated with legislative appropriations. This responsiveness makes it a particularly effective tool for economic stabilization and immediate relief (Ganong & Liebman, 2018).

SNAP's automatic stabilizer feature can complement a basic income program by providing support that adapts to business cycles. While a basic income program provides a fixed amount of monetary transfer, it does not provide a flexible, responsive mechanism that automatically increases support during economic downturns. SNAP's ability to quickly adjust benefits acts as a supplementary safety net. The combination would create a more robust social support system. SNAP's automatic stabilizer feature can complement a basic income program.

Housing Assistance

Housing voucher programs, such as Section 8, are designed to help low-income individuals and families afford housing in the private rental market. These programs are intended to address the gap between what individuals can afford to pay for housing and the actual market costs of renting. A guaranteed income does not necessarily address the geographic variations in housing costs. Housing assistance can complement a basic income program by addressing the varying pressures in different housing markets.

The housing voucher program has positive impacts on housing outcomes for low-income households. The program relieves the housing cost pressure and lowers the likelihood of missing rent payments (Newman et al., 2024). Housing vouchers can also alleviate economic hardship during an economic downturn. As local housing markets expand or contract, the level of assistance can be adjusted to provide housing support. This flexibility helps address housing market volatility by offering the resources for housing stability. By integrating a basic income program with geographically and macroeconomically adaptive housing assistance, housing assistance programs can build a resilient social support system that reflects the complexities and variations of housing markets across different regions.

- Cash Transfer Programs

Supplemental Security Income (SSI)

Established in 1974, SSI is a federal cash transfer program that provides a guaranteed minimum income for elderly, blind, and disabled individuals who cannot fully participate in the labour market. In Fig. 8.4, Supplemental Security Income (SSI) does not appear to reduce poverty significantly compared to other programs due to its low benefit levels[4] and narrow eligibility criteria. The maximum benefit is below the federal poverty line, and therefore, it often leaves recipients in poverty, particularly in high-cost areas. However, it plays a crucial role in supporting some of society's most vulnerable individuals.

SSI was created as part of President Nixon's broader welfare reform efforts aimed at ensuring a guaranteed minimum income for all families through the Family Assistance Plan (FAP). This initiative also sought to federalize inconsistent state-level aid systems and simplify administrative processes. Although the FAP ultimately failed to pass Congress, SSI was able to survive due to political compromise, as it targeted sympathetic groups, making it more politically acceptable.

In 2023, SSI provided monthly payments of $914 to 7.4 million people (SSA website). SSI serves as the sole income source for 57% of them (U.S. Census Bureau, 2023). In 2023, the federal government spent $65 billion on the program, or 1.9% of the entire budget. SSI offers financial stability and predictability by guaranteeing a steady income. In comparison to non-SSI households that have similar incomes, SSI recipients tend

[4] The benefit level is $914 per month for an eligible individual and $1,371 per month for an eligible couple in 2023 (Social Security Administration, 2023).

to borrow less often, and when they do, they typically borrow smaller amounts (Bauer, 2023).

The standard tax credit cannot fully address SSI's targeted financial support for individuals facing additional challenges. To prevent harm, the standard tax credit program should complement SSI instead of replacing it and ensure their overall financial stability remains intact. This integration ensures that guaranteed income serves as a foundational safety net, while SSI continues to provide targeted assistance, thus maintaining its role as a lifeline for individuals with disabilities or other qualifying conditions.

Temporary Assistance for Needy Families (TANF)

TANF (Temporary Assistance for Needy Families) does not have a significant impact on reducing poverty, as shown in Fig. 8.4. TANF is a federally funded, state-administered program designed to provide financial assistance and support services (e.g. job training, pregnancy prevention) to low-income families with children. Since its inception in 1996, the TANF budget has remained at $16.5 billion and eroded by inflation. The funding structure causes critical issues. It does not increase automatically in response to rising demand, economic downturns, or population growth. Once a state exhausts its annual TANF funds, it cannot provide additional benefits, regardless of how many families qualify for assistance. As a result, the program cannot provide a safety net when people need it the most, and the benefit levels during economic downturns often fall below the poverty line.

Not only that, but the strict work requirements and time limits of the program create significant challenges for families trying to achieve financial stability through TANF. In fact, these work requirements are not effective. According to the Department of Health and Human Services, the national average work participation rate for TANF in 2022 was only 35.6%. Furthermore, TANF does not necessarily focus on financial aid. States flexibly use the funding for services like childcare, child education, and job training instead of giving direct cash assistance. The Department of Health and Human Services reports that only 22% of the total TANF and TANF-related state budget of $31.3 billion is allocated for "basic assistance" (also known as direct financial support).

Advocates for TANF argue that the federal government needs to increase the budget substantially and adjust it for inflation annually. However, only about 0.3% of the adult population receives TANF (Pavetti et al., 2021), so it would be challenging to increase its budget and change the rules to make a real impact.

TANF is ineffective. Pavetti et al. (2021) summarize the program in their paper title, "TANF at 24: A Weaker Cash Safety Net Reaching Fewer Families and Doing Less to Lift Families out of Deep Poverty". The combined federal and state budget of $31.3 billion could be redirected and used more effectively to reduce poverty. Therefore, I advocate abolishing outdated, non-functional, and stigmatizing TANF.

Conclusion

Implementing a basic income program requires a comprehensive analysis of existing tax and social welfare systems, as well as the political and economic realities at play. The idea of "targeting within universalism" presents a helpful approach that integrates a universal program with targeted assistance for those who need it the most. Additionally, the principle of UBI can inform the future directions of current safety net systems.

A feasible path forward for the United States, as suggested in this chapter, is to transform the existing standard deduction in the federal tax system into a refundable standard tax credit of $13,000 per adult and $2,000 per child annually, and the amount should be indexed annually. This approach, estimated to cost around $525.4 billion (or less than 8% of the federal budget in 2024), would provide a universal income floor while leveraging existing administrative structures. It could be integrated with the current Supplemental Security Income (SSI) program and complemented by the Earned Income Tax Credit (EITC) to encourage work. The lack of responsiveness of basic income to economic fluctuations can be improved by supporting in-kind programs like SNAP, which are known to adapt well to these changes. In contrast, ineffective and stigmatizing programs like TANF should be phased out, with their resources redirected to enhance effective income maintenance programs.

Challenges persist, especially in reaching non-filers and ensuring universal coverage. However, lessons from the COVID-19 pandemic, such as the expanded Child Tax Credit and economic impact payments, show that these challenges can be addressed through effective inter-agency coordination and administration.

A basic income program should be integrated into the existing welfare system by building on its strengths, addressing its gaps, and aligning with the core principle of UBI. Therefore, the design of a basic income program must adapt to each country's unique social, economic, and institutional context. While the integration of a basic income program into broader welfare systems will vary across countries, it should provide a consistent experience of UBI by transforming welfare systems to better meet the challenges of future economies and ensure financial security for all.

References

Bastian, J. (2024). How would a permanent 2021 child tax credit expansion affect poverty and employment? *National Tax Journal, 77*(2), 263–311.

Bauer, A. (2023, November 15). *Updating SSI would improve the economic resilience of low-income women.* Center for American Progress.

Bellafiore, R. (2019, May 21). The earned income tax credit (EITC): A primer. *Tax Foundation.*

Center on Budget and Policy Priorities. (2020). *Aggressive state outreach can help reach the 12 million non-filers eligible for economic impact payments.* Center on Budget and Policy Priorities.

Chang, Y., Han, J.-S., & Kim, S.-B. (2024). Negative income tax and universal basic income in the eyes of Aiyagari. *Macroeconomic Dynamics, 28*(4), 813–825.

Duncan, G., Ziol-Guest, K., & Kalil, A. (2010). Early-childhood poverty and adult attainment, behavior, and health. *Child Development, 81*(1), 306–325.

Furman, J. (2021). Enhancing micro and macro resilience by building on the improvements in the social safety net. In O. Blanchard & D. Rodrik (Eds.), *Combating inequality: Rethinking government's role* (pp. 237–243). MIT Press.

Ganong, P., & Liebman, J. B. (2018). The decline, rebound, and further rise in SNAP enrollment: Disentangling business cycle fluctuations and policy changes. *American Economic Journal: Economic Policy, 10*(4), 153–176.

Goldin, J., & Michelmore, K. (2022). Who benefits from the child tax credit? *National Tax Journal, 75*(1), 123–147.

Greenstein, R. (2019). *Commentary: Universal basic income may sound attractive but, if it occurred, would likelier increase poverty than reduce it.* Center on Budget and Policy Priorities.

Hernandez, D. C., & Jacknowitz, A. (2014). The role of the supplemental nutrition assistance program in food security and health outcomes. *PMC, 8*(4), 456–469.

Holmes, N., & Berube, A. (2015, November 20). *The earned income tax credit and community economic stability.* Brookings Institution.

Hoynes, H., & Rothstein, J. (2019). Universal basic income in the United States and advanced countries. *Annual Review of Economics, 11*(1), 929–958.

Internal Revenue Service. (2023). Publication 554 (2023), *Tax guide for seniors.* U.S. Department of the Treasury.

Langetieg, P., Payne, M., & Plumley, A. (2017). *Counting elusive non-filers using IRS rather than census data*. Internal Revenue Service. https://www.irs.gov/pub/irs-soi/17resconpayne.pdf
Lee, S. (2018). Attitudes toward universal basic income and welfare state in Europe: A research note. *Basic Income Studies, 13*(1), 20180002.
Mankiw, N. G. (2021). How to increase taxes on the rich. In O. Blanchard & D. Rodrik (Eds.), *Combating inequality: Rethinking government's role* (pp. 137–140). MIT Press.
Newman, S., Leventhal, T., Holupka, C. S., & Tan, F. (2024). Experimental evidence shows that housing vouchers provided measurable benefits, including parent stress reduction. *Health Affairs, 43*(2) Housing & Health, 278.
Pavetti, L., Safawi, A., & Trisi, D. (2021). TANF at 25: A weaker cash safety net reaching fewer families and doing less to lift families out of deep poverty. *National Tax Journal, 74*(3), 763–789.
Robert Wood Johnson Foundation. (2023). *Work requirements: What are they? Do they work?* Robert Wood Johnson Foundation.
Santens, S. (2022, May 1). Negative income tax is not cheaper than universal basic income (UBI), nor is guaranteed income more progressive by excluding the rich..
Skocpol, T. (1991). Targeting within universalism: Politically viable policies to combat poverty in the United States. In C. Jencks & P. E. Peterson (Eds.), *The urban underclass* (pp. 411–436). The Brookings Institution.
U.S. Census Bureau. (2022). *Poverty in the United States: Table B-7. Effect of individual elements on supplemental poverty measure rates: 2021 and 2022*. Retrieved December 3, 2024, from https://www.census.gov/library/publications.html
U.S. Census Bureau. (2023, September 12). *Poverty in the United States: 2022: Table B-8: Effect of individual elements on the number of individuals in poverty using the supplemental poverty measure: 2021 and 2022.*
U.S. Department of Agriculture, Food and Nutrition Service. (2023). *Characteristics of supplemental nutrition assistance program (SNAP) participants: FY 2022*. Food and Nutrition Service.
USAspending.gov. (n.d.). *Budget function explorer*. Retrieved November 3, 2024, from https://www.usaspending.gov/explorer/budget_function
Widerquist, K. (2017). The cost of basic income: Back-of-the-envelope calculations. *Basic Income Studies, 12*(2).
Widerquist, K., & Sheahen, A. (2012). The basic income guarantee in the United States: Past experience, current proposals. In M. Murray & C. Pateman (Eds.), *Basic income worldwide: Horizons of reform* (pp. 11–32). Palgrave Macmillan.
Zwolinski, M., & Fleischer, M. P. (2023). *Universal basic income: What everyone needs to know*. Oxford University Press.

CHAPTER 9

Conclusion

Roberto Merrill and Catarina Neves

This edited book features recent work on some pressing normative and empirical debates about Unconditional Basic Income. It draws from several disciplines, with contributions from philosophy, political science and economics.

Divided into two parts, the first one, entitled *Ecological and Moral Dimensions of Basic Income*, features contributions from three authors—James P. Mulvale, Thiago Souza and Michael W. Howard—who engage with the fundamental question of whether we can call UBI green. Interestingly, while taking different approaches and having fundamentally different goals, the three chapters all delve around the notion of degrowth, a debate that has exploded, as evidenced by recently published papers on the topic in the natural sciences, but also in ecological economics and political science (Durand et al., 2024; Gomez-Baggethun, 2022; Schmelzer et al., 2022; Hickel, 2020; Kallis et al., 2018; Jackson, 2009). But while the debate is fervently ongoing, the three authors look for ways

R. Merrill (✉)
Escola de Letras, Artes e Ciências Humanas, Departamento de Filosofia, Universidade do Minho, Braga, Portugal

C. Neves
Ethics Institute, Utrecht University, Utrecht, Utrecht, The Netherlands

R. Merrill, C. Neves (eds.), *Determining the Value of Universal Basic Income*, Exploring the Basic Income Guarantee,
https://doi.org/10.1007/978-3-032-04004-6_9

in which BI supporters can participate in the discussion. In doing so, the three chapters help us navigate three fundamental questions:

1. Can a UBI be a green policy?
2. Can a UBI be consistent with a degrowth society?
3. Can UBI be part of a politically attractive set of policies for a green transition?

None of the papers presents a decisive answers to these questions, but they do provide clues, while illustrating new research pathways that are required if we wish to answer them. On question 1, the minimalist argument of Michael W. Howard could justify a green BI, even if only a partial one (dropping the commitment with the notion of a 'basic' income), while the policy of Marica in Brazil, as presented by Thiago Souza, in Chap. 2, can already be an example of an environmental policy. While none of the authors claims this to be a bulletproof argument for those wishing to claim UBI as green, they do compellingly show how such a possibility can take place. Moreover, Souza's conceptual framework hints at six pillars that help us judge if a given UBI policy or pilot is green—from an environmental or ecological standpoint—highlighting some of the key features that Howard, in Chap. 3 also introduces in his paper, namely issues around funding, workers' decisions and bargaining power, consumption, among others.

On question two, the debate remains to be settled. It is worth praising the authors' attempts to contribute to the discussion on degrowth. And both Souza and Howard seem to share intuitions that a UBI can be an important policy for an efficient implementation of working time reduction (WTR), a requirement for a degrowth transition. However, Howard highlights the thorny issue of scale, namely how endorsing WTR in the Global North can compromise the extent to which wealthier countries can have financial resources to ensure the transfers required for the Global South to adapt but also mitigate the climate crisis. As mentioned, these transfers are not only required instrumentally, but also morally, given the wealth and the big historical share of responsibility for global emissions that wealthier countries hold compared to the Global South. Moreover, both authors seemed to be concerned about the impacts of UBI on green consumption. This highlights the fundamental trade-off a UBI faces between promoting autonomy and freedom, and what the green transition might demand, including restrictions in what we might be able to buy and produce. On this issue, they both seem to claim we need more empirical data to understand the impact of UBI on consumption.

Finally, on the question of political feasibility, while Howard does not advance any view, although he acknowledges the need to work out how attractive a UBI can be in the context of the green transition, Mulvale, in Chap. 1, takes a particular stance on this question, by arguing that both empirical data (i.e. on the need to degrow) and moral arguments (i.e. on why a basic income can enhance freedom or community) will be required to sway people towards implementing it. In doing so, it reinstates the claim that we cannot rely on evidence alone, especially if our aim is to implement a basic income that promotes a degrowth transition at a global scale.

Besides giving us clues to answer these three questions, the chapters also clearly delineate future interdisciplinary research agendas.

Firstly, any attentive reader will acknowledge Howard's plea that more research is required on the relationship between a BI and consumption. If a BI increases consumption, namely from unsustainable products (i.e. high-intensity farming, single-use plastics, fast fashion, ...), it will be very difficult to argue for it, and conditional cash transfers might be preferable from the standpoint of the climate crisis. As Howard rightly points out, this is not only an empirical question. It also deserves attention by philosophers, namely in telling us how much freedom, and what conception of freedom, we should be endorsing when discussing a UBI in the midst of a climate crisis. We would add that a discussion on welfare and a good life should also be featured, even if we have to tackle the contradiction between UBI's unconditional nature and a potentially perfectionist account of the good, and claims for sufficiency and consumption corridors (Gough, 2023).

But the three chapters also make a very stark distinction between consumption and production, exception granted to Howard's debate on WTR policies and transfers at a global scale. In fact, more needs to be said about how a UBI can help shape production decisions and practices—if at all—and, in doing so, contribute to a reduction in products and services produced, and hence potentially consumed. Worker decisions—to work less hours, or to change occupations altogether, by, for example, moving away from carbon-intensive occupations—can all impact the productive landscape, and hence determine consumption decisions. Maybe less environmentally sound products are available; or perhaps they are costlier, whereas other sustainable consumption products are cheaper. The point is that if we have a better grasp of UBI's potential in shaping production decisions, concerns with consumption might be less warranted, at least for those in favour of green growth. More research is thus needed to understand UBI's potential impact on the productive decisions of workers, and whether UBI can be the best strategy, or at least a fairly efficient complement to other proposals, when it comes to implementing changes on the production side of the economy.

Another interesting research agenda is raised in Chap. 3, particularly the discussion around UBI justified by automation and the requirements of the ecological transition. While it is easier to see why a UBI implemented in a context of productivity increased by automation (i.e. since production levels could increase or be more efficient, hence not jeopardizing revenues required for funding the welfare state, a UBI, but also required transfers for climate transition in the Global South), it is less clear whether this would amount to a desirable UBI from the standpoint of justice, freedom and ecology. Current large language models (e.g. GPT-4) consume big amounts of energy, with AIcompanies investing heavily on energy sources, thus increasing their emissions.[1] While decoupling can help, we might not be able to do it fast enough to accommodate the speed of technological development that is contributing to the developments in AI. Moreover, even if we could, concerns about the distribution of jobs can still be raised, especially if some jobs will likely not be able to be automated, either because they can't or because we don't want them to be (i.e. care work). When working out how such a distribution can take place, a UBI will certainly be important, but more needs to be said of how we should do it, and why.

The three chapters also help us consider new ways of thinking about UBI, and what design options we should choose. Souza's framework and its application to the cases of Marica and the Alaska Permanent Dividend

[1]There are increasing concerns that the recent technological developments will increase energy consumption, rather than help reduce emissions, especially considering the rising surge in CO_2 emissions from energy consumption from AI-companies, related to the development of LLMs—large language models like Chat GPT (the recent 2024 Forbes Magazine paper on the topic by Ariel Cohen https://www.forbes.com/sites/arielcohen/2024/05/23/ai-is-pushing-the-world-towards-an-energy-crisis/ or Nature's article discussion on the same issue by https://www.nature.com/articles/d41586-024-03408-z Katherine Bourzac).

While there is still uncertainty about the full scope of the effects, is still worth taking these alarms into account, especially degrowth advocates claims that historical technological adoption has led to an increase in energy, rather than a decrease, due to a number of effects, including so-called rebound effects (Hickel, 2020).

Fund provide hints at what design decisions we should go for if we wish to have a more ecological basic income. Further work could be build on the tool, and potentially argue whether certain features should be deemed as constraints to the UBI one wishes to implement. Such a route will imply considering trade-offs, and potentially jeopardizing some of the features that make characterize UBI in its 'purest' form (i.e. consider Marica's local currency model, which does not fulfil the unconditional desideratum of UBI to its fullest). However, it is plausible to consider that this is required in a context of ecological transition. Perhaps more importantly, acknowledging the former can help us consider democratic decision processes, in which, together and armed with good moral reasons, we argue on what cluster of values we wish to prioritize and which ones we are willing to forego when deciding to implement a UBI in the context of the ecological crisis.

Finally, while all the chapters discuss UBI in the context of green growth or degrowth, they either discuss UBI's ecological impacts in general, without much specificity (i.e. Chaps. 2 or 3) or when they do so, they restrict their analysis to UBI's impacts on climate, and thus to CO_2 emissions We would like to agree with Howard on the need to do more work on UBI's impact across planetary boundaries.[2] Current ecological evidence supports the view of planetary boundaries as a better illustration of the complexity of the Earth's ecosystem and the extent of our influence on it. As such, if we are committed to a discussion of UBI in the current ecological crisis, we should follow these pleas, and broaden the scope, to understand in what way a UBI can influence our impacts beyond the climate.

* * *

[2] Planetary Boundaries are nine processes that regulate the stability and resilience of the Earth system. Keeping within the nine boundaries is required for humanity to 'thrive, develop' and to ensure the livelihood of future generations, given that 'crossing the boundaries increases the risk of generating large-scale abrupt or irreversible environmental changes'. They are interdependent and interrelated. The nine boundaries are: climate change, novel entities, stratospheric ozone depletion, atmosphere aerosol loading, ocean acidification, biogeochemical flows, freshwater change, land-system change, biosphere integrity. In: https://www.stockholmresilience.org/research/planetary-boundaries.html [accessed on 7 January 2025].

The second part of this volume, entitled *Political Feasibility and Global Perspectives*, features the additional four chapters of the book. For the most part, they provide insights into methodological issues that are cornerstones of any UBI discussion around experiments or policy adoption. Three major methodological advices can be plucked out from the four chapters, with significant overlaps in the opinions of the authors.

The first relates to the inclusion of several voices in the discussion of basic income. While Sara Bizarro, in Chap. 5, claims that any UBI policy proposal has to include a multistakeholder analysis, Evelyn Forget claims that qualitative analysis that uses storytelling and storylistening requires being attentive to several voices, often from marginalized populations. Despite common, these radical inclusion proposals are worth reinstating. These relate to fundamental issues around equal representation, espistemic justice, but are also important for instrumental considerations, including how to get a UBI implemented, or how to better grasp the insights of a basic income. As Forget mentions in an illuminating passage in her Chap. 6, depending on who is interpreting the data, failing to consider different voices (and their stories) implies not understanding how the impact UBI has on one value—i.e. independence—can be very differently perceived and apprehended. In a nutshell, *independence* means very different things for a white, wealthy, male individual versus a member of an impoverished and historically marginalized indigenous communities. Thus, the concerns of deep diversity should be taken seriously by UBI advocates for moral reasons, and hence multistakeholder approaches, which are justified for scientific and political strategy reasons, should be as radically inclusive as possible.

The second methodological insight has to do with the importance of context. In Chap. 7, Pedro Goulart and Carla Costa argue that critical socio-economic indicators can help us predict whether a UBI pilot will be successfully implemented, leaving open the question of whether success implies replication or good results (i.e. defined based on the questions asked). Their analysis is centred on the assumptions that existing literature on the pros and cons of UBI is focused on concerns with the efficiency of targeted welfare programmes, the cost and financial feasibility of a UBI, and the policy's potential to encourage workers' large-scale exit from the labour market. Hence, we need to look at the context of a country to determine whether welfare programmes are efficient or not; whether labour markets and workers' conditions are more or less prone to generate massive exits when a cash transfer is implemented; and whether the country's financial health will be able to accommodate an ambitious programme such as a large-scale cash transfer. While in Chap. 8, Soomi Lee focuses on the cost and related concern with funding of a basic income, highlighting that any UBI proposal needs to be considered alongside the tax and welfare-state context where it will be implemented. Her chapter argues that the most desirable proposals (especially in the United States) will likely follow the 'targeting with universalism' approach, where a means-tested guaranteed income is adopted alongside other social programmes. Besides claiming that this will probably be the most fiscally sound proposal, Lee argues that those wishing to implement a UBI, should be mindful of political feasibility issues, alongside financial ones. The former, requires considering how support for UBI tends to be lower in countries with robust safety nets. While we can plausibly speculate that this is also due to the fact that in such countries citizens believe poverty and insecurity are adequately covered, Lee offers another explanation, namely that in such countries citizens might fear that UBI will replace existing programmes. Hence, UBI advocates need to grapple with how UBI is embedded in the welfare state, further reinforcing Chap. 7's main claim of the importance of context.

Finally, the third advice is a long-standing concern of UBI advocates, and related to political feasibility. While context is key for considering an experiment or UBI policy, Sara Bizarro warns us of how intended and unintended consequences play a crucial role in political strategizing for UBI. She requests that we go beyond the efficacy of the policy on stated intended goals, and consider unintended consequences from the onset, by enlarging the group of voices involved in the debate. But her account is more than a plea for multistakeholder analysis. It also seems to evoke a certain scepticism of standard evidence-policymaking procedures. In her chapter, she claims that the stated intended goals of policymakers can often occlude other goals, namely unintended and hence presumed-to-be-out-of-responsibility outcomes. The latter can be detrimental to the lives of many individuals, to the point that a policy should have been modified or not adopted, but can also be used to either justify or reject a policy later on, closing the debate on what—if revised—could be a sound policy option. This is a particular concern for UBI, as highlighted in the chapter. Take UBI labour market impacts: for the most part, large-scale equilibrium impacts will not be able to be determined with pilots (Widerquist, 2018). But we have some evidence to estimate possible scenarios, which can be transparently discussed, and perhaps even mitigated, or strategically obscured from the debate.

Tying It All Together: Two Parts, Common Learnings for the UBI Debate

This edited volume's two-part structure can feel challenging to navigate, as if two distinct sets of claims, arguments and proposals are put forth in the seven chapters comprising the book. In the first part, three approaches to the green-UBI debate, while the second part focuses on methodology and political feasibility. While there are certainly more commonalities found in the chapters within each section, we close by proposing that we take the findings of the volume together. This will hopefully show the lessons, tensions and limitations that run through the entire book, but it will also highlight potential new research pathways.

The chapters all seem to share a concern with the political feasibility of UBI. The first three chapters argue that this concern needs to come in tandem with concerns about the ecological transition, given the pressing urgency of the crisis we are facing. But doing so requires that we consider the methodological and strategic advices from the last four chapters of the book. When considering UBI's impact on work, one is set to understand how different people across the globe will experience and perceive such impacts; when discussing how we can ensure a global transition, and global safety nets for climate transition, we need to consider the fiscal context of each country, and even within the global North, the scope and capacity for implementing a UBI (or for transferring resources for the Global South to do so) are distinct. These are strategy and feasibility concerns, which also hold normative weight. Can we ignore the concerns and narratives of women who, while championing the valuing of care work in a more ecological world, fear that a basic income can do nothing to distribute care work more equitably along gender lines? (Robeyns, 2008) Or can we take out from the equation the huge debts of some southern European countries, and their high poverty rates, when discussing their responsibility towards the Global South, alongside other Global North countries, whose financial situations are starkly different? And if there are potential 'oblique effects', in Bizarro's terms, from a basic income on consumption, and if these can be detrimental to the ecological transition, how do we consider them, alongside positive consequences on poverty alleviation? If we take the methodological concerns of the second part of the book seriously, we enlarge the scope of the debate included in the first part of the volume.

Another interesting possibility afforded by reading the chapters together relates to a proposal for designing UBI pilots and policies. Both Chaps. 3, 7 and 8 seem to imply that we might need to consider several criteria for conducting a pilot, while Chaps. 5 and 6 argue for inclusive multistakeholder and qualitative-narrative approaches to design and policy evaluation. If we consider these arguments, a UBI pilot should focus on more than discussing the unconditionality and universality of the policy, or the individual character of the disbursement. Concerns with fiscal capacity, or with the structure and conjectural impacts of the job market, should figure more prominently on the decision to implement a pilot, especially if the experiment is run in the hope of creating momentum and providing robust evidence to move towards a larger-scale experiment, or even towards a UBI implemented in the country. But Souza's paper can be stretched further. Perhaps his six-pillar framework can be a call for more than just using it to ex-post evaluate a UBI pilot; instead, some of these criteria can constrain pilot and perhaps policy design, signalling that the demands of ecology cannot be overturned. Of course, more needs to be said of this possibility, which offers a new interesting research pathway. But it is worth noting that the chapters of this volume enlarge what is often considered to be the aims of UBI and even of pilots, telling us to look beyond it, and take the requirements and conditions of the context more heavily into account.

The readings of the two parts together opens up additional new opportunities and research options. First, is exploring the possibility that UBI is a transitional policy towards a more ecological future. While Souza briefly mentions this, it is worth considering this further, and how UBI framed and instituted as a transitional policy can be impacted by the concerns of the second part of the book. In this case, we can hypothesize that storytelling and listening or the socio-economic context are both important before, but all through the policy implementation, to ensure that we are aware of how the policy's intended transitional objectives are running, and if new adjustments need to be made, or more importantly, when the policy is becoming redundant and we have successfully *transitioned.* Moreover, narratives might be key to understand how *being a transitional policy* is understood and apprehended, avoiding that those who are already excluded, marginalized and impoverished are not disproportionately affected in a negative way. Second, It is also worth considering that the discussions of Bizarro on side effects might be as or even more relevant. One needs to consider as much as possible the oblique effects, to understand what possible visions of the future might underlie different political constituents' support (or objection) to UBI as a transitional policy.

Furthermore, and still on the matter of unintended consequences, both Chaps. 5 and 7 seem to be concerned with labour markets and social inclusion through the market. But many of the discussions of the first three chapters of the volume, and their ecologically inspired frameworks, take a different view of social inclusion. One where labour market participation might either not be as relevant, or even rejected altogether. In an era of both automation, but also of ecological urgency, we need to consider carefully what social inclusion means in the UBI debate, something which, while not entirely new in the discussion, might require additional work given current developments.

Finally, if we read the chapters of the book together, we also understand the large geographical scope that the authors take, and the radical inclusion account that many chapters also respect. Throughout the book, the authors engage with evidence from UBI experiments across the Globe, showing a rich set of data that spans several countries. Moreover, some chapters include narratives and views that consider marginalized voices (i.e. indigenous communities, namely in Canada), women, or the least privileged in a significant way. Given that some of the most interesting developments in UBI debates and policy are taking place in the Global South (i.e. Brazil, South Korea), but also that there might be instrumental, and perhaps even moral, arguments to prioritize a UBI in the Global South, as Howard's contribution on Chap. 3 seems to suggest, the book's expansive geographical scope is a welcomed development, and one that should be more actively pursued. We are thus very grateful to the authors of this volume for their overall contribution, but also for the expansive outlook provided on the basic income debate.

References

Durand, C., Hofferberth, E., & Schmelzer, M. (2024). Planning beyond growth: The case for economic democracy within ecological limits. *Journal of Cleaner Production, 437*, 140351.

Gomez-Baggethun, E. (2022). Rethinking work for a just and sustainable future. *Ecological Economics, 200*, 107506.

Gough, I. (2023). Sufficiency as a value standard: From preferences to needs. *Ethics, Policy & Environment*, 1–22.
Hickel, J. (2020). *Less is more: How degrowth will save the world*. Random House.
Jackson, T. (2009). *Prosperity without growth: Economics for a finite planet*. Routledge.
Kallis, G., Kostakis, V., Lange, S., Muraca, B., Paulson, S., & Schmelzer, M. (2018). Research on degrowth. *Annual Review of Environment and Resources, 43*(1), 291–316.
Robeyns, I. (2008). Introduction: Revisiting the feminism and basic income debate. *Basic Income Studies, 3*(3).
Schmelzer, M., Vetter, A., & Vansintjan, A. (2022). *The future is degrowth: A guide to a world beyond capitalism*. Verso Books.
Widerquist, K. (2018). *A critical analysis of basic income experiments for researchers, policymakers, and citizens*. Springer International Publishing.

Index[1]

A

B

C

[1] Note: Page numbers followed by 'n' refer to notes.

R. Merrill, C. Neves (eds.), *Determining the Value of Universal Basic Income*, Exploring the Basic Income Guarantee,
https://doi.org/10.1007/978-3-032-04004-6

Kolibri 360 GmbH
Ferdinand-Jühlke-Straße 7
99095 Erfurt, Deutschland
produktsicherheit@kolibri360.de